VOTING GREEN

Your Complete Environmental
Guide to Making Political
Choices in the '90's

JEREMY RIFKIN
AND
CAROL GRUNEWALD
RIFKIN

DOUBLEDAY
New York   London   Toronto   Sydney   Auckland

PUBLISHED BY DOUBLEDAY
a division of Bantam Doubleday Dell Publishing Group, Inc.
666 Fifth Avenue, New York, New York 10103

DOUBLEDAY and the portrayal of an anchor with a dolphin
are registered trademarks of Doubleday,
a division of Bantam Doubleday Dell Publishing Group, Inc.

Book design by Patrice Fodero

Library of Congress Cataloging-in-Publication Data
Rifkin, Jeremy.
Voting green : your complete environmental guide to making
political choices in the 1990s / Jeremy Rifkin and Carol Grunewald
Rifkin. — 1st ed.
p.   cm.
1. Environmental policy—United States—Citizen participation.
2. United States—Economic policy—1981–   3. Elections—United
States.   I. Rifkin, Carol Grunewald.   II. Title.
HC110.E5R53   1992
333.7′.0973—dc20   91-39060
                                                              CIP

ISBN 0-385-41917-1

1   3   5   7   9   10   8   6   4   2

May 1992

Steven Paul Grunewald
with love

ACKNOWLEDGMENTS

During this project, we consulted with dozens of people who have committed their lives to ensuring that the world of the future will be just, peaceful, sustainable, and humane—in a word, Green. We would like to thank them all for their work and inspiration.

In particular, we would like to thank our tireless and persistent research director Erik Jansson for searching for needles in haystacks —and finding them. We owe a big debt of gratitude to Anna Awimbo, Jennifer Beck, Kathy Johnson, and Joe Mendelson. Without their energetic and painstaking effort, the biggest Green congressional scorecard ever compiled could not have been completed.

Carolyn Bennett, Beulah Bethea, Clara Mack, Helen Mathis, and Regina Thompson put in hours of extra work for which we are very grateful. Special thanks also to college interns Nicole Kerber and Jill Rice for their long hours of research.

The following people contributed their advice, supplied information, or helped us in myriad other ways, and we appreciate their efforts: the Animal Welfare Institute staff; Richard Ayres of the Clean Air Coalition; Jeb Brugman of the Center for Innovative Diplomacy; Rear Admiral Eugene Carroll, Jr., and Captain James Bush of the Center for Defense Information; Carol Capps of Church World Service/Lutheran World Relief; Judy Corbett of the California Local Government Commission; Scott Denman of the Safe Energy Communication Council; Brock Evans of the National Audubon Society; Greenpeace staff including: Alexandra Allen, Rick Hind, and Susan Sabella; Sam Harris of RESULTS; Doug and Steve

Hellinger of The Development GAP; The Humane Society of the United States; Andrew Kimbrell of The Foundation on Economic Trends; Howard Lyman of the National Farmers Union; Jim Maddy of the League of Conservation Voters; Pat Mooney and Cary Fowler of the Rural Advancement Fund International, Katy Moran of the Smithsonian Institution; Mark Satin of *New Options*; Nancy Skinner, City Council Member, Berkeley, California; Martin Teitel of the C.S. Fund; Michael Totten of the International Institute for Energy Conservation; Jeff Tyrens of the Center for Policy Alternatives; the Wilderness Society staff; Larry Williams of the Sierra Club, and our good friends Mark and Claudia White.

For donating their work to this project we would like to thank cartoonists: Cameron Cardow of the *Regina Leader Post*, Bill Day of the *Detroit Free Press*, Brian Duffy of the *Des Moines Register*, Paul Fell of the *Lincoln Journal*, Eric Sakach of The Humane Society of the United States, Scott Willis of the *San Jose Mercury News*, and Matt Wuerker of *Easy Reader*.

We also want to thank our agents, Jim Stein and Michael Carlisle, for their support and belief in the book. And last, but not least, we would like to thank our editor, John Duff, for his thoughtful and insightful stewardship of *Voting Green*.

Contents

SECTION III: VOTING GREEN

"I pledge allegiance to the Earth, and to the flora, fauna, and human life that it supports; one planet, indivisible, with safe air, water, and soil, economic justice, equal rights, and peace for all."

—Pledge of Allegiance to the Family of Earth,
Bella Abzug

SECTION I

GREEN POLITICS

GEOPOLITICS

BIOSPHERE POLITICS

INTRODUCTION:
THE EMERGENCE OF
GREEN POLITICS

The past few years have been marked by triumph after triumph for the United States in the world. After forty-six years of conflict with the Soviet Union, the United States has won a final and decisive victory in the Cold War. The Berlin Wall has been taken down. The Eastern Bloc and Baltic countries have broken away from the Soviet Union and are moving toward democracy and market economies. The Soviet Union, once our archenemy, no longer exists. The prospect of a nuclear confrontation has dimmed. The United States armed forces won a quick and decisive military victory in the Middle East, restoring confidence in the government's war machine.

Yet, even as we bask in the glory of our President's "new world order" we sense, though vaguely, that things are not quite right, not quite what they seem on the surface. Other realities haunt us —realities not easily remedied by the dispatch of troops to the Middle East or the collapse of the Soviet Union.

Our winters are getting milder, our summers warmer. It's not raining as much as it used to. We're afraid of the sun and anxious about staying out too long without covering up.

Our families seem more vulnerable to a range of environmentally induced diseases. At the same time, new diseases and syndromes are emerging, some without a name or an apparent cause. We're unsure what to eat or drink or what to avoid. We're warned to check underneath our homes' foundations for deadly radon to check our drinking water for toxic chemicals, and not to let our children play near high voltage electrical wires for fear that low-level radiation may be harmful to their health.

We hear fewer songbirds in the early morning hours. The wild creatures—the grizzly bear, the timber wolf, the lynx—are dwindling toward extinction. We put them on official government lists to mark their passing.

We're running out of soil in the farm belt and running out of drinking water in the West. The country is running short on domestic reserves of oil and natural gas, becoming more dependent on foreign exports to survive.

We are losing the next generation to drugs, boredom, and despair. Teenage drug addiction is on the rise. So too are teenage suicides. Our educational system is falling apart. Many of our students cannot read or write or even distinguish between the Midwest and the Middle East.

No one feels safe walking after dark. Few neighborhoods are secure. Violent crimes are increasing in every region of the country. There are now more than 200 million handguns in the United States—one for every man, woman, and child. People are guarded and scared. Children rarely play out in the streets or on the front lawns. Many neighborhoods are desolate. People have retreated inside behind locked doors. Countless others are homeless, living exposed on the open streets.

Our cities are in disrepair. Some have declared bankruptcy. Our national highways, once a mark of our greatness, are riddled with potholes, and there's too little money to restore them.

Millions of Americans are out of work. Those who have a job complain of being overtaxed and underpaid.

In the summer of 1991, we welcomed our troops home from the Persian Gulf with an exuberant ticker-tape parade. Large numbers of people came out to pay tribute. Yet, barely half of the country's eligible population bothered to come out to the polls to vote in the last national election. We have little regard for our elected officials and even less respect for the two major political parties. Most Americans feel that their opinions don't count, that they can't compete with the corporate lobbies and special interests whose millions of dollars of campaign contributions appear to swing elections. Voters watch as their elected officials bail out the rich bankers and financiers in the savings and loans fiasco, while refusing to ease the burden of increasing health care costs for the average citizen.

Questions about our quality of life are beginning to emerge. Parents worry about the future and the world their children will inherit. Beneath the surface of our national complacency, gnawing doubts are beginning to arise about who we are as a people and what direction we should be charting as a nation. Our national leaders seem to have few answers. They operate the ship of state as if oblivious to troubled waters. Most seek the entitlements that go with power, but refuse to lead. Many become pawns of the powerful moneyed interests who are never far removed from the councils of government.

This, then, is the condition we find ourselves in on the eve of the 1992 presidential election. Our elected officials, for the most part, prefer to campaign around the theme of business as usual. Few significant differences separate the two major political parties. Both parties are deeply entrenched in the status quo, unwilling to heed the rumblings of discontent looming on the political horizon.

Still, history teaches us that political vacuums are rarely left unfilled. Already there are signs of a new politics emerging in the land. Its stirrings are tentative, its mark still faint and barely detectable. Yet there is no doubt that the outline of a new political movement is beginning to form, its contours shaped by the discontent of millions of American voters and molded by new challenges facing America and the world in the coming century.

The new politics has its roots in the growing environmental and economic crisis and the cultural transformation that is accompanying it. Millions of Americans have begun to make fundamental changes in their personal lifestyles—changes that reflect a new way of living and acting in the world. Now these personal transformations are being politicized for the first time as many American voters seek fundamental changes in the political process that are compatible with their own changing sensibilities.

Green politics is about to emerge in America as a powerful new political force. It is an intergenerational politics that is already beginning to unite the sixties generation with their sons and daughters just now coming of age in the nineties. The two generations share a new vision of the world and their place in it and are determined to imprint their own political will on the body politic.

Thomas Paine, the great American revolutionary, once said: "Every generation must be free to remake the world anew." There are signs of a new world in the making. At the local and state level, a new generation of elected officials is beginning to pay attention to the revolution afoot. In Congress, there now exists a scattering of proto-Green representatives and senators. The Green vote is growing. In the next few years it may well influence the direction of our national politics and the course of world events.

THE GLOBAL
ENVIRONMENTAL CRISIS

The new Green political vision differs fundamentally from the conventional politics to which we have long been accustomed. Traditional party politics has galvanized largely around questions of economic power—of who should control the means of production and how the material gains should be distributed among groups and constituencies. Questions of entitlement and economic justice, of privilege and exploitation, of empowerment and disenfranchisement have dominated political discussion and the political agenda for as far back as anyone cares to remember. Groups in society have been divided along economic lines since the early days of the Republic. Class, gender, race, religion, ethnicity, and geography have all been used as convenient markers to separate the haves from the have-nots in industrial society.

For more than 200 years people have struggled to secure their rights of expression and participation so that they might share in the economic fruits of American society. Today that struggle continues as women, union workers, the poor, and people of color all vie for recognition, each seeking a voice, a vote, and a role in the economic process.

While the issues of economic power and economic justice continue to hold meaning, deeply affecting the political dynamics of our society, a new historical reality is beginning to impose itself, forcing us to broaden our very conception of politics to include new categories of thinking and acting in the world.

A new genre of environmental threats and challenges have arisen in the past several decades that transcend the narrow eco-

© WILLIAM K. DAY, TRIBUNE MEDIA SERVICE.

nomic arena within which conventional politics takes place. Global warming, ozone depletion, deforestation, species extinction, desertification, and soil erosion are affecting the very biochemistry of our planet and with it the conditions that dictate the survival of our species and civilization.

Global warming threatens to destabilize every bio-region on Earth in the coming century. Already, the scientific establishment is predicting climate changes of unprecedented magnitude, changes that could lead to a worldwide loss of agricultural production, rising oceans, the flooding of low-lying countries, superhurricanes, and the wholesale destruction of entire ecosystems.

The atmospheric ozone layer is now being depleted at a rate of 4 to 5 percent a decade over the United States, and government experts are predicting millions of additional cancers and deaths from exposure to deadly ultraviolet radiation. Ultraviolet rays also greatly diminish the growing capacity of plants and seriously weaken the immune systems of humans and animals, raising the specter of both famine and pestilence in the years ahead.

The world's remaining forests are being cut down to make way for cattle pastures and cultivation, and to provide lumber for the growing commercial and residential markets in the wealthy nations as well as fuel for the poor of the third world. The clear-cutting and burning of trees releases million of tons of carbon dioxide into the atmosphere, contributing to the warming of the planet. Since trees absorb carbon dioxide from the atmosphere, the worldwide loss of forests exacerbates the greenhouse effect by eliminating the most important sink for atmospheric CO_2.

Mass deforestation also has led to the erosion of the soil base on every continent. The roots of trees anchor the soil. When the trees are cut down, the soil is exposed and blows or is washed away. Entire land surfaces of the planet are now falling victim to erosion and spreading desertification.

The loss of forest ecosystems, the pressures of development, and the poisoning of the air, soil, and water with spent energy and toxic chemicals are destroying the wildlife of the planet. We are losing a species to extinction every sixty minutes, and by the turn of the century we may well experience the loss of more than 15 percent of the entire plant and animal kingdom. Many of these species play a critical role in the survival of human civilization, providing us with food, fiber, pharmaceuticals, and myriad other useful substances and products.

These global environmental threats are unprecedented in human history. They represent the inverse history of the Age of Progress. During the industrial era, the powerful nations of Europe, the Americas, and the Far East used an array of sophisticated technologies and institutions to convert the earth's bounty into consumable wealth—and then discarded waste—at a speed that far exceeded the biosphere's ability to recycle the pollutants and replenish the natural stock. Now the accumulating environmental bill of the industrial era threatens the future sustainability of the very ecosystems from which all economic activity is extracted and upon which our economic survival depends.

The worldwide environmental crisis affects every member of our species. No single individual, group, or nation, regardless of economic status or privileged political position, can escape the global consequences of these overarching new environmental realities. Their impacts will continue to be felt by every human being and by every other species with whom we share this planet.

In the years to come, every one of our economic and political decisions will be tempered and qualified by the constraints imposed by an increasingly weakened biosphere—the thin chemical envelope that extends from the ocean depths to the stratosphere and which sustains all life on Earth. The shift in emphasis from the economy to the ecosystem underlies the new Green political vision emerging in the United States and other countries around the world.

Environment: The Framework for Politics

The Republican and Democratic parties continue to think of the economy as an autonomous force, largely unbeholden to the forces of nature. The environment, therefore, is regarded as just another issue and relegated to the margins of the political world. The conventional wisdom notwithstanding, a growing number of elected officials inside the major parties, as well as leaders within many of the country's constituent groups, are beginning to view the environment as the essential framework for both economic activity and political decision making. They understand that the health of the environment is essential to the health of the economy and the well-being of every person, not a mere incidental concern as so many party regulars have argued in the past.

When the environment is compromised, so are we. When we despoil the biosphere—fill its oceans with poison, choke its atmosphere with deadly gases, denude and parch its soil—we reap the consequences. They flow back into the very sinew of our physical being. We are made up of the chemical and mineral elements and gases of the biosphere. We take into ourselves, into our organs and tissue, into our flesh and fluids, the stuff of the biosphere. As we degrade and pollute it, we become degraded and polluted in the process. When we expropriate and exploit the biosphere, reduce and diminish its grandeur, we become reduced and diminished as well.

Our damaged environment, once a subject of concern only to ecologists and environmental activists, now concerns us all. Farmers worry about the environmental toll on their land of using high-

© David Catrow, Copley News Service.

input petrochemical fertilizers and chemical pesticides. Consumers are increasingly concerned about dangerous chemicals in food and household products. Families are plagued by rising health care costs, in part induced by a range of illnesses triggered by pollutants and toxic chemical emissions. Many workers are deeply concerned about their own work environments and are demanding greater protection from exposure to dangerous pollutants on the job. At the same time, industrial workers also fear loss of employment in the wake of a growing public demand to safeguard the environment by shutting down polluting factories. Neighborhood citizens' groups are beginning to form across the country to protest plans to place incinerators, landfills, and toxic and radioactive dumps in their backyards. Native Americans are demanding an end to the commercial exploitation of their lands by multinational corporations and the restoration of their ancestral right to enjoy what were once sacred commons. Students are becoming increasingly concerned about the earth they will inherit and are organizing around long-term environmental problems that will affect their generation in the coming century. Religious leaders are exhorting the faithful to enter into a new covenant with God's creation and serve as stewards of the environment. Many feminists are calling for a more empathetic and nurturing approach to science, technology, and the natural world. Animal rights activists are drawing the public's attention to the plight of millions of animals who are suffering from abuse and neglect in medical laboratories, municipal pounds, intensive-confinement farms, and in the wild. Environmental activists are marshaling public support behind efforts to protect entire species and ecosystems. The peace and disarmament community is troubled by increasing international tensions spawned by critical shortages of oil, fresh water, arable land, and rare minerals, and warn of the increased likelihood of resource wars in the coming decades.

Already there are signs that existing constituencies and issue groups view the environment as a shared framework for exploring mutual interests and concerns. They are beginning to understand that the environment is both their common ground and a point of reference that can unite their separate struggles into a new and powerful political force.

While the new Green vision places the environment at the center of public life, making it the context for both the formulation of economic policies and political decisions, the new Green perspective differs from conventional politics in still another important way. Most party politicians continue to think of the earth as little more than a reservoir of commercial and strategic resources having either market or military value. The old political consciousness is still wedded to a strictly utilitarian approach to the natural world. Its adherents believe that "man" is the center of the universe and that the world was made solely for human use. The new Green politicians, on the other hand, are beginning to think of the earth as a living entity, a complex biochemical organism whose continued functioning depends on proper stewardship.

FROM GEOPOLITICS TO BIOSPHERE POLITICS

The two major parties continue to emphasize geopolitical concerns in their foreign policies, believing that a combination of military muscle and market strength is the best guarantor of individual and national security.

President Bush's "new world order" is a classic example of the old geopolitical way of thinking. In 1991, the President risked the lives of half a million American servicemen and -women, spent tens of billions of dollars, and caused the death of more than 150,000 Iraqis in the war in the Gulf to ensure the continued flow of Mideast oil to the U.S. market. Few Americans entertained any illusions as to the primary reason for our intervention in the Middle East. Yet, had the previous Administration and Congress agreed to implement a domestic energy conservation program for the United States, including a hike in automobile fuel efficiency of only 13 miles per gallon, the United States would not have needed a single gallon of oil from the Middle East and might have avoided a military confrontation altogether.

The emerging Green voters and politicians, although still heavily influenced by geopolitical notions of security, have begun to sense that the more serious threat to the individual and to the national security interests of the United States lies not in the geosphere but in the biosphere. The looming environmental threats to the planet cast a dark shadow over the prospect of human survival in the coming century and comprise a new security threat unparalleled in human history.

The shift in political thinking from geopolitics to biosphere politics and from military security to global environmental security is likely to be a long and drawn-out process. Still, signs of the new biosphere consciousness are already apparent in some of the defense bills being introduced into Congress. Green legislators argue that the nation ought to take advantage of the post–Cold War era by converting our entrenched military-industrial complex into an ecologically sustainable Green economy, and they are drafting legislation to ease the transition for industries, workers, and communities. Other legislation is being introduced to curtail the worldwide arms trade and reduce the spread of nuclear, chemical, biological, and conventional weapons. Green legislators would like to see the country marshal its resources and energy to restore and defend the biosphere.

Preserving the biosphere against the forces of military and commercial exploitation will require a new way of thinking and acting in the world. We will need to transcend the narrow bounds that divide us into constituencies, classes, genders, races, and nationalities, and begin thinking and acting as a species.

Addressing the new spate of global threats and challenges will require collective action by the human race, entered into jointly in every neighborhood of the biosphere. The almost exclusive attention on individual rights, which has so dominated the political thinking of the modern era, will have to be buttressed by a new emphasis on collective responsibilities if we are to have any chance of addressing the issues of biosphere security that threaten the very survival of the planet and human civilization.

Defending the Commons

Acting politically on behalf of the species and the biosphere requires a fundamental restructuring of our modern worldview. As noted earlier, the Green perspective on politics begins with a very different relationship to the earth.

In the conventional political framework, the earth is viewed largely in terms of enclosed areas and commercial property. Over the course of the past five centuries, humanity has increasingly enclosed sphere after sphere of the global commons, transforming the earth's biosphere into a latticework of private domains whose value is measured almost exclusively in commercial terms. The land surface of our planet has been divided and subdivided in recent centuries, with nation-states, corporations, and individuals all claiming ownership over bits and pieces of the earth's integrated ecosystems. The oceans have also been partially enclosed, with each nation claiming economic sovereignty over 200 miles of ocean extending out from its coast—an area comprising 36 percent of the high seas.

In this century, the nations of the world enclosed the atmospheric commons, transforming the skies into commercial air corridors, negotiable in the marketplace. More recently, the electromagnetic spectrum has been divided up and leased out to service a range of electronic and communications technologies. And now, even the gene pool is being commercially enclosed. Legislation has been passed and court decisions rendered in the United States, allowing corporations to patent and own genetically engineered microbes, plants, and animals.

The very idea of owning large parts of the biosphere is anathema to the new Green worldview. Indeed, as long as the biosphere remains divided, enclosed, and commercially exploited for private gain, it will be virtually impossible for the human species to join together in common stewardship of the earth. The commercial self-interests of nations, multinational corporations, and individuals will continue to thwart the public will.

In the new world of Green politics, humanity's relationship to the earth is fundamentally altered. The notion of the earth as a commercially exploitable private space gives way to the idea of the biosphere as an indivisible community made up of all of the various forms of life on earth. In the new spatial scheme of things, each ecosystem and local biome is a microcosm of the biosphere, a small part of the whole, whose health and well-being help condition the health and well-being of the entire planet.

Political boundaries, in a biosphere world, are drawn along very different lines than in a geopolitical world. Nation-state boundaries have been the result of market-driven forces and military might. Borders were designed with commerce in mind. In the new species-oriented politics, political boundaries would be designed with ecosystems—not economic systems—in mind. Because political decisions and economic activity in every locale inevitably affect the entire biosphere of the planet, political identification and loyalty need to be centered as much in the local biome and in the biosphere as in the nation-state.

The fledgling Green political movement often uses the aphorism, "Think globally, act locally." Protecting the biosphere requires acting in an ecologically responsible fashion in every region of the biosphere. For this reason, the local community is likely to play a new and expanded political role in the years ahead.

The local community, long the centerpiece of social life, lost much of its power and presence in the current century as human allegiances were drawn to the marketplace at one pole and the state at the other. The community has become a less essential part of people's day-to-day life.

As the ecosystem replaces the economic system as the context for social and political life in the coming decades, however, the local community will become an ever more important arbiter and intermediary, continually adjusting the needs and interests of society to the prerequisites and constraints imposed by local ecosystems. In the Green era, community boundaries also will be broadened to encompass the larger ecological community to which human society is bound and on which it is dependent.

Already, scattered localities throughout the country are beginning to take seriously the new concept of community. Fort Collins, Colorado, for example, is attempting to create an integrated Green community with the ecosystem as the underlying framework and common bond. The city council and the local citizenry have begun to convert backyards, parks and other urban spaces back to their natural state to attract wildlife into their midst. The city, which has wildlife biologists on its payroll, has been certified as an urban wildlife sanctuary.

While local communities are beginning to assume a new level of responsibility for the local biome, they are also beginning to adopt a new biosphere-oriented political consciousness. Many are seizing the initiative from the federal government and forging agreements with other cities around the world to combat a range of global environmental challenges including the greenhouse effect, ozone depletion, and deforestation.

Some legislators in Congress, buoyed by the new Green surge within the electorate, are beginning to introduce legislation to address the needs of the biosphere. New international compacts and treaties are also being proposed to enhance efforts to preserve the global environment.

At the same time, legislation is being introduced that would, for the first time, begin to reverse the historical trend toward the increasing commercial enclosure of the global commons for private gain. Congress recently passed legislation to preserve the continent of Antarctica as a global commons and to prohibit the commercial exploitation of its land mass by international mining and oil interests. Other bills have been introduced to encourage "debt for nature" swaps and to establish ecological preserves in developing nations. In return for retiring debts, developing countries agree to prohibit commercial development of parts of their rain forests and other valuable ecosystems, leaving them as protected commons. Legislation has also been proposed to prohibit the enclosure of the gene pool by halting the patenting of genetically engineered animals. Still other bills have been introduced to prevent the military enclosure and exploitation of the outer space commons.

In the United States, hundreds of millions of acres of land are publicly owned and administered as a shared commons by the federal and state governments. In the American West alone, the federal government administers nearly 300 million acres of public lands—a domain that makes up 48 percent of the land mass of the American West and 19 percent of the total land mass of the contiguous forty-eight states.

Unfortunately, private business interests have been able to exert tremendous influence over the use of public lands, often securing their commercial use for a fraction of their fair market value. Western ranchers lease millions of acres of public rangeland for a fraction of the land's worth on the open market. Lumber companies lease public forestlands in Alaska and the Northwest for nominal fees while reaping huge profits. The same story is repeated over and over again with offshore oil rights and coal leases, mineral and mining rights, and the like. U.S. and foreign corporations have been raiding the public commons of our country, plundering and depleting the rich natural endowment of the continent for the better part of two centuries.

Some members of Congress have introduced legislation to protect public lands from unsustainable commercial development and exploitation. Unlike the more traditionally minded politicians who have long viewed public lands merely as exploitable commercial domains, the new Green-oriented minority in Congress argues for a new spirit of public stewardship over the remaining land commons of the United States.

Bills have been introduced to raise fees for grazing livestock on Western public land to more accurately reflect the land's true value and to reduce overgrazing, which has already seriously damaged the ecology of the range. Other bills would stop the practice of selling off public lands to mining companies and prospectors for speculation and development. This legislation would impose environmental restrictions to minimize adverse impacts and include provisions requiring reclamation of the land after mining is completed. Other bills have been put forth to protect wildlife in national wildlife refuges from a range of commercial and recreational activities, including hunting and trapping, and to curtail destructive government predator-control programs on public lands. Companion bills have been introduced into the House and the Senate to establish an "American Heritage Trust" to acquire additional lands, thus expanding the public land commons in the United States.

While these gestures are still limited in number, they point to a new direction in American politics: one based on reopening the global commons.

This new willingness to restore the global commons signals a fundamental shift in our collective loyalties and responsibilities. Increasingly, in the years ahead, a new generation of voters and politicians will likely identify more and more with the shared interests of the commons and take seriously their responsibility to serve as stewards over both the public domain of the United States and the biosphere of the planet.

THE GREENING OF SCIENCE AND TECHNOLOGY

Nowhere is the new Green perspective more in evidence than in the changing attitudes about science and technology. In today's highly secular world, science and technology have come to play a unique role in the body politic. We often look to science and technology as our salvation, much the way earlier generations looked to God. For the most part, the assumptions and values that underlie modern science and technology have gone unchallenged in the political arena. The direction of science and technology has also gone largely unattended, the electorate content to leave such questions in the hands of scientists, engineers, and corporations. Now, a growing number of Green voters and politicians are questioning both the orientation and direction of modern science and technology, arguing that the environmental crisis facing the world today is attributable, in large measure, to the ways science and technology have been pursued in the modern world.

The origin of modern science dates back to the seventeenth century and the works of Francis Bacon. Bacon surveyed ancient Greek and medieval science and found them wanting. In the past, he argued, science was far too interested in the "why" of things, at the expense of the "how" of things. Bacon was more pragmatic and interested in an approach to science that would "enlarge the bounds of the human empire to the effecting of all things possible." He found the tool he was looking for in the scientific method, an approach to understanding and unlocking the secrets of nature that would "establish and extend the powers of dominion of the human race itself over the universe." Bacon approached nature as an adversary and boasted that through the use of the scientific method, we would have "the power to conquer and subdue" nature and "to shake her to her foundations." His aggressive approach to nature has conditioned our relationship to the biosphere during the whole of the modern age.

Now Green voters and more than a few Green legislators, are calling for a new approach to science, one more compatible with our new sense of participation and partnership with the natural world. Although the powers that be continue to entertain the myth that modern science is "objective" and "value free," Green thinkers argue that the approach to science we have come to rely on in the modern era is narrowly conceived and based on power, domination, detachment, and expediency.

While the political establishment continues to pour money into "big science" and to encourage research into powerful new technologies like supercolliders, nuclear fusion, star wars weaponry, and genetic engineering, some members of Congress and state legislators are proposing an alternative science agenda that emphasizes cooperation with, rather than control over, the environment. Bills are being introduced and laws passed at both the local and federal levels to explore the fields of ecology, soft energy paths, and preventive medicine—all scientific pursuits based on developing an understanding of the myriad relationships that bind human beings and society to the natural world.

At the same time, the new Green awareness is beginning to extend to questions of the proper role and direction of technology in the modern world. Often, the introduction of new technologies more intimately affects our private and public lives than any other phenomenon. Yet, technology decisions have, for the most part, been made in corporate board rooms, outside the political arena. Many of the powerful technological introductions of the twentieth century were never subject to political discussion or congressional debate. Little public discussion or political debate accompanied the introduction of the automobile, nuclear power or the electronic computer. Still these technologies have had a dramatic and enduring effect on the environment and the political and economic dynamics of the country.

Today's new Green voter is likely to be less sanguine about all

© 1991, USA TODAY. Reprinted by permission.

of the supposed benefits of new technology and more concerned about the secondary impacts and consequences that new technologies are likely to have both on the environment and society. The new voter no longer blindly accepts the proposition that "if it can be done, it should be done." Nor is the Green voter likely to agree with the long-held popular assumption that technology itself is "neutral" and that the only question of political significance is how it is to be regulated and who is to be in charge.

Many Green voters understand that all technologies represent power and are, therefore, never neutral. A bow and arrow gives a person more power than his throwing arm. A train provides more locomotive power than one's feet and legs. A computer amplifies human memory. Tools, then, are power, and power is never neutral, because in the mere act of using tools, power is being exercised over someone or something in the environment.

A nuclear power plant, Green thinkers contend, is inherently powerful and poses grave risks to the environment and human health regardless of whether it is regulated and controlled by a government elite or a corporation or democratically controlled by the local community in which it operates.

The question, then, for the Green voter and politician is how much power is appropriate? Are there tools that are so inherently powerful that the mere act of using them poses a potential danger to the biosphere, other creatures, and our own species? The gas-fueled automobile, high-input petrochemical farming, nuclear power plants, and genetic engineering are all technologies whose benefits need to be weighed against the powerful damage they inflict on the biosphere and the creatures that live within its protective sheath.

Green voters and politicians advocate appropriate technologies —technologies whose inherent power is compatible with the power distribution in the surrounding environment. Appropriate techniques are in scale, both spatially and temporally, with their environmental milieu. They are easily integrated with the rhythms of the environment and its carrying capacity. They are enmeshed with their surroundings and help sustain rather than drain the environment.

For example, compare the Sears Tower in Chicago with a passive solar home. The first structure is out of scale with the natural environment and requires an inordinate amount of energy to function—the Sears Tower uses more energy in twenty-four hours than the entire city of Rockford, Illinois, with a population of 137,000 people. The solar home, in contrast, is structurally designed to be compatible with the rhythms and flows of the natural environment in which it operates. It is sustained by the environment, but does not drain the environment.

Today a growing number of Green voters are seeking a voice in technology decisions, demanding that the political process be used to decide whether or not new technologies should be introduced and under what conditions, rather than leaving such decisions up to the corporations and the marketplace, as has been so often the case in the past.

Congress and state legislators are also becoming involved in techno-politics. Genetic-engineering, nuclear power, and other high-input technologies are being subjected increasingly to public attention and scrutiny as a new generation of Green voters assumes its responsibility to participate in decisions regarding the introduction of new technologies.

Legislators, prodded by Green constituencies and public-interest groups, are also beginning to introduce bills to stimulate research, development, and commercial introduction of appropriate technologies that are compatible with the requisites of the environment. In the past few years alone, bills have been proposed (and in some instances passed) to foster the development of sustainable agriculture technologies and new energy-saving technologies—technologies of appropriate scale that help sustain the workings of the biosphere.

GREEN ECONOMICS

Nothing so distinguishes a Green voter as his or her views on economics. Traditional economists continue to labor under the assumption that the economy operates as a semi-independent force in the world. They view the environment less as a limiting condition and more as an open-ended stock of inputs that can be harnessed with human ingenuity and innovative new technologies to create an ever expanding store of wealth. They would agree with John Locke, the Enlightenment political philosopher, who argued that "land left wholly to nature, is called . . . waste." Natural resources, they contend, only become valuable when transformed by humankind to create productive assets. By this way of thinking, the more efficient the economic system becomes at transforming nature's "waste" to productive wealth, the more material benefits will accrue to the advantage of every member of society. Virtually every economist views the gross national product (GNP) as a measure of the wealth generated in goods and services over a twelve-month period.

The Green economic perspective begins with an entirely different premise. Everything in a state of nature is not unproductive waste, as Locke and others have long contended, but rather a storehouse of value. Human ingenuity and technology transform that value into assets, goods, and products by extracting, collecting, and converting nature's resources. In the process, the environment itself is diminished and degraded, and waste accumulates. Even the assets, goods, and products are only temporary. Eventually they are discarded back into the environment as waste—some of which is recycled back into the earth, the rest irretrievably lost in spent energy or entropy.

In the new Green way of thinking, gross national product is more an index of the temporary value of productive wealth generated by society, measured against the natural resources used to make it and the pollution created in the process. The greater the GNP, the more depleted and polluted the environment becomes.

The very idea of economic "growth" is a misnomer, according to Green thinking. Economics is more about borrowing than about growth. We borrow from nature's storehouse, transforming living things and inanimate material into useful products that we use for a short time before discarding them back into the natural environment. Everything, from an economic point of view, is borrowed from the environment—our food, tools, goods, and other accoutrements. And to the environment everything is eventually returned.

Green economics, then, is based on borrowing from the biosphere. Being wholly dependent on nature and indebted to it, all economic activity brings with it an inherent obligation of repayment. Paying back one's debt to the biosphere means serving as a steward and caretaker of creation, and using as little of nature's resources as absolutely necessary to lead a healthy existence. It also means sharing the earth's bounty more equitably among our fellow human beings and the other creatures with whom we share the planet.

The depletion of the earth's ecosystems and the deterioration of the biosphere affect the poor most of all. As resources become more scarce and expensive, the least fortunate are the first to experience the consequences of the shortfall. They are the first to be let go in the production process as environmental scarcity forces economic slowdowns. They are the hardest hit by rising prices for energy and other scarce resources. They are also least able to protect themselves against the ravages of pollution. Toxic dumps, landfills, open sewers, and contaminated drinking water are a recurrent theme in the shantytowns and urban ghettos of the world.

Still, with precious few exceptions, members of the Republican and Democratic parties continue to align themselves with "old-fashioned" economics, believing in unlimited economic growth, with little understanding of, or regard for, the environment from which all wealth is generated. While the Republicans put more emphasis on the marketplace, entrepreneurial incentives, and corporate profit margins, and the Democrats prefer to concentrate on the questions of economic justice and greater worker and community participation in the production and distribution process, both parties give unqualified allegiance to unlimited economic growth as the solution to the human crisis. They continue to reason that the more productive wealth the society can generate, the more there will be to go around—sometimes known as the "trickle-down theory of economics." The truth lies elsewhere. The more wealth that is generated, the fewer resources are available to provide for the needs of others—now and in the future.

The Green voter prefers to recast the modus operandi of economics from one of "unlimited growth" to one of "economic sustainability." Living within our means, in the Green way of thinking, means living within the carrying capacity of the earth's ecosystems. Sustaining the economy is only possible, in the long run, by sustaining the environment from which we gain our sustenance.

Fragments of Green economic thinking are beginning to find their way into national legislation, offering hope for a fundamental transformation in economic theory and practice in the decades ahead. Several legislators have introduced innovative foreign aid bills based, in large part, on the principles of environmentally sustainable development and local self-reliance. The bills promote small-scale economic development projects, including "micro-enterprise" lending programs to encourage entrepreneurship, self-employment, and the formation of small businesses in village communities. Other legislation emphasizes the development of solar and other renewable energy technologies and greater reliance on bicycles as means of transportation.

Many of these new development assistance bills require that aid be directed to the poorest of the poor and mandate that those who are to receive the aid be consulted in the design of the assistance program and be responsible for running it. Particular emphasis is placed on the involvement of women, who make up a majority of the labor force in virtually every developing nation but who have been traditionally ignored in aid assistance programs. Virtually all of these new Green-oriented development programs emphasize a sustainable relationship between the economy and the ecosystem and focus on proper resource management and pollution abatement.

Some legislators have introduced bills designed to promote sustainable economic activity in the domestic economy. For example, legislation has been introduced that would eliminate the clear-cutting of America's forests and instead promote an environmentally sustainable approach to forestry practices. Other legislators have introduced bills to encourage greater energy conservation in government, industry, commerce, and the residential sectors. In the field of transportation, a few elected officials have suggested development of solar and electric automobiles and greater reliance on alternative means of transportation, including the bicycle. (More than 50 percent of all commuting trips in the United States are less than 5 miles, a distance easily traveled by bicycle.) The low-input sustainable agriculture provisions of the 1990 Food and Agriculture Act also reflect the new Green economic thinking.

REDEFINING PROGRESS

While Green economic thinking is beginning to emerge in Congress, the two major political parties are still a long way from replacing the economics of unlimited growth with the economics of sustainability. Much of the intransigence is due, in no small part, to the clichéd and outworn notions of progress still adhered to by most elected officials in the United States. For most of the modern era, we have defined progress almost exclusively in terms of increased material production. Greater progress has always meant optimizing the use of resources and maximizing the consumption of goods and services. In a world plagued by resource shortages, global environmental threats, and growing population pressures, the conventional notion of progress appears more as a prescription for disaster than a hopeful beacon of a better future.

By contrast, the Green concept of progress is based on the assumptions of economic sustainability rather than unlimited growth and consumption. Progress, in the world of Green politics, is defined as new scientific, technological, and economic initiatives that enhance the well-being of the community, conserve the resources, steward the environment, and protect the interests of future generations of human beings and other species.

The theme of ecological progress was explored by a handful of legislators in 1990 during consideration of new clean air legislation. While industry lobbies and their political allies on Capitol Hill and in the White House argued that economic growth, profits, and employment would all suffer if tough new clean air statutes were adopted, a few members of Congress challenged the old shibboleths, arguing that progress means more than simple output. They reminded their colleagues of the increased health bills that accompany air pollution, as well as the toll atmospheric pollution is taking on the nation's environment and infrastructure. They warned of the long-term biospheric, economic, and social consequences of failing to address the worsening air pollution crisis. They pleaded on behalf of the interests of future generations whose quality of life would be seriously compromised by failure to act now. And finally, a few legislators introduced bills to ease the transition for workers whose jobs would be lost by new clean air provisions that were being considered. In short, they argued for a new perspective with regard to progress. They asked their colleagues to go beyond the narrow confines of short-term economic performance and corporate profit and consider the overall well-being of the community, the conservation and stewardship of resources, and the rights and interests of future generations.

Just a few years ago, the very idea of balancing increased production and short-term profit with the need to preserve and protect the environment would have been unthinkable. But today, a new generation of Green activists, voters, and politicians are beginning to alter fundamentally the political debate around the question of appropriate future directions for the economy and society.

BEYOND RIGHT AND LEFT

Conventional politics is still trapped inside old, outmoded categories. Politicians in both the Republican and Democratic parties continue to talk in terms of right/left, conservative/liberal splits, even as the electorate becomes increasingly uninterested and unresponsive to these traditional political labels. Most voters (and nonvoters) find it more and more difficult to identify themselves as either liberal or conservative. These categories, once a lightning rod sure to evoke the passions of the electorate, are now largely ignored by a growing number of Americans. That's because many of the issues of interest to American voters transcend the old forms of classification. Nowhere is this more true than when it comes to the protection of the environment.

A majority of Americans, regardless of their party affiliation or past ideological orientation, are in favor of tough new legislative initiatives to clean up the environment. According to a Harris Poll conducted in 1990, three out of every five Americans are now deeply concerned about the environment. In a survey conducted by the Associated Press, 79 percent of all the respondents said that pollution now threatens their quality of life. Interestingly, an ABC/*Wall Street Journal* Poll in 1990 "found no difference in the degree of support for environmental protection between Democrats and Republicans." A majority of Americans from both political parties said they are prepared to make significant economic sacrifices, if necessary, to address the growing environmental threats. In a Gallup Poll conducted in 1990, 71 percent of those surveyed believed that protecting the environment should be given priority, even if it meant "stifling economic growth." In a Harris Poll, 95 percent of those surveyed said they would even be willing to trade a loss of jobs and the closing of polluting plants, if necessary, to clean up the air. Clearly, a majority of the public, Republicans and Democrats alike, are beginning to shift political perspective, aligning themselves with the new Green vision of progress with its emphasis on the quality of life and the protection of the biosphere.

The old politics lent itself to conservative/liberal categorization. As long as the economy was the exclusive framework for political decision making, it is not surprising that the question of economic privilege vs. economic rights dominated political debate, separating the rich from the poor, managers from workers, and so forth. Today, the ecosystem is increasingly challenging the economic system as the framework for political decision making, portending a basic change in political orientation in the United States. As environmental concerns shift from the political margins to the political center and from issues to framework, voters are going to be forced to make political decisions based on how they perceive their shared relationship to each other, the environment, and other living creatures. Already a new political spectrum is emerging between those who view their fellow human beings, other species, and the environment in strictly utilitarian terms, as resources to exploit for short-term material gain, and those who view human beings, other species, and the environment as an overarching biotic community to which we are each indebted and beholden as members and active participants. The former would enclose the entire biosphere, turning every nook and cranny in the global commons into a commercially exploitable private domain. The latter would begin to open up the global commons and pursue a political agenda based on sustainable and humane stewardship of the earth and its inhabitants.

The new spectrum is beginning to influence and shape the course of politics at both the federal and state levels. The new political thinking has already become a factor in animal-protection issues. Conservative and liberal members of Congress have repeatedly joined together in introducing bills designed to protect the inherent rights and interests of other creatures. A flurry of bills have been introduced in the 101st and the 102nd Congresses to

curtail the unnecessary use and inhumane treatment of laboratory and farm animals as well as animals in the wild. One bill would allow individuals and organizations to bring suit in court on behalf of animals whose rights to humane treatment and protective care are being violated by the government's failure to enforce the Animal Welfare Act. Another bill would require veal producers to provide more humane living conditions for veal calves. Some legislators have introduced bills to protect specific endangered species, including African elephants, whales, and wolves. Others have sought passage of legislation to protect the biodiversity of entire ecosystems. Bills to ensure a "no net loss" of ancient forests and wetlands have been introduced in Congress, as have bills to prohibit driftnet fishing on the high seas.

Champions of animal rights and biodiversity in Congress and in the statehouses argue that other sentient creatures have intrinsic value, not just utility value, and should be treated with dignity and respect. Opponents of animal-rights legislation argue that other creatures are important only in as much as they are useful in some way to humankind. Their suffering is of little concern or consequence as long as it advances the welfare of society.

The issues of animal rights and biodiversity are only a few of the many concerns that are beginning to unite politicians and voters of formerly opposing political ideologies in a new Green political vision. In the years ahead, the emerging Green consciousness is going to exert greater pressure on the political process, with voters increasingly identifying themselves along the new political spectrum that runs the gamut from market-driven utilitarianism at one pole to ecological stewardship at the other.

SECTION II

green

LEGISLATION

ISSUES, BILLS AND SPONSORS

Voting Green

Recent events in the Soviet Union and throughout Eastern Europe are a powerful reminder that the people can and do make history on occasion, often in the face of what appear to be overwhelming odds. Today a new generation faces a threat of far greater magnitude than any other in our short history as a species. Addressing the global environmental crisis will require nothing short of a transformation of political will, a collective determination by the human species to fundamentally restructure our worldview, our lifestyle, and our institutions to accommodate the needs of an imperiled biosphere.

The elements of a new Green politics are already in the making. They exist in scattered bills and pieces of legislation that have been introduced in Congress and in the statehouses and municipal governments across the country. Together they represent the beginning of a revolutionary new vision of politics that transcends traditional party platforms and the conventional approach to political decision making in this country.

In preparing this environmental guide to making political choices in the 1990s, we read through thousands of pieces of legislation in search of a "Greenprint" for political change. We selected 264 bills introduced in the 101st Congress (1989–1990) and the first quarter of the 102nd Congress (January through June 1991) that together form the basis of a Green political agenda. It should be pointed out that we were unable to include every single Green-oriented bill. In some instances, we may have overlooked a bill that deserved recognition. In other instances, our judgment of what qualified a bill to be Green may have differed from the views of others. To ensure fairness and impartiality, we sought out the recommendations of a range of activist organizations well versed in Congressional matters and Green sensibilities.

Most of the Green bills discussed in the following pages have not been passed into law. Many have never even come to a vote or been passed out of committee onto the floor of the House or Senate for consideration. The political leadership of both major parties has often ignored and, on occasion, vigorously opposed these Green bills. In a few instances, the compelling need for the legislation has been so evident, and the public pressure has been so great, that Congress has been forced to act in spite of opposition by industry and the recalcitrant, antienvironmental stance of the Bush administration.

Quite frankly, we were surprised and encouraged by how many Green bills existed, some of them far reaching and visionary. At the same time, we have felt a growing sense of frustration knowing that many, if not most, of these bills will languish or die in committee unless an aroused electorate demands their passage.

We have prepared this guide to give Green voters the information they need to vote Green in the upcoming 1992 election.

In this section of the book, Section II, we have divided the 264 Green bills into fourteen issue categories and devoted a chapter to each issue to fully explore the Green legislative approach. The categories are: global warming, ozone protection, energy, transportation, defense, international development, foreign policy, the global commons (oceans and Antarctica), agriculture, public lands, forests and wetlands, animal rights, genetic engineering, and endangered species and biodiversity.

We conclude each chapter with a roster listing the recommended Green position on each issue under consideration. Section II concludes with a listing of 102 voting-Green positions, which together amount to a Green platform for the 1992 election. Only a few of the 102 voting-Green positions have been voted into law. Of the bills that have become law, virtually all of them need to be either strengthened or expanded. Together, these 102 voting-Green positions provide a litmus test of Green thinking on issues by which to judge candidates in the upcoming national elections.

GLOBAL WARMING: THE GREENHOUSE EFFECT

Our planet functions much like a living organism. It is an extremely complex, self-regulating system of interrelated biochemical processes. Vital to the equilibrium of these processes are stable temperature and climate. The earth's surface temperature has not varied more than about 4 degrees Fahrenheit since the last ice age, 18,000 years ago.

Now, a growing number of scientists are projecting a 4°–9°F rise in the earth's surface temperature over the next fifty years as we continue to spew carbon dioxide (CO_2), methane, chlorofluorocarbons (CFCs), and nitrous oxides into the atmosphere, blocking solar heat from escaping the planet—the so-called "Greenhouse effect." A change in temperature of this magnitude in less than one human lifetime may well exceed the temperature change that has occurred over the entire last geological epoch.

Ten years ago global warming was of interest to only a small coterie of atmospheric scientists and meteorologists and little discussed in policy circles. Today global warming has emerged as a grave potential threat to the earth's environment and the survival of human civilization. The National Academy of Sciences and more than half of the world's Nobel laureates have warned that global warming looms as the most serious environmental threat of the twenty-first century.

The effects of global warming could be far reaching. Thermal heat expansion may result in a 3 to 5 foot rise in the sea level around the world. Island nations and low-lying countries may well be swallowed up by the rising oceans. Radical shifts in temperature are likely to change rainfall patterns, affecting agricultural production on every continent. The Midwestern farm belt in the United States may face increasing droughts and spreading desertification, threatening the food supply for Americans and peoples of other countries. Cities like New York and Chicago may have tropical climates by the middle of the next century. Mighty lakes and rivers could be reduced to giant mud flats, interrupting transportation and destroying aquatic life. A new generation of superhurricanes could wreak havoc on port cities, destroying coastlines and wetlands.

According to the Bellagio Report, a study undertaken by some of the world's leading climatologists in 1987, the greenhouse effect is likely to result in massive forest dieback by the end of the first decade of the twenty-first century. Forests will not be able to migrate fast enough to keep up with the shift in their temperature range. Writing in the journal *Science,* Richard Akerr points out that "each 1 degree centigrade of warming pushes climatic zones 100 to 150 km [60–95 miles] northward." Consider the impact on one ecosystem alone. Within sixty years, the climate that nurtures Yellowstone National Park will have shifted well into Canada. Trees are not capable of migrating at the speed set by the greenhouse phenomenon. In every region of the globe, entire ecosystems—trees, insects, microbes, animals—will be trapped by these rapid shifts in climate and left behind to die.

Already, governments around the world are grappling with the potential consequences of global warming, attempting to fashion new laws and statutes to mitigate the effects of a rapidly rising temperature on the earth's environment. Their task is formidable. To significantly reduce the emissions of global warming gases would require wholesale changes in our way of life and a fundamental reorientation of the global economy. Still, we may have little or no choice if we are to stave off a dramatic change in world climate and prevent a potential ecological catastrophe in the twenty-first century.

TURNING DOWN THE HEAT

The U.S. Congress has begun to take up the challenge of global warming. Although none of the proposed legislation has addressed the fundamental need to restructure the industrial way of life that is the source of increasing greenhouse gas emissions, some of the bills introduced point in the direction of a more sustainable Green future.

A handful of legislators have emerged in the House and Senate as prophetic voices, leaders in what may well turn out to be the most important political initiative in world history.

Rep. Claudine Schneider's (R-RI) omnibus bill, the Global Warming Prevention Act, has become the standard-bearer, marshaling 144 cosponsors in the House of Representatives in the 101st Congress. Its scope is impressive, covering everything from energy efficiency standards in federal buildings, to a tax on the import of tropical wood products from developing nations.

Among other things, the legislation would reduce CO_2 levels by at least 20 percent by the year 2000 "through a mix of federal and state energy policies." To achieve that goal, Rep. Schneider outlined a series of statutory initiatives. The Secretary of Energy is directed to establish "energy efficiency goals" to save energy in "federally owned or leased buildings as well as federally assisted housing." The secretary is further instructed to use "renewable forms of energy," when possible, in buildings. The bill also calls for the establishment of "a uniform nationwide home energy rating system." The bill even calls on the Secretary of Energy to "promulgate energy efficiency standards for incandescent and fluorescent lamps. . . ." No small item, since lighting accounts for 25 percent of electricity use in the United States. The new generation of compact fluorescent lights consume 75 percent less electricity and last ten to thirteen times longer than comparable incandescent bulbs. Each new compact fluorescent bulb will "save the consumer over 25 dollars and prevent the combustion of 1000 pounds of carbon dioxide. . . ."

The Schneider bill also includes provisions to reduce auto energy use and emissions, including car-pooling arrangements, the mandating of high-occupancy vehicle lanes, and the encouragement of mass transportation.

Every state is required to "reduce by 10% or more the total amount of energy consumed" by the year 2000, using October 1, 1990 as the base year.

The Secretary of Agriculture is required to implement an accelerated urban tree-planting program to reduce CO_2 emissions.

The Secretaries of State and Treasury and the administrator of the Agency for International Development are instructed to "promote multilateral tropical forestry programs in developing third world nations." At the same time, the Secretary of Commerce is mandated "to impose a tropical wood tax upon products containing specified woods."

The Foreign Assistance Act of 1961 would be amended under this bill to "prohibit assistance for large-scale production of energy." The new emphasis in aid is to be "least cost energy planning," including small-scale renewable energy technologies.

The Schneider bill also requires that the various development banks that receive U.S. support emphasize nonmotorized transport, renewable-energy technologies, and conservation programs in their development loans, to minimize the emission of carbon dioxide in third world nations.

To provide an incentive for developing nations to conserve their forests, Schneider included provisions authorizing the Secretary of the Treasury "to modify loan terms on up to one half of the sovereign debt owed the United States by developing countries" in return for agreements to adopt forest and energy conservation programs.

A GLOBAL RESPONSE

In the Senate, **Sen. Albert Gore (D-TN)** introduced the World Environment Policy Act to curb global warming. While the bill failed to pass, it sparked considerable debate, educating many in

Catastrophic Impacts of Global Warming

- "An estimated 100 billion dollars will have to be spent on seawalls and coastline protection against rising sea levels."

- "Farming would shift northward as would agricultural pests and pathogens—many resistant to current pesticides—as temperatures and droughts increase. Some regions would suffer crop losses of up to 80%."

- "Heat waves will drive up electricity demand eventually leading to the need for upwards of 400 thousand megawatts of extra power plants at a cost of $325 billion. By 2055, utility bills could climb by as much as 75 billion dollars per year solely to pay for the additional generating capacity."

Practical Solutions

- "Detailed government and private studies show the U.S. economy could maintain robust economic growth while achieving 200 billion dollars per year in energy savings through continued investment in efficiency technologies."

- "Only one tree is replanted in the United States for every four that die or are cut down. As a result of a loss of shade in our communities more fossil fuels are burned to operate air conditioners. An estimated 160 million trees could be selectively planted around buildings and on streets, cooling communities, saving billions of dollars per year in air-conditioning costs, and reducing carbon dioxide emissions by tens of millions of tons per year."

—*Rep. Claudine Schneider (R-RI)*

the Senate about the complex problems of global warming. Many of Gore's recommendations paralleled those of Rep. Schneider's bill and other bills introduced in both chambers of Congress. Some of his proposals, however, were unique and potentially far reaching.

For example, Gore called for the establishment of a Council on World Environmental Policy, to be chaired by the administrator of the Environmental Protection Agency (EPA), to replace the existing President's Council on Environmental Quality. The new council would recognize the global nature of the new generation of environmental threats facing the planet and the need to marshal a global political response. Global warming represents a unique environmental threat whose impacts spill over national boundaries to affect the entire planet. The Council on World Environmental Policy would be responsible for "coordinating policy responses to world environmental problems." The council would also ensure that all federal agencies establish criteria "to minimize the impact of federal policies on the world environment." To underscore the importance of global warming and other global environmental threats, the bill "authorizes the President to appoint an ambassador to represent the United States in negotiations relevant to global environmental issues."

The Gore bill, like the other global warming bills, includes specific statutory provisions for the phasing out of chlorofluorocarbons. The bill also emphasizes the need to control methane emissions. Methane is one of the most potent global warming gases and many scientists believe it will pose a greater threat than CO_2 by the middle of the next century. The bill directs the administrator of the EPA to report on "the contribution of methane gas to global climate change" and to find "new methods of controlling methane emissions."

Interestingly enough none of the global warming legislation has addressed the issue of cattle and global warming head-on. The world's 1.2 billion cattle emit approximately 100 million tons of methane, or 20 percent of all the methane released into the atmosphere. The United States is the number one beef-producing nation in the world and the largest consumer of beef products. Members of Congress have been reluctant to suggest a curtailment in beef production for fear of raising the ire of the powerful cattle and

Think Globally, Act Locally

- In 1990, the state of Connecticut passed into law the first global warming legislation in the nation. The legislation "prevents electrical utilities from supplying new or renovated buildings with electric heating after 1993 unless they have been analyzed for compliance with energy efficiency standards." A key provision of the act allows state regulators to charge higher utility rates to owners or occupants of buildings that waste energy.

- The state of Massachusetts passed a bill to reduce the greenhouse effect. The legislation includes a provision that would "provide developers of large new projects with financial incentives (bonuses and assessments) to design their buildings in an energy-efficient manner." The bill would also "encourage energy conservation measures in homes through a home energy rating system that would single out the most energy-efficient homes for special distinction, and encourage more favorable mortgage terms for these homes."

- The World Congress of Local Governments for a Sustainable Future has initiated an urban CO_2 project to reduce global warming emissions. Ten major world cities, including cities in the United States, will work together to achieve a 20 to 25 percent reduction in CO_2 emissions. The cities will evaluate innovations in "land use planning, energy, transportation, waste management, construction practices, and education" with an eye toward significantly reducing CO_2 emissions in the years ahead.

• • •

beef-industry lobbies. Then too, beef consumption and especially hamburger consumption is a way of life in America, and few members of Congress are willing to be branded "antibeef."

The World Environment Policy Act also includes provisions covering fuel efficiency standards for automobiles, the imposition of a gas-guzzler tax, environmental guidelines covering World Bank loans, a sophisticated recycling initiative, and protocols governing the conservation of tropical forests. The latest version of the bill even contains a provision urging the "Nobel Commission to consider awarding a Nobel Prize for achievements in preservation of the world's environment."

Sen. Timothy Wirth (D-CO) introduced his own global warming bill, entitled the National Energy Policy Act, in the 101st Congress. The bill passed the Senate, but the House version, introduced by **Rep. Les AuCoin (D-OR)**, was not brought to a vote. Wirth reintroduced his bill in the 102nd Congress in 1991. The Wirth bill contains tough new guidelines governing energy efficiency standards in federal buildings, setting an example for the commercial and residential sectors. The bill sets a "deadline by which each federal agency must install energy conservation measures in its federal buildings."

The Wirth bill is particularly innovative on the issue of technology transfer. It directs the Secretary of Energy to "expand the transfer of energy efficient and renewable energy technologies to lesser developed countries; and promote the development of such technologies in those countries." Wirth's bill sets a goal of 20 percent reduction of CO_2 emission levels by the year 2000.

On the other hand, the bill also contains a provision calling on the Secretary of Energy to "report to Congress on the extent to which nuclear fission generated electricity can safely and reliably supply electricity and reduce greenhouse gases." Most environmental groups oppose any government effort to revive nuclear research and development in the fight to reduce global warming. So, while the Wirth legislation contains many admirable provisions, his inclusion of nuclear power makes the bill unacceptable from a Green perspective.

Sen. Patrick Leahy (D-VT), introduced still another global warming bill in the 101st Congress entitled the Global Environmental Protection Act. While his bill included similar provisions on nuclear power, it placed special emphasis on federal lands protection. The bill would require the federal government "to undertake a systematic and comprehensive survey of all federal lands and structures . . . to ascertain their vulnerability to changes associated with global environmental changes."

In two follow-up bills introduced in the same session of Congress, Leahy zeroed in on agriculture and forestry policies. One bill would "develop a program to determine potential impacts of cli-

No Nukes

In June 1989, at a congressional hearing on global warming and alternative energy technologies, Bill Keepin of the Rocky Mountain Institute presented the results of a study analyzing the feasibility of nuclear power as an energy source. His findings shatter any illusion that nuclear proponents might entertain about the prospects of a nuclear future. According to the study, even under optimal conditions—including quick construction and minimum cost —it would be necessary to construct a new 1,000 megawatt nuclear power plant "every 1.6 to 2.4 days for the next 38 years" to meet electricity demands worldwide. A massive construction schedule of this scale would cost trillions of dollars and would bankrupt civilization well before the switch was triggered on a majority of the plants. And even if all the fossil fuel–burning plants were replaced with nuclear plants, it would only reduce global emissions by approximately 7 percent since fossil fuel–burning plants are responsible for only a small part of the worldwide emission load.

• • •

mate on agriculture and forestry" and help American agriculture develop new programs to cope with the problems brought on by global warming. The bill mandates establishment of an Office of Climate Change inside the U.S. Department of Agriculture "to coordinate policy, planning, research, and response strategies relating to climate change issues." The Secretary of Agriculture is directed to conduct specific studies on: (1) the effects of global warming on rice production; (2) the effects of global warming on major U.S. crops; (3) methane emissions from irrigated rice production; (4) emissions from nitrogen-intensive crops; and (5) forest emissions. The bill also "amends the Forest and Rangelands Renewable Resources Research Act of 1978 to include the effects of weather, climate, and air pollution on forests and rangelands."

The other Leahy bill strengthens U.S. assistance in tropical forestry and energy efficiency and focuses "on those key . . . developing countries that could have a substantial impact on reducing greenhouse gas emissions."

"A 4-degree rise in average temperature could cut rice production in half. Because rice is the staff of life for 70 percent of the world's population, global warming could devastate the world's food supply and result in widespread hunger and famine."

—Sen. Patrick Leahy (D-VT)

Other global warming bills have pursued different avenues. Sen. Max Baucus' (D-MT) bill, the Global Environmental Protection Act of 1989, contains many of the same provisions as the other proposed legislation, with some interesting exceptions. The bill directs the EPA to promulgate standards requiring a 25 to 35 percent reduction in CO_2 emissions by the year 2000 in the cement, iron and steel, pulp and paper, and synthetic fiber manufacturing industries. The bill also requires that all new homes be equipped with furnaces, air-conditioning, and hot water heaters that satisfy "the carbon dioxide emission limitation achieved by the best available residential control technology."

"Not many Americans realize that we are adding 6.14 tons of CO_2 to our atmosphere per person every year in America as a result of our electrical generating, refining, transportation, and manufacturing processes. . . . In Japan . . . comparable emissions are only 2.5 tons per person, less than half of our emissions."

—Rep. Jim Cooper (D-TN)

A CARBON TAX

In 1988, the Prime Ministers of Norway and Canada proposed a "law of the air" treaty to protect the atmosphere from global warming and ozone depletion. The two countries suggested that a world atmosphere fund be established, financed by a tax on fossil fuels consumption in the industrial countries. The money accrued would, in turn, be used to help finance energy efficiency programs, the transition to renewable energy sources, and the research and development of alternatives to chlorofluorocarbons (CFCs).

Rep. Fortney (Pete) Stark (D-CA) introduced a carbon tax bill in the House to the applause of many environmentalists and the ringing condemnation of the oil, coal, and natural gas lobbies. The bill calls for a tax to be levied against producers or importers of primary fossil fuels to encourage energy conservation and a movement toward renewable energy technologies. According to Stark, "the carbon tax is estimated to bring in $7 billion in the first year growing by $7 billion per year. When phased in over 5 years, the carbon tax will bring in $35 billion per year with a 5-year revenue total of $105 billion. This will go a long way toward dealing with federal red ink."

The "White House Effect"

During the 1988 presidential election campaign, George Bush remarked "those who think we are powerless to do anything about the 'Greenhouse effect' are forgetting about the 'White House effect.' " The then-Vice President promised that upon his election, he would make global warming a top priority of the new Administration. After taking office, the President reneged on his campaign promise, effectively sabotaging efforts to develop a concerted national and international response to the greenhouse effect. Former White House Chief of Staff John Sununu publicly questioned the conclusions of every major scientific organization in the world on the issue of global warming, including the U.S. National Academy of Sciences, the National Oceanic and Atmospheric Research Institute, the World Meteorological Organization, the National Aeronautics and Space Administration, and the government's own Department of Energy national laboratories. Sununu argued that global warming is still largely conjecture and requires more study, but no action of any consequence.

While other industrial nations, including Japan, Germany,

© M. WUERKER.

Canada, France, Great Britain, Italy, Sweden, the Netherlands, and Australia, all announced specific plans to cut greenhouse gas emissions over the coming decade, the United States stands alone among the industrial powers in refusing to take remedial measures —this despite the fact that the United States is the leading contributor to global warming.

In 1990, at our international conference on global warming hosted by President Bush in Washington and attended by world leaders from many nations, the White House distributed a confidential briefing memo to its own delegates entitled "Debates to Avoid." The memo warned not "to discuss whether there is or is not warming, or how much or how little warming. In the eyes of the public we will lose this debate. A better approach is to raise the many uncertainties that need to be better understood on this issue." When asked if the President had reversed himself on his earlier commitment to address global warming, presidential spokesman Marlin Fitzwater said, "The people who think this is a problem that needs to be solved today don't understand it. They're wrong." Asked about Bush's pledge to use the "White House effect," Fitzwater replied, "I don't know if he said those words during the campaign, but if so, he changed his mind."

WORKERS VS. THE ENVIRONMENT

Environmental issues like global warming have often pitted workers against environmentalists. Over the years, many important environmental bills have been defeated or seriously compromised because of organized opposition by labor unions, corporate management, and local communities adversely affected by the imposition of environmental safeguards. The conflict between labor and environmentalists has been particularly contentious over proposed legislation to protect the atmosphere from pollutants, including greenhouse gases. Now, some members of Congress are beginning to draft legislation to bridge the gap between workers and environmentalists. They argue, with justification, that workers should not be unfairly singled out and made to suffer for environmental problems over which they have little or no control. Indeed, many labor union leaders argue that workers and their families are likely to be the first victims of toxic poisoning and suffer the most from the ill effects of working with or living near dangerous chemicals and other pollutants. Unfortunately, when new environmental legislation mandates changes that result in plant shutdowns or loss of jobs, these same workers and their families become victims a second time. After being exposed to polluted work environments for years, they suddenly find themselves without jobs, forced onto unemployment lines or the public dole. They are generally abandoned by the larger community and the government.

The newly emerging Green consciousness extends traditional environmental sensibilities to include the economic well-being of workers and their communities. In the new scheme of things, the environment is perceived as the total community that sustains human, animal, and plant life. Preserving the economic well-being

A Superfund for Workers

"Many workers see the growing environmental clashes and they are angry and frustrated. They hold deep pro-environmentalist convictions. But none can advocate the elimination of his or her job. If they switched jobs they would have to cut their income in half, and probably lose all their benefits. Not many families can afford to do that. They do not like being exposed on the job and they do not like what their facilities are doing to the environment. But they are not about to commit economic suicide. . . . I have had the great fortune to travel around the country and promote a discussion of . . . a Superfund for Workers. This concept—which calls for full pay and benefits and tuition for any workers losing their job for environmental reasons—has been positively received. . . . I have watched our older members who served in World War II, in Korea, recognize the roots of this proposal in the GI Bill of Rights. They remember that our society was capable of reconverting itself after the war and finding the funds to provide income and education for millions of returning soldiers. . . .

"Our younger workers with families see a different part of this vision. . . . They see it as a way to escape from the toxic filled world of traditional work. They are hungry for the chance to enter colleges and gain access to a new kind of work. They would jump at the chance to get paid to go to school. . . .

"Our vision entails a substantial pool of capital to fund this transition. Clearly, we are talking about tens of billions of dollars. But we know that the money is there. It is amazing how easily $500 billion is found to pay for the profligate practices of the savings and loan pirates . . . we certainly should be able to treat our working people as well. . . ."

—*Anthony Mazzocchi,*
Secretary/Treasurer,
Oil, Chemical and Atomic
Workers' International Union

of working people and their families is as important as preserving the well-being of the ecosystems in which they live.

Sen. Robert Byrd (D-WV) and **Rep. Robert Wise (D-WV)** both introduced provisions to deal with worker displacement expected to result from the implementation of the Clean Air Act of 1990.

Sen. Byrd's proposed legislation would "minimize the effects on individuals employed as coal mine workers who are terminated from their employment as a result of the enactment into law of the provisions . . . of the Clean Air Act." The proposal, which provides for up to four years of employment compensation as well as additional compensation while engaged in retraining or educational programs, was defeated in the Senate by a vote of 50 to 49.

Rep. Wise offered an amendment to the Clean Air bill—which passed by a vote of 274 to 146—that "would extend unemployment benefits by up to six months and provide up to two years of retraining for workers who suffer unemployment or a reduction of wages as a consequence of the implementation of the bill's provisions." The program would be funded at $50 million per year for a five-year period.

Ironically, President Bush initially opposed the Wise amendment, threatening to veto Clean Air legislation if it were included. This from the man who said during the campaign:

"I want to be known as the environmental President. I also want to be concerned about a person's ability to hold a job and have a job. The jobs of many thousands of people . . . in whole communities are at stake."

Later, during conference negotiations, Bush backed down, realizing that Congress was adamant about providing for displaced workers. A modified version of the Wise amendment was finally incorporated into the clean air legislation and was signed into law by the President.

The Wise and Byrd proposals are harbingers of a new commitment to incorporate the needs of workers into environmental legislation.

GLOBAL WARMING: THE GREEN VOTE

☑ Reduce CO_2 emissions by at least 20 percent by the year 2000 through energy conservation programs and switch to renewable sources of energy.

☑ Require the Secretary of Agriculture to accelerate the government's tree-planting program in the United States. Instruct the Secretary of State to promote tropical forestry conservation programs in developing nations.

☑ Appoint an ambassador to represent the United States in negotiations on global warming.

☑ Establish federal standards governing energy conservation in all federal buildings and facilities and all new homes and offices.

☑ Encourage the transfer of energy efficient and renewable energy technologies to developing nations.

☑ Impose a carbon tax on producers and importers of primary fossil fuels to encourage conservation and a shift to renewable sources of energy.

☑ Extend unemployment benefits, financial assistance, and training for workers displaced as a consequence of implementing global warming legislation, the Clean Air Act, and other environmental laws.

Restoring the Ozone Layer

"Mr. President, the air in this historic chamber all of us in here now are breathing into our lungs, has over six times as many chlorine atoms as it did 40 years ago when this chamber was built or, for that matter, 3 billion years ago in this particular spot on the surface of the earth. It is not surprising that in a period of only 40 years, the air everywhere on earth could be changed so dramatically as to increase the concentration of a basic element—chlorine—by 600 percent . . . because 40 years ago, we began using a new family of chemicals called chlorofluorocarbons. . . . It is these chlorine atoms in the stratosphere which are responsible for eating away a hole in the ozone layer above Washington, D.C., Tennessee, West Virginia, China [and] everywhere else on the face of the earth."

—Sen. Albert Gore (D-TN)

In 1985, scientists discovered a vast hole in the ozone layer over the Antarctic. Ozone in the upper atmosphere serves as a protective shield, blocking excessive amounts of harmful ultraviolet radiation from penetrating the earth. Researchers soon discovered that man-made chemicals known as chlorofluorocarbons (CFCs)—already identified as potent global warming gases—were responsible for destroying the ozone. The CFCs migrate to the upper atmosphere where they are broken down by the sun's rays, releasing atoms of chlorine, which, in turn, destroy ozone.

DEADLY RAYS

By 1987, the loss of ozone had increased to 60 percent over the Antarctic. More troubling, scientists discovered still another hole in the ozone over the mid-northern hemisphere. The National Aeronautics and Space Administration (NASA) went on to predict a 10 percent depletion in the ozone layer worldwide by the year 2050. The Environmental Protection Agency (EPA) warned that a loss of ozone of that magnitude would result in millions of additional cases of skin cancers annually from exposure to increased amounts of ultraviolet radiation. The statistics are numbing. Melanoma, an often fatal form of skin cancer, will increase from 31,000 to 126,000 cases, with 7,000 to 30,000 more deaths. Common skin cancers will increase from 3 to 5 million additional cases, with 52,000 to 252,000 more deaths. Eye cataracts will increase between 555,000 to 2.8 million additional cases.

Ultraviolet radiation also damages the immune systems of animals and humans making them more vulnerable to outbreaks of long-established diseases as well as new pathogens. According to the EPA, the cost in medical bills could exceed a cumulative total of $3.5 trillion by the mid twenty-first century.

Ultraviolet radiation also endangers plants. At the University of Maryland, botanist Alan Teramura, found that excessive ultraviolet radiation resulted in tissue and cell damage in two thirds of the two hundred plant species he tested. According to one recent study conducted at the University of Oregon, a 15 percent reduction in atmospheric ozone by the year 2050 could cause crop losses in excess of $2.5 billion a year in the United States alone.

Increased ultraviolet radiation is likely to have the most harmful effect on plankton, the microscopic marine organisms that are the base of the ocean food chain. A recent study in the Antarctic reported serious ultraviolet radiation damage to plankton, raising questions about the survival of aquatic life in the world's oceans.

TOO LITTLE, TOO LATE

World leaders were sufficiently alarmed by the revelations concerning ozone depletion that they signed an international treaty in 1987, called the Montreal Protocol, which mandated a worldwide phaseout of some of the more dangerous CFCs. The protocol initially called for a 20 percent reduction in the use of CFCs, by 1994 and a 50 percent reduction by 1999. In 1990, however, the protocol was revised to accelerate the CFC phaseout. Currently, the international agreement calls for a 100 percent ban on the production and use of CFCs by the year 2000. The United States is a party to the Montreal protocol; President Bush agreed to the accelerated phase-out in 1990.

Environmental scientists have warned repeatedly that the phase-out schedule being set is still too slow and that many CFC chemicals that should be on the phase-out list are not included at all. The warnings have proved justified. Government officials and the public were shocked by new scientific findings released in 1991 by the National Aeronautics and Space Administration (NASA) showing that the ozone layer is disappearing twice as fast as previously believed. According to Robert Watson, the director of the ozone program for NASA, the ozone layer worldwide is now depleting at a phenomenal rate of 8 percent per decade, whereas earlier estimates in 1988 had shown ozone decreasing at 2 to 4 percent per decade. Watson said that losses of 3 to 4 percent persist over most of North America through late May every year, posing a direct and immediate threat to all life on the continent.

EPA officials now admit that the Montreal Protocol, even as amended, is woefully inadequate to deal with the enormity of the environmental crisis unfolding in the wake of ozone loss. Eileen Claussen, director of EPA's atmospheric program, acknowledged that "even after you do all the things we've agreed to do [in the Montreal Protocol] you still, over the next 50 years or so, end up

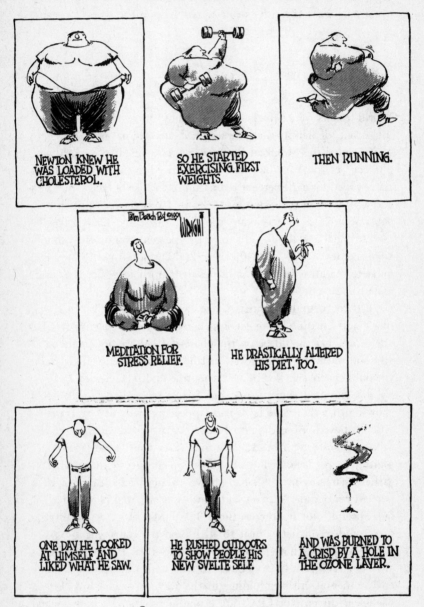

© DON WRIGHT, THE PALM BEACH POST.

with another 12 million skin cancer cases and another 210,000 deaths."

A RACE AGAINST TIME

Several members of Congress have proposed legislation to address the crisis. Some of the bills have been tough and uncompromising, reflecting the critical nature of this unfolding environmental catastrophe. Unfortunately, the chemical industry, aided and abetted by the White House, has put every conceivable obstacle in the way of an accelerated timetable. The chemical companies have argued that they need more time to phase in substitutes to CFCs and warned that any speedup in the schedule would hurt the economy. While their voice has prevailed at The White House, some members of Congress, including those of President Bush's own party, have continued to push their colleagues to act before it's too late and the damage becomes irreversible.

In 1989, **Sen. John Chafee (R-RI)** introduced the Stratospheric Ozone and Climate Protection Act in the 101st Congress in order to speed up the timetable for the complete phaseout of the five most damaging chlorofluorocarbons. Chafee's bill called for a 20 percent reduction in the use of CFCs by 1992, a 50 percent reduction by 1995, and a complete elimination by 1997.

The bill would have prohibited the release or venting of any CFCs into the open atmosphere after January 1, 1993. Strict provisions governing the recapture, recycling, and safe disposal of CFCs are mandated. To encourage other nations to follow suit, the Chafee bill would ban the importation of ozone-depleting chemicals and any products "made with or containing such chemicals."

In introducing the comprehensive legislation, Chafee warned his colleagues that "nothing less than total elimination of these harmful chemicals will suffice. We need a crash program to find and use safe substitutes as quickly as possible. We have a crisis on our hands and business as usual will not be tolerated."

In the House of Representatives, **Rep. Jim Bates (D-CA)** introduced similar hard-hitting legislation during the 101st Congress. Bates reminded his colleagues that if the current timetable is adhered to—calling for a phaseout of CFCs by the year 2000—the several intervening years of delay "would mean that peak ozone destruction would persist for another fifty years."

Frustrated over government inaction, internecine party politics, and the influence exerted by corporate lobbies in Washington, municipalities seized the initiative on the ozone issue under the banner "think globally, act locally." Irvine, California, and Newark, New Jersey, passed "comprehensive bans on the use, sale, and manufacturing of ozone-depleting compounds within their juris-

• • •

THINK GLOBALLY, ACT LOCALLY

On October 4, 1989, Newark, New Jersey, established a comprehensive policy regulating and banning the use of ozone-depleting compounds within its municipal jurisdiction. The ordinance:

- bars the sale, purchase or use of food-packaging materials made with any ozone-depleting substance
- bars the manufacturing use of any ozone-depleting substance
- bars installation of building insulation containing any ozone-depleting compounds
- requires refrigeration and air conditioner repair and recycling facilities to capture and recycle ozone-depleting CFCs
- bars the retail sale of ozone-depleting coolants for refrigeration or air-conditioning units
- restricts use of Halon fire extinguishers in testing or firefighting training to instances required by law or to those with proper city permits
- imposes fines up to $1000 for each violation, and each additional day of noncompliance

dictions." Albuquerque, New Mexico, passed an ordinance "requiring the recycling of CFCs in auto air conditioners and refrigeration units." In Kalamazoo, Michigan, the city established "a refrigeration roundup program to collect used refrigerators, recover the CFCs for recycling, then sell the old refrigerators for scrap."

Some state governments have been equally aggressive. Maryland grants a 100 percent tax credit to gas stations that purchase CFC-recycling equipment. Hawaii, Maine, New York, and Vermont passed laws barring the sale of auto air conditioners containing CFCs starting in 1993.

Vermont's action, the first state initiative against ozone depleting chemicals used in automobile air conditioners, sent a powerful message across the country. State legislators, not often known for their courage, were suddenly willing to buck powerful corporate interests in matters of grave environmental import. Some members of Congress became emboldened by the local and state initiatives. Both **Sen. James Jeffords (R-VT)** and **Sen. John Kerry (D-MA)** introduced bills into Congress calling for a ban on the sale of any automobile containing an air conditioner using CFCs. This proposed ban was more than a symbolic gesture. According to the World Resources Institute, 450 million tons of CFCs were purchased worldwide in 1985. Over 75 million tons of the total chemical production was used in automobile air conditioners.

Other bills were introduced in Congress to place an excise tax on manufacturers of ozone-depleting chemicals in an effort to pressure the companies to shift to alternatives. A bill introduced by **Rep. Fortney Stark (D-CA)** would place an excise tax on any ozone-depleting chemical sold or used by manufacturers. A tax would also be levied on any substance sold or used by an importer "if its manufacture or production included the use of any ozone depleting chemical." **Sen. Albert Gore (D-TN)** introduced a bill stipulating that the revenue accrued from the excise tax be placed in a special Ozone Layer Conservation Trust Fund "for developing chemical and technological alternatives to ozone depleting chemicals. . . ."

Sen. Gore also introduced several other innovative bills designed to grapple with the ozone-depletion crisis. The most controversial called for the authorization of funds to be used "for the purpose of assisting developing nations in their efforts to comply with the Montreal Protocol." The signatories to the Montreal Protocol had recognized that the burden of addressing the ozone problem had to be equitably shared among nations. The United States is responsible for more than 20 percent of the total global emissions. Other wealthy industrial nations contribute much of the rest. Yet the consequences of ozone depletion are felt throughout the biosphere.

While all of the industrial nations agreed to the establishment of a development fund to help the poorer nations introduce substitutes for CFCs, and the Senate overwhelmingly approved a U.S. funding contribution of $25 million a year for three years, the White House nixed the plan. Only after intense pressure by European allies, including then Prime Minister Margaret Thatcher of Britain, did Bush relent and agree to contribute the United States' fair share to the global fund.

Rep. Stark has also introduced legislation to label all products that contain CFCs or that have used CFCs in the production process. Stark argues that consumers have the right to know what they're buying so as to be able to make informed choices. He hopes that product labeling will spur environmentally conscious consumers to seek alternatives to CFCs in their purchases.

The Congress bowed to Administration and industry pressure in 1990, passing a weak CFC phase-out plan as part of the Clean Air Act. This plan will phase out CFCs by the year 2000 (allowing their continued use for three to five years longer than the bills previously described). Three halons and carbon tetrachloride will also be phased out under the slower timetable. Methyl chloroform production will be phased out by 2002. Hydrochlorofluorocarbons, chemicals that are less ozone depleting than CFCs, but still damaging, will have their production levels frozen in 2015 and will not be phased out until 2030. The bill also includes serious loopholes. For example, exceptions are allowed for CFCs, halons, and carbon tetrachloride for "certain exports to developing nations." The President is also allowed to make exceptions for national security purposes.

Despite the overwhelming threats that ozone depletion poses to the biosphere and the security of present and future generations, the White House and industry have been determined to place narrow geopolitical and commercial interests above even the fate of the earth, demonstrating their lack of understanding of the grave realities confronting human civilization and the planet we live on.

RESTORING THE OZONE LAYER: THE GREEN VOTE

☑ Phase out all chlorofluorocarbons, halons, methyl chloroforms, tetrachloride, hydrochlorofluorocarbons, and other ozone-depleting chemicals by 1997.

☑ Impose an excise tax on the manufacturers of ozone-depleting chemicals to encourage producers to shift to alternatives.

☑ Establish a fund to assist developing nations in their efforts to switch from ozone-depleting chemicals to safe substitutes.

☑ Label all products that contain CFCs or that have used CFCs in the production process to encourage Green consumers to seek alternatives in their purchases.

ENERGY ADDICTION

"The energy bill for the U.S. amounts to 11% of the U.S. Gross National Product. By contrast the energy bill in Japan amounts to only 5% of the country's Gross National Product."

—Lawrence Berkeley Laboratories Study, 1987

Fossil fuels are the lifeblood of the modern age. The entire industrial infrastructure runs by the grace of the carbon tars of an earlier era. The United States is the largest consumer of fossil fuels in the world. With about 5 percent of the world's population, the United States is currently using up 24 percent of the total commercially produced energy consumed in the world. In 1987, the United States consumed 75 quadrillion BTUs of energy—more than Canada, the United Kingdom, France, Japan, Italy, West Germany, and the Netherlands combined. When U.S. energy consumption is compared to that of developing nations, the differences are even more compelling. For example, in Haiti, energy consumption per capita is 68 pounds of coal per year, while the per capita consumption of energy in the United States is equivalent to 23,000 pounds of coal per year.

Americans not only use more fossil fuel energy than any other people in the world; we also waste more energy. Americans use twice as much energy per capita as many other industrial nations. Fossil fuel energy is hemorrhaging through the American infrastructure, spilling out and overflowing in every sector.

Now, in the wake of the Gulf War and the increasingly grim projections about global warming, some members of Congress are beginning to turn their attention to the issue of energy conservation and alternative energy technologies. Many elected officials are angry over the years of intransigence in the 1980s when the Reagan administration systematically gutted important energy conservation programs begun during the first energy crisis in the 1970s. The national effort to become energy self-sufficient, which had made significant progress in the last year of the Carter administration, was cast aside during the Reagan years. Energy conservation programs were abandoned. So too were the many programs aimed at developing renewable resources and other alternative energy technologies. By the end of the 1980s, the United States found itself more dependent on foreign oil than it was before the OPEC oil embargos. Meanwhile, previous gains in energy efficiency had leveled off or, in some instances, were showing reversals. The Reagan and Bush administrations focused their attention on increased domestic fossil fuel production, even championing the opening up of pristine wildlife refuges in Alaska and increased offshore oil drilling.

By the time Saddam Hussein invaded Kuwait, the United States was once again virtually dependent on Mideast oil and prepared to commit tens of billions of dollars and the lives of half a million men and women to insure a steady oil supply. Ironically, any one of a number of legislative initiatives to conserve energy might have made it unnecessary to send troops to defend U.S. oil interests in the Middle East. For example, had the Congress and the White House simply raised fuel efficiency standards on American automobiles from 27 miles per gallon to 40 miles per gallon during the 1980s, the United States would not have to rely on a single gallon of oil from the Middle East today.

The Green contingent in Congress is emphasizing energy conservation, increased energy efficiency, and renewable energy technologies over increased production of fossil fuels and expansion of nuclear power to solve America's energy needs in the coming decades. Their enthusiasm for Green alternatives has been spawned, in part, by public pressure. According to a 1991 national opinion survey, seven out of ten Americans believe that immediate action

BY PERMISSION OF MIKE LUCKOVICH AND CREATORS SYNDICATE.

RUNNING OUT OF FOSSIL FUEL

According to a study conducted by the Complex Systems Research Center at the University of New Hampshire, between 1995 and the year 2005 the United States will be using more energy to explore for new oil and gas deposits than the wells produce. By the year 2020 the United States will have exhausted its remaining oil and gas reserves. By 2025 nearly 88 percent of the world's oil and gas supplies will be effectively depleted.

• • •

should be taken to curb global warming and said they would be willing to pay $11 more per month for fossil fuels to reduce energy use and carbon emissions. By a three-to-two margin those polled said they favor a 10-cents-per-gallon gas tax, with the proceeds earmarked for an environmental trust fund. Six out of ten Americans favor a gas-guzzler tax and nine out of ten support reestablishing tax credits for consumers who opt for using solar, wind, and other alternative energy technologies. Many of the new bills being introduced in Congress reflect the growing Green awareness on the part of American voters.

SETTING AN EXAMPLE

The federal government is the largest single consumer of energy in the United States, spending 8.7 billion dollars on fuel in 1989. Nearly 3.5 billion of that total was spent on energy in buildings. Federal agencies have also been the most negligent of any sector in introducing energy conservation measures. The Alliance to Save Energy, a public interest group in Washington, estimates that "in 1989 industry averaged $7,000 in expenditures per building on energy conservation while the federal government only averaged $90 per building."

Rep. Philip Sharp (D-IN) has introduced a bill that would require federal agencies to retrofit their facilities. Under this proposal, "agencies which do not meet the requirements will be prevented from spending funds on construction or acquisition of buildings." Sharp's bill also provides cash bonuses that "reward agency personnel that do outstanding jobs of improving energy efficiency." Another Sharp bill establishes a deadline by which "all federally owned and leased space under construction must meet federal building standards for energy efficiency."

Sen. Arlen Specter (R-PA) has joined Sharp and others in the Congress pushing for greater energy conservation within the federal government. He introduced his own energy conservation bill, which, among other things, calls for the creation of "a $500 million revolving fund . . . to be established to assist federal agencies in implementation of their [energy saving] plans." **Rep. Jan Meyers (R-KS)** introduced a companion bill in the House.

Sen. Joseph Lieberman (D-CT) offered his own bill to address the need for energy conservation within federal agencies. Many of the suggestions mirror those introduced by others, including **Sen. John Glenn (D-OH)** and **Sen. John Chafee (R-RI)**.

Lieberman points to the tremendous dollar savings that would accrue in a systematic federal effort to conserve energy. According to Lieberman, "a 25% reduction in federal energy consumption can save the taxpayer $1 billion a year." The Department of Energy projects that an initial investment of $336 million dollars in federal energy-conservation programs over five years would result in a potential payback in energy savings of $32 billion over twenty years; or a savings of one hundred dollars for every dollar of investment.

GETTING ALONG ON LESS

While many bills focus on energy savings inside the federal government, others have addressed a need for energy savings in the private sector, especially in housing. Worldwide, homes and apartments use up one sixth of the total energy output, or more energy than is produced in the Middle East in a single year. The average American home uses up the energy equivalent of 1,253 gallons of oil at a cost of $1,123 each year. Altogether, U.S. homes and apartments spew more than 770 million tons of CO_2 into the atmosphere each year operating space and water heaters, appliances, lighting, air-conditioning and refrigeration units, and the like.

Currently, less than 40 percent of the 12 million houses that use oil heat have been retrofitted with energy efficient oil burners, despite the fact that retrofitting saves approximately 16 percent on energy bills.

According to an article published in *Scientific American,* the technology is now available to construct energy efficient buildings that would save enough energy in fifty years to avoid building "85 power plants, and the equivalent of two Alaskan pipelines." A rigorous national campaign to improve energy efficiency in the home, office, industry, and on the road could reduce the national energy bill from $400 billion to $270 billion and greatly reduce the emission of CO_2 and other greenhouse gases into the atmosphere. Yet, as former Congresswoman Claudine Schneider pointed

---

THINK GLOBALLY, ACT LOCALLY

- Minneapolis has initiated a program called "Operation Insulation," which provides free home consultation for major weatherization retrofits. A fixed fee for work needed is set by the city, and the city contracts with contractors to install the insulation.

- Santa Monica launched an "Energy Fitness Program" to provide "door-to-door energy audits and installation of low-cost weatherization devices." In one year, the city conducted over 12,000 audits and installed thousands of weatherization devices. The program saved more than $314,000 in utility bills for the homes covered.

- San Francisco has passed ordinances covering both residential and commercial energy conservation retrofits. More than 25,000 residential units have already been retrofitted. The retrofitting of commercial buildings has saved San Francisco businesses more than $50 million dollars in energy costs in the first five years of the program.

- The State of Washington has enacted a new housing code that requires new houses under construction to be more than twice as efficient as homes built under the State's 1977 code.

- Iowa requires its utilities to spend between 1.5 and 2 percent of their operating revenues on energy conservation programs.

—Local Government Commission Report

• • •

out at congressional hearings on the greenhouse effect, "less than 2% of the upwards of $50 billion per year in federal energy subsidies goes to promote greater reliance on energy efficiency."

Rep. Philip Sharp (D-IN) and **Sens. Timothy Wirth (D-CO)** and **Arlen Specter (R-PA)** are among those who have made legislative proposals to tighten energy conservation standards for homes, commercial buildings, and offices. Sen. Wirth's proposal calls on the Secretary of Housing and Urban Development to promulgate energy efficiency standards for all federally assisted housing. Sen. Specter has introduced legislation that would require the

Secretary of Energy to establish "an insulation value rating system for homes and commercial windows and require that all windows display a label disclosing the rating of the window." Specter's bill also includes "measures to require the establishment of home energy rating systems and financing incentives to encourage construction of energy efficient homes."

After mortgage payments and/or rental costs, energy costs represent the largest expense for home owners and renters—averaging 20 percent of the cost of housing. Unfortunately, most home buyers or prospective renters have no way of accurately measuring the energy efficiency of houses despite the fact that buying a home is the largest single purchase for most American families. These new legislative initiatives would help home buyers and renters make intelligent choices using energy conservation standards as a key determinant in their purchasing decisions.

THE POOR SUFFER THE MOST

Energy considerations are even more important for low-income families because their energy bill often makes up over one third of their entire housing expense. **Representatives Philip Sharp (D-IN)** and **Cardiss Collins (D-IL)** have introduced legislation to address the special needs of low-income families. Collins' bill directs the Secretary of Housing and Urban development to "establish public housing energy conservation performance standards." Sharp's bill "mandates that states participating in the low income Weatherization Assistance Program ensure that: (1) Weatherization assistance benefits accrue primarily to low income tenants; (2) Such tenants are not subjected to rental increases unless they are demonstrably unrelated to weatherization measures." Sharp's bill would also have the federal government pay part of the cost of making schools and hospitals more energy efficient.

According to recent studies, a national program of home energy conservation could slash our national housing costs by a staggering $25 billion a year. The Alliance to Save Energy estimates that if the steps outlined in these various congressional bills were adopted into law, the energy savings alone would allow 250,000 additional families to become home owners for the first time, and allow more than 2 million low-income renters to pay their monthly housing bills. The energy savings of these measures would be equivalent to 400 million barrels of oil.

It All Adds Up

Heating and cooling costs are only part of the energy equation inside the home. For the most part, home appliances manufactured and sold in the United States are energy guzzlers and add to the energy bill of every family and the collective energy bill of the nation. Several years ago the Congress passed a national appliance energy conservation act requiring major appliances to be 15 to 25 percent more energy efficient in 1990 than they were in 1985. The legislation, which was vetoed by President Reagan, would have cut consumer energy bills by $28 billion by the year 2000 and eliminated the need to construct 22,000 megawatts of electrical generating capacity—thus, greatly reducing the amount of fossil fuel burned and the amount of CO_2 released into the atmosphere. The bill was passed overwhelmingly by the 101st Congress and finally became law.

Renewable Energy

The dual threat of diminishing fossil fuel deposits and global warming is forcing greater attention on alternative sources of energy. Nothing so divides the new Green politicians from the older generation of elected officials than the question of energy sources. The conventional politicians have, by and large, lined up with the oil companies, the nuclear industry, and the automotive companies in support of increased oil exploration and a greater reliance on nuclear power. The Green-oriented officials, on the other hand, are increasingly touting the advantages of solar, wind, geothermal, and other renewable energy sources that are both less damaging to the environment and sustainable.

Solar and other renewable energy sources now provide more than 8 percent of the energy needs of the United States and could supply more than 20 percent of the nation's energy requirements by the year 2000 and more than 50 percent by the year 2030.

TAKING THE "SOFT PATH"

Several bills have been introduced in Congress to spur the development of "soft path" energy technologies. **Rep. Philip Sharp (D-IN)** and **Sen. Wyche Fowler (D-GA)** introduced the Renewable Energy and Energy Efficiency Technology Competitiveness Act, a modest bill which was passed by Congress and signed into law on December 11, 1989. The law requires the Secretary of Energy to submit to Congress a research and development program to include work on biofuels, hydrogen energy systems, solar buildings energy systems, ocean energy systems, and geothermal energy.

• • •

"The development and marketing of these ["soft-path" energy] technologies can make major contributions to eliminating our trade imbalances—by reducing our need for oil imports and increasing our exports of energy technologies. The potential for marketing photovoltaic devices alone is huge in developing countries.

Many of these resources . . . can provide a virtually inexhaustible energy supply with no adverse effects on the environment. . . . They can stem the greenhouse effect and arrest global warming. They can also lessen our need to turn to nuclear energy. . . . These clean sources of energy will also have direct economic benefits. We can potentially save billions on pollution control, cleanup and health care costs. We can also abate extensive damage to our natural resources—from our farms to our lakes and forests."

—*Sen. Wyche Fowler (D-GA)*

BY PERMISSION OF BOB SCHOCHET.

The legislation also authorizes funds for wind energy research, photovoltaic energy programs, solar-thermal energy, and the like. The law requires the Department of Energy to enter into joint ventures with industry to facilitate the commercial expansion of renewable energy technologies.

Sen. Mark Hatfield (R-OR) and Rep. Ron Wyden (D-OR)

have introduced joint legislation to encourage the export and use of renewable energy technologies in developing nations. The new Green approach to energy assistance to third world nations stands in sharp contrast to the conventional approach favored over the past forty years, with its emphasis on large centralized energy projects, including nuclear power plants and hydroelectric dams. The Hatfield/Wyden bills would amend the Foreign Assistance Act of 1961 to include renewable energy programs under the special projects of the Overseas Private Investment Corporation. The legislation also amends the Export-Import Bank Act and the Small Business Act "to include loans to small businesses for the promotion of renewable energy technology for export. . . ." At least 5 percent of all funding for energy-related projects would have to be given to renewable energy programs. Hatfield's bill further directs the Secretary of the Treasury, the International Monetary Fund, and the Inter-American Development Bank "to provide financing for renewable energy development."

• • •

MONEY TO BE MADE

- "The international market for wind turbines today is roughly $200 million per year and is expected to rise to $1 billion per year by 1994 and $3–6 billion by the year 2000. In the last seven years, however, the share of the U.S. wind machine market captured by foreign imports has gone from 0 to 70%."

- "The international market for photovoltaics is currently $500 million and is expected to increase to $5.4 billion by the year 2010."

—*Rep. Philip Sharp (D-IN)*

Energy: The Green Vote

☑ Require all federal agencies to retrofit their facilities and provide cash bonuses to agency personnel who implement innovative new energy conservation programs.

☑ Promulgate uniform energy efficiency standards for all federally assisted housing. Require the establishment of an energy rating system for all homes so that buyers can make informed choices.

☑ Expand the government's research, development, and commercialization program on alternative energy technologies, including solar, wind, hydrogen, geothermal, and biofuels.

☑ Amend the Export-Import Bank Act and the Small Business Act to include loans to small businesses for the promotion of renewable energy technologies for export. Direct the Secretary of the Treasury, the International Monetary Fund, and the Inter-American Development Bank to provide financing for renewable energy development.

TRANSPORTING AMERICA

Today 34 percent of all American households own one automobile or light truck, 36 percent own two and 16 percent have three or more. Every day 30,000 new drivers and 28,000 new cars are added to the road. Between 1936 and 1985 American automobiles burned over 3 trillion gallons of fuel, making the automobile the largest single consumer of nonrenewable energy in the twentieth century.

Every gallon of gas burned releases 19 pounds of carbon dioxide. In a twelve-month period, the average automobile spews more than 5 tons of CO_2 into the atmosphere. With more than 144 million automobiles and light trucks on American roads today, auto emissions account for 16 percent of all the carbon dioxide emitted into the atmosphere, making the car a primary contributor to global warming.

The automobile is also responsible for 60 percent of the total air pollution in most U.S. cities. Cars emit 69 percent of all the lead, 70 percent of all the carbon monoxide, and are responsible for 60 percent of the ground ozone. Every day 250,000 tons of carbon monoxide, 25,000 tons of hydrocarbons, and 8,000 tons of oxides of nitrogen are spewed out from auto exhausts.

The automobile is the centerpiece of the American transportation system. Its widespread use was made possible by the creation of an innovative highway grid across the United States that was laid down, at the taxpayers' expense, over the past forty years. The Interstate Defense Highway Act, signed into law in the Eisenhower administration, called for the establishment of a network of highways to connect every locale and region together into a single web. Completed in the 1980s, at a cost of $379 billion dollars, it is the greatest public works project in the history of civilization.

The highway culture fundamentally altered the economic, social, and cultural dynamics of the country. It helped create the suburban lifestyle and spawned new commercial innovations including the shopping mall, fast-food restaurants, and industrial office parks. Americans took to the road, ferrying back and forth between home, office, shops, and schools. We became the most traveled people in history.

Today we are paying the real price for our love affair with the automobile. This form of individualized transportation is draining the earth of its remaining fossil fuel reserves and adding massive volumes of carbon to the atmosphere, threatening the future stability of the earth's biosphere and human civilization.

Not surprisingly, the psychology of automobile ownership reflects many of the values of modern society, values that have helped to undermine our sense of relationship and obligation to our fellow human beings and the natural world. The very word *automobile* is a hybrid of the words *autonomous* and *mobile.* In the modern world we have come to value personal autonomy and mobility above all other considerations. We have little allegiance or sense of obligation to "place," preferring always to be "on the go." The idea of being rooted in a community, surrounded by myriad relationships with our fellow human beings and the environment in which we dwell, seems strangely out of place in the fast-paced highway culture.

Automobile ownership brings with it a set of values that are often at odds with the Green vision. Anyone who's ever spent time behind the wheel knows that driving an automobile conveys a sense of power, control, detachment, isolation, and privacy—values that have been used so effectively in the modern age to mold and manipulate nature to suit short-term expedient ends.

The automobile, perhaps more than any other single technology, represents the values of individual self-interest and convenience at the expense of the common good. It's interesting to note that more than half the automobile trips we take are less than 3 miles, a distance that could easily be walked or bicycled in less than an hour. Still, while the car is often used merely as a convenience, it is also often indispensable. Our transportation system is so tied to the automobile and the highway culture that most Americans have little choice but to continue using their cars to commute to work or to shop.

Breaking the hold of the gas-burning automobile and highway culture is an essential task of the new Green politics. Convincing the public to transcend their autonomous mode of private travel and join together in car pools, public transport, bicycling, and walking is an enormous task—part of the psychological reorientation that would be necessary to create a Green consciousness in the United States.

FUEL EFFICIENCY

Some legislators have begun to draw public attention to the automobile culture and the destructive role it plays in undermining the environment and human relationships. In Congress, the battle lines have been drawn around the question of automobile fuel efficiency standards. The automotive industry has systematically opposed congressional efforts to raise the current fuel efficiency standards for cars, arguing that higher standards can only be achieved by reducing the size and weight of automobiles. Industry is launching ambitious advertising and public relations efforts to convince the public that small cars will compromise safety standards. Advocates of higher fuel efficiency standards refute such claims as ill founded and untrue and argue that we have no choice but to increase fuel efficiency if we are to have any chance of dealing with our ongoing dependency on foreign oil and the emerging global warming crisis.

Several bills have been introduced into Congress to raise fuel efficiency standards. In the House, Rep. **Barbara Boxer (D-CA)** has introduced the Motor Vehicle Fuel Efficiency Act with fifty-seven cosponsors. The bill establishes "new average fuel economy standards for passenger automobiles and light trucks" and calls for

---

Safety vs. Fuel Efficiency

When Corporate Average Fuel Economy (CAFE) standards were first passed in 1974, the automobile companies argued, as they do now, that the increase in fuel efficiency standards would mean smaller, less-safe cars. The Ford Motor Company said at the time: "This proposal would require a Ford product line consisting of either all sub-Pinto size vehicles or some mix of vehicles ranging from the sub-subcompact to perhaps a Maverick."

The Chrysler Company argued that the increase in fuel efficiency standards: "would outlaw a number of engine lines and car models, including most full-sized sedans and station wagons."

Their predictions turned out to be false. The companies have also proved wrong on the issue of auto safety. Traffic fatalities have been reduced from 3.5 per hundred million vehicle miles traveled in 1974, just before the first CAFE standards were set, to 2.4 fatalities per hundred million vehicle miles traveled today.

• • •

a 60 percent increase in fuel efficiency over the 1988 standards by the year 2001.

On the Senate side, **Sen. Richard Bryan's (D-NV)** bill to raise fuel efficiency standards has become the lightning rod for the battle between industry and environmentalists over the future of the automobile. The bill would require automobile manufacturers to raise the average fuel economy of their fleets by at least 20 percent above the 1988 average beginning with the 1996 model year and by 40 percent beginning in the model year 2001. These percentage increases translate to an average fuel efficiency of 34 miles per gallon by 1996 and 40 miles per gallon by 2001. Currently the average fuel efficiency is set at 27.5 miles per gallon. If enacted into law the Bryan legislation would save a staggering 49.1 billion gallons of fuel by the year 2001 and would reduce carbon dioxide emissions by 483 million tons.

Upon reintroducing his legislation in 1991, Sen. Bryan made note of America's growing dependence on Mideast oil.

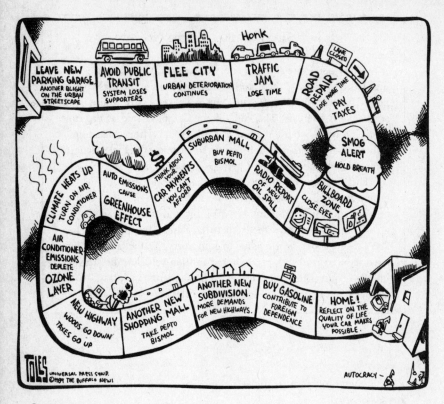

"We now import well over 40 percent of the oil we use, and we import more of our oil from the Persian Gulf than we did at the time of the 1973 embargo."

At the same time, said Bryan,

"The fuel economy of passenger vehicles has declined at a rate of 4 percent in just the last two years."

Bryan and other members of Congress are anxious to wean America off its dependency on Mideast oil. They point out that the new auto fuel efficiency standards being proposed would save more than 2 million barrels of oil per day by the year 2005 "or over four times the amount of oil we imported from Iraq and Kuwait prior to the invasion."

Other innovative bills have been introduced into Congress to encourage greater fuel efficiency and reduce auto emissions. Several members of Congress have proposed a gas-guzzler tax to be imposed on the automobile companies for every gas-guzzling car they produce. **Rep. James Scheuer (D-NY)** has proposed legislation that would make the purchaser of an automobile liable for carbon dioxide emissions. If the buyer's car exceeds the carbon dioxide emissions for its size class, he would have to pay a fee. If, on the other hand, the automobile's carbon dioxide emissions were below the standard set for its size class, the purchaser would receive a rebate.

GROUP TRAVEL

While auto efficiency and emissions standards have taken up a great deal of time and attention in Congress, several members of Congress have also introduced bills to encourage employers and communities to change driving habits, emphasizing carpooling and mass transit. These bills would amend the Internal Revenue Service code to exclude from an individual's gross income employer subsidies for carpooling and mass transit. **Sen. Daniel Moynihan (D-NY)** explained the need for such legislation in a speech on the Senate floor.

> "Current tax law produces a significant bias against the use of mass transit: an employer can provide unlimited free parking to employees without tax consequences to them, but if the same employer wants to provide subway, bus, or other mass transit benefits, any benefit over $15 a month produces a tax liability for the employee. . . . Vanpooling benefits have been fully taxable since 1986 when the statutory exclusion for them was allowed to expire. The juxtaposition of unlimited employee tax benefits for parking and very limited or nonexistent tax benefits for mass transit produces a tax policy encouraging automobile use. . . . Is it fair for a highly paid executive to receive tax-free parking benefits worth as much as $3,000 a year, while a clerical worker owes taxes on transit passes or the value of a ride in a company-provided van pool?"

Moynihan's bill would raise the amount of mass transit benefits that an employer can provide on a tax-free basis from $15 to $60 per month which, according to the sponsor, "is the average cost nationwide for monthly mass transit commuting." Sen. Moynihan's bill would also reinstate the tax-free provision for carpooling provided by an employer. Similar bills have been introduced by Sens. **Alan Cranston (D-CA)** and **William Armstrong (R-CO)** and by Reps. **Thomas Foglietta (D-PA), Robert Matsui (D-CA), Barbara Kennelly (D-CT), Dean Gallo (R-NJ),** and **Charles Rangel (D-NY).**

GREEN TRANSPORTATION

Rep. George Brown (D-CA) and **Sen. John Rockefeller (D-WV)** both introduced bills to establish research and development programs for electric vehicles. Rockefeller's bill would provide financial assistance to electric vehicle demonstration projects. It also authorizes the Secretary of Transportation to "undertake a program of joint ventures with nonfederal persons to accelerate the infrastructure development required to support the use of such vehicles." The National Electric Vehicles Act is aimed at "no less than an automobile revolution" says Rockefeller. To achieve that revolution, the bill covers every step from laboratory research on batteries to the equipping of service stations to service electric vehicles, to cost-shared, on-the-road demonstrations.

RIDING THE RAILS

Despite the commercial success of Amtrak and other regional mass transit systems, the federal government has been reluctant to support research and development aimed at encouraging mass transportation. Now, with the energy crisis and global warming threats becoming more pronounced, legislators are beginning to look to mass transit as a viable alternative to the automobile. **Rep. Bill Green (R-NY)** has introduced a bill that would increase the gasoline tax "for purposes of providing additional revenue for the Mass

THINK GLOBALLY, ACT LOCALLY

- Montgomery County, Maryland, has instituted both developer requirements and a ride-share ordinance to cut down on car trips. Developers must prepare a ten-year trip reduction plan that includes personalized ride-sharing assistance, shuttle van services, transit pass subsidies, and other innovative measures. The ride-share ordinance requires new employers to achieve a specified increase in transit use by their employees. In just one year, the ordinance resulted in a 31 percent increase in the number of carpools, and a nearly 60 percent increase in rail commuters.

- In Bellevue, Washington, developers are required to appoint a "transportation coordinator" to assist employees in securing alternative modes of transportation, including ride sharing and public transit.

• • •

Transit Account in the Highway Trust Fund." The federal excise tax on gasoline would be increased by 10 cents, from 9.1 cents to 19.1 cents per gallon. Three cents of the total increase would be earmarked for the Mass Transit Account of the Highway Trust Fund and 7 cents would go to fund the deficit reduction. The new tax would raise an additional $3 billion for mass transit to assist localities around the country.

Another bill, introduced in the House by **Rep. Al Swift (D-WA)**, would require the Federal Railway Administration "to establish a National High-Speed Rail Transportation Policy to promote the commercialization of high-speed rail transportation systems in the United States." High-speed rail already exists in other industrial nations. Japanese and French high-speed rail systems are already transporting passengers at speeds of 200 to 300 miles per hour. Swift hopes that the United States will join the ranks of the high-speed rail nations by the turn of the century. In the meantime, private investors in Texas have announced plans to go ahead and introduce a high-speed rail system across Texas.

Today some cities in the United States are beginning to restore and rebuild their light rail systems. In the late 1970s Portland, Oregon, made a decision to build a rail system rather than a ten-lane freeway. The light rail system known as MAX extends 12 miles east from Portland and carries more than 7 million passengers a year. Other cities including Los Angeles, San Diego, Buffalo, San Jose, and Sacramento have introduced or expanded light rail service in recent years, greatly reducing the use of automobiles, the burning of fossil fuel, and the emission of carbon dioxide and other gases.

• • •

THINK GLOBALLY, ACT LOCALLY

In Seattle, Washington, an estimated 2 percent of commuters now bicycle to work along one of the city's many bicycle trails. The city has passed several ordinances designed to accommodate the growing bicycle traffic. City building codes require one bicycle parking space for every ten automobile spaces. In addition, showers are being installed in office buildings to accommodate bikers. In Palo Alto, California, the city council has implemented similar measures to accommodate a growing legion of bicycling commuters, including:

- a two-mile "bicycle boulevard" featuring barriers that block cars but permit bikers
- a requirement that newly paved streets must meet the more stringent standards of smoothness required for bicycle traffic
- a requirement that employers must install one shower for every ten thousand square feet of office space
- special "detection loops" buried at intersections to allow bikers to activate traffic lights

GREEN COMMUTING

Even bicycling, long used in other industrial and developing nations as a major form of transportation, is slowly taking hold in American cities plagued by increased traffic jams and squeezed by the price of energy and the increase in urban smog. **Rep. Joseph Kennedy (D-MA)** has introduced the Bicycle and Pedestrian Transportation Improvement Act. The legislation requires states to "obligate not less than 3% of the funds apportioned to federal aid to highway systems, to bicycle transportation and pedestrian walkways."

The Bicycle and Pedestrian Transportation bill, which has seventeen cosponsors, represents the kind of Green vision that would have been unheard of in the halls of Congress just a few decades earlier. The new thinking emphasizes small appropriate technologies and public forms of transportation that are sustainable and minimize damage to the environment.

· · ·

NEO-TRADITIONAL TOWNS

Community developers are beginning to plan residential communities that minimize the need for motorized transportation. The "neo-traditional town" is an innovative attempt to restore existing communities and create new ones based on many of the most effective features of nineteenth-century towns. The neo-traditional town movement is based on the concept of closely integrating offices, shops, and housing in compact areas easily accessible by bicycle and pedestrian paths. The new development offers a clear alternative to the conventional suburban highway culture with home, office, and shops all widely separated and accessible only by automobile and freeways. Neo-traditional towns like Seaside and Charleston Place, Florida, and Mashpee Commons on Cape Cod appeal to the new Green consciousness with their emphasis on appropriate scale and the reestablishment of livable communities.

Transporting America: The Green Vote

☑ Raise the average automobile fuel efficiency standards to 34 miles per gallon by 1996 and 40 miles per gallon by the year 2000.

☑ Impose a gas-guzzler tax on the automobile manufacturers, with revenues passed on as rebates for purchasers of fuel efficient cars.

☑ Amend the Internal Revenue Service code to exclude from an individual's gross income employer subsidies for carpooling and mass transit.

☑ Establish a government research and development program for electric and solar vehicles.

☑ Increase the excise tax on gasoline with part of the revenue going to the Mass Transit Account in the Highway Trust Fund, the additional funds to be used to assist mass transit in localities around the country.

☑ Require the Federal Railway Administration to establish a National High-Speed Rail Transportation Policy to promote the commercialization of high-speed rail systems in the United States.

☑ Earmark at least 3 percent of the funds apportioned to federal aid to highway systems for bicycle lanes and pedestrian walkways.

TURNING ARMS INTO A GREEN DIVIDEND

> The global arms trade is estimated to be about $50 billion per year. Three fourths of that trade is with developing nations. Over 66% of the global arms trade is supplied by the United States and the Union of Soviet Socialist Republics. Those weapons have been used to kill over 20 million people in some 200 developing nations.
>
> —The Gaia Peace Atlas

For most of the twentieth century, domestic politics has revolved around the competition between guns and butter. Today that polarity has given way to a new debate: guns vs. the environment. The anticipated "peace dividend" from reduced U.S. defense spending on the Cold War—though not a panacea—can make a significant contribution to addressing environmental problems currently facing America and the planet. While the Gulf War temporarily blocked efforts in Congress to significantly reduce military spending, many members of Congress believe that the end of the Cold War will inevitably lead to a reduction in military spending over the coming decade.

The peace dividend, however, could easily be squandered or nibbled away by special-interest pleading or pork barrel projects. This is likely to happen if we fail to articulate clearly a vision of national priorities. Fortunately, a consensus is beginning to emerge. As the Cold War fades, Americans are turning their attention to a new security threat—the first truly planetary environmental crisis in human history. In the past few years the public has become increasingly aware of the greenhouse effect, ozone depletion, the energy crisis, acid rain, deforestation, and mass extinction of species. In a 1988 public opinion poll, conducted by the American Talk Security Project, more than 77 percent of the respondents said they regarded global environmental problems as "a very serious threat" to national security.

Securing the biosphere will be expensive. The Environmental Protection Agency estimates that it will cost $110 billion dollars to clean up the worst hazardous waste sites in the country. Disposing of radioactive waste will take another $30 billion over the next five years. Reducing acid rain will cost taxpayers and industry an additional $30–40 billion. Reclaiming strip-mined land will cost $7 billion. Our total environmental bill is estimated at more than $300 billion, and that assessment is likely to increase dramatically in the years ahead.

Shifting our economic priorities from military security to environmental security is the critical political task of the coming decade. That shift will be a formidable task. The American economy has been entrenched in military production for more than a half century. There are currently 20,000 major defense contractors and 100,000 subcontractors working on Pentagon projects. According to the Center for Defense Information, in 1989 some 8 million Americans received full- or part-time paychecks associated with some form of military activity: 3.2 million in defense-related industrial employment; 2.2 million on active duty in the armed services and 1.6 million in the reserves; and 1.1 million in Department of Defense civil service. A University of California study found that the military owned industrial equipment, land, and buildings valued at $475 billion—an amount equivalent to half the holdings of all U.S. manufacturing corporations. Currently, more than 45 percent of all U.S. public and private research and development monies go to military-related activity.

The military-industrial complex has swollen to the point that, "if it were a separate nation, it would rank 13th in the world's top twenty powers." The military-industrial complex dwarfs other sec-

tors and now consumes more than 6 percent of the nation's total
energy.

• • •

GUNS VS. ENVIRONMENT

According to the Worldwatch Institute, for the $100 billion
cost of the Trident II submarine and the F-16 jet fighter programs,
the U.S. government could clean up more than 3,000 of the worst
hazardous waste sites. For the cost of the Stealth Bomber Program,
estimated at $68 billion, the government could pay for two thirds
of the projected cost of the Clean Water Program over the next ten
years. For the $39 billion earmarked for the Strategic Defense Ini-
tiative program in fiscal years 1988–92, we could dispose of all the
nonmilitary highly radioactive waste in the United States. If the $6
billion cost of developing the Midgetman Intercontinental Ballistic
Missile was transferred to biosphere protection, it could pay for a
year of cutting U.S. sulfur dioxide emissions by 8–12 million tons,
significantly reducing the acid rain problem. For the price of three
B-1B bombers, the federal government could finance its entire Renewable Energy Research Program for two years. Three weeks of
worldwide military spending could pay for primary health care for
all of the children in the third world and prevent more than 5
million deaths. Four days of total global military spending—estimated at about $8 billion—could finance a five-year action plan to
protect the world's remaining tropical rain forest. Two days of
global military spending transferred to biosphere security efforts
could finance a year's worth of efforts to halt third world desertification. The cost of one nuclear weapons test alone could pay for the
installation of 80 thousand hand pumps, giving third world vil-
lages access to clean water.

PUNISHING THE WRONGDOERS

Members of Congress are beginning to respond, on a number of
fronts, to the new public pressure to reduce American military

spending and the threat of military conflict around the world. Several bills have been introduced to curtail the international weapons trade. **Rep. Howard Berman (D-CA)** and forty-five cosponsors have introduced the Missile Technology Control Act. The legislation would require the President of the United States "to impose sanctions on any company he finds in violation of the Missile Technology Control Regime," a pact signed in 1987 in which participating countries agreed "to prevent their own companies from exporting equipment or technology that could contribute to the acquisition of nuclear-capable missiles" which can carry long-distance payloads. Unfortunately, many countries are not strictly enforcing the pact.

Berman's bill, which passed in the House, imposes specific sanctions against companies violating the pact. "First, denial of U.S. export licenses; second, denial of U.S. government contracts; and third, a ban on imports into the United States from any such company." Similar bills have been introduced by **Rep. Fortney Stark (D-CA)** in the House and by Sens. **John McCain (R-AZ), Albert Gore (D-TN),** and **Jeff Bingaman (D-NM)** in the Senate.

Rep. Jim Moody (D-WI) has introduced a bill in the 102nd Congress that would prohibit the Export-Import Bank of the United States from "using any of its funds or borrowing capacity to extend credit for the sale of defense articles and services to any country." The bill has fifty-six cosponsors.

CHEMICAL AND BIOLOGICAL WEAPONS: THE POOR MAN'S NUCLEAR BOMB

Renewed interest in chemical and biological weapons has sparked much concern in the halls of Congress in recent years. Chemical weapons were first used in World War I. Their impact was so horrific that the nations of the world held back from using them again in World War II, for fear of reprisals. This informal agreement was shattered in the 1980s during the Iran-Iraq conflict

---

PROFITING IN MASS DESTRUCTION

"[Former] CIA Director William Webster, testifying before a congressional committee, said, by the year 2000 at least 15 developing countries will be producing their own ballistic missiles. An unprecedented 20 countries may already be manufacturing chemical weapons, while at least ten countries may be attempting to develop biological weapons. Over the past 15 years the number of countries with nuclear weapons capability has almost doubled from the initial five with the addition of India, Israel, South Africa, and Pakistan. Several other countries are attempting to develop nuclear weapons capability . . . the convergence of missiles and chemical and nuclear weapons in the third world puts the means of massive destruction not only in more hands, but it puts them into the hands that are most likely to use them. . . . if the United States does not take the lead in controlling missile proliferation, there will be no limit to the spread of these weapons. China, Argentina, and Brazil will continue to develop and sell their missiles; private companies in the West, attracted by big profits, will set up front companies that will circumvent lax export restrictions; and the Soviet Bloc will supply their clients."

—*Sen. Jeff Bingaman (D-NM)*

• • •

when both nations employed chemical weapons. Today many nations, including the United States and Russia, have chemical weapons arsenals. Because chemical weapons are cheaper than nuclear weapons, requiring less infrastructure and technology, there is a growing fear that developing nations might look to them as a way to exercise greater geopolitical power in their regions of the world. Fortunately, the logistical requirements to support large-scale chemical warfare are beyond the means of most nations.

Meanwhile, interest in biological weapons has also been rekindled in the wake of the genetic engineering revolution. Biological weapons can be viral, bacterial, fungal, rickettsial, or protozoan. They can be used to destroy animals, crops, and people. Biological agents can mutate, reproduce, multiply, and be spread over a large terrain by wind, animal, and insect transmission. Once released, many biological pathogens are capable of developing viable niches and maintaining themselves in the environment indefinitely. Traditional biological agents include *Yersinia pestis* (the plague), tularemia, Rift Valley fever, *Coxiella burnetii* (Q fever), Eastern equine encephalitis, and smallpox.

THE BIOTECH ARMS RACE

Biological warfare has never been widely used because of the expense and danger involved in processing and stockpiling large volumes of toxic materials and the difficulty in targeting the dissemination of biological agents. However, in a May 1986 report to the Committee of Appropriations in the U.S. House of Representatives, the Department of Defense pointed out that recombinant DNA and other genetic engineering technologies are finally making biological warfare an effective military option.

With recombinant DNA technology it is now possible to develop "a nearly infinite variety of what might be termed designer agents." The DOD report concludes that the new developments in genetic engineering technology enable "the rapid exploitation of nature's resources for warfare purposes in ways not even imagined ten to fifteen years ago."

Under the rubric of defense research, the U.S. Department of Defense launched a significant research and development effort in the 1980s. In 1981 the Pentagon budget for "defensive biological warfare research" was only $15.1 million dollars. By 1986 the DOD budget had grown to $90 million. The various branches of the armed services now work with virtually every major pathogen in the world, from exotic viral diseases to newly discovered viruses such as AIDS. The DOD claims that most of the work is unclassified and intended to provide the military with defensive protection in the form of vaccines and antidotes. Despite DOD assurances that its biological warfare program is defensive in nature and not in violation of the Biological Weapons Convention signed by the United States and many other nations in 1972, observers are alarmed over the increased commitment of DOD funds for genetic engineering research.

While Congress has made serious attempts to outlaw new chemical weapons it has been less willing to challenge the DOD and the White House on biological weapons research and development. Still, some members of Congress have pushed ahead on the international front, determined to make sure that chemical and biological weapons technology is not spread to other nations, creating a new and deadly arms race.

ELIMINATING INVISIBLE WEAPONS

Rep. Dante Fascell (D-FL), along with forty-two cosponsors, introduced the Chemical and Biological Warfare Elimination Act in the 101st Congress. The bill, which passed in the House by a voice vote, requires the President of the United States to impose sanctions against foreign persons "if he determines that they knowingly contributed to the efforts of a country to acquire or use chemical or biological weapons." The bill also calls for sanctions against any person "that has used such weapons in violation of international law." Such sanctions include "(1) Denial of U.S. procurement contracts for goods or services from such foreign persons and (2) prohibition against importation of products from such persons. Countries found using chemical or biological weapons are to have the following sanctions imposed on them: (1) Prohibition against arms sales and security sensitive goods and technologies; (2) Prohibition of the export of U.S. goods and technology (except agricultural products); (3) Import restrictions; (4) Denial of foreign assistance; (5) U.S. opposition to loan or financial assistance from international and U.S. financial institutions; and (6) The suspension of diplomatic relations." Similar legislation was introduced into the House by **Rep. John Porter (R-IL)** and **Rep. Mel Levine (D-CA)** and in the Senate by **Sen. Claiborne Pell (D-RI)** and **Sen. Robert Dole (R-KS).** The Dole bill would impose trade sanctions against companies that knowingly export material know-how and equipment which could contribute to the proliferation of chemical and biological weapons capability.

Rep. Robert Kastenmeier (D-WI) and **Sen. Herbert Kohl (D-WI)** introduced a joint bill in Congress entitled the Biological Weapons Anti-Terrorism Act, which passed in both the House and the Senate and was signed into law by the President. The act amends the federal criminal code to "impose criminal penalties upon anyone who knowingly develops, produces, stockpiles, transfers, acquires, retains, or possesses any biological agent, toxin, or delivery system for use as a weapon, or assists a foreign state or any organization to do so."

DEMILITARIZING THE OUTER SPACE COMMONS

In March 1983, President Reagan announced a new military initiative designed to open up outer space to military exploitation. The Strategic Defense Initiative, popularly referred to as the Star Wars Program, immediately became the centerpiece of the Reagan administration's geopolitical strategy. The President outlined an ambitious program to establish a defense shield around the earth that could intercept and destroy incoming Soviet missiles from staging areas in outer space. Using space battle stations, the Pentagon envisioned employing a new generation of energy directed weapons —X ray, microwave, laser, electromagnetic, and particle beam weapons—to destroy Soviet missiles shortly after launch or while traveling through outer space on their flight path to America and Allied targets. Every missile that evaded the "peace shield" would be shot down as it reentered the earth's atmosphere.

The enclosure and militarization of space has become the latest goal in the "nuclearization" of the global commons. During the 1980s billions of dollars were invested in the Star Wars program despite the fact that many distinguished scientists viewed the concept as theoretically suspect and technologically unfeasible.

The militarization of outer space is part of a 500-year quest by the modern nation-states to enclose and militarize every available commons on the planet. Today the earth's land masses, oceans, air corridors, electromagnetic spectrum, and gene pool have all been transformed into militarily significant battlegrounds. Now military planners hope to extend their domain to the last remaining global commons, outer space, providing an overarching battlefield to play out the deadly geopolitical game of nuclear warfare.

Some members of Congress have actively opposed the militarization of space. They argue that the space commons should remain a nuclear-free zone and not be enclosed by weapons of mass destruction.

Rep. Les AuCoin (D-OR) and **Sen. Tom Harkin (D-IA)** introduced companion bills in the 101st Congress to outlaw the use of outer space for military purposes. The Outer Space Protection Act prohibits the use of funds by federal agencies for (1) The testing, production, or deployment of any weapons system designed to be based in outer space; (2) The testing of any weapons system to determine its capability to damage or destroy any object in outer space; or (3) The launch of any spacecraft that carries weapons capable of inflicting death or injury on people. The bills gained twenty-six cosponsors in the House and thirteen cosponsors in the Senate. In introducing the legislation, Sen. Harkin spoke eloquently of the need to reverse the arms race and turn away from the narrow geopolitical thinking that has turned nation against nation during the nuclear age:

"The challenge for us, as the twentieth century draws to a close, is to prove that we have learned something from four decades of the arms race on earth. Will we continue our old ways, filling outer space with weapons of war, or will we learn from history the futility of an unconstrained competition in weapons? . . . Either we move one step closer to nuclear war or we move one step back from it. An arms race in space is not inevitable. If it is to occur, it will occur because we have chosen it."

SAYING NO TO STAR WARS

While AuCoin's and Harkin's bills attempt to keep military weapons out of the space commons, Rep. **Ronald Dellums (D-CA)** and Rep. **Barbara Boxer (D-CA)** introduced an amendment to the fiscal year 1991 defense authorization program to "terminate the organization within the Department of Defense known as the Strategic Defense Initiative Organization." The bill would also reduce the funds available for the Strategic Defense Research Program by $2,238,000,000 to a ceiling of $1,300,000,000. Though ultimately defeated, the Dellum/Boxer initiative garnered a surprising 137 votes in the House.

ADDING UP THE COSTS

Several other bills have been introduced in Congress the intent of which is to reduce U.S. reliance on military approaches to global security while bolstering programs that encourage new forms of international cooperation, including assistance for sustainable development and environmental preservation.

Rep. Paul Kanjorski (D-PA) introduced the War Cost Disclosure Act, which requires the President to provide Congress with a war impact statement prior to seeking a declaration of war from Congress. The report would include a statement of "the circumstances necessitating the introduction of U.S. Armed Forces; the level of U.S. and foreign casualties expected; the estimated scope, duration, and cost of the hostility; the proportion of the total cost that will be paid by U.S. allies; [and] what Federal programs should be cut and what Federal revenues should be increased to pay for military actions. . . ."

The Kanjorski bill would place greater responsibility on the President and Congress before the outbreak of war to address the full range of implications and consequences of military action. It would also force both the White House and Congress to justify the need for armed intervention and weigh the benefits against the short- and long-term costs involved. This kind of cost-benefit analysis in advance of a declaration of war would likely create a sobering counterpose to the sabre-rattling that generally precedes armed conflict.

BEYOND WAR

Perhaps the most radical and far-reaching departure from traditional geopolitics has come in the form of a resolution introduced jointly by **Rep. Matthew McHugh (D-NY)** and **Sen. Mark Hatfield (R-OR)**. The resolution, entitled the Harvest of Peace, is cosponsored by 169 representatives and 25 senators and calls for a fundamental shift in our concept of security, away from military might and geopolitical advantage and toward peaceful cooperation and biosphere protection. This Green-oriented resolution calls for a worldwide reduction in military spending of 50 percent by the year 2000. The resolution also calls for "reducing military assistance and arms sales to developing nations; encouraging the peaceful settlement of conflict; providing increased assistance to developing nations to overcome hunger and poverty, reduce debt burdens, promote human rights, ensure sustainable development, and protect the environment; increasing support domestically for programs that address human needs; helping defense industries and their employees convert to productive non-defense work; and reducing the federal deficit."

Another Green-oriented peace bill introduced by **Rep. Andrew Jacobs (D-IN)** and **Sen. Mark Hatfield (R-OR)** would amend the Internal Revenue Service code "to provide that a taxpayer conscientiously opposed to participation in war may elect to have such taxpayer's income, estate, or gift tax payments spent for non-military purposes; to create the United States Peace Tax Fund to receive such tax payments; to establish a United States Peace Tax Board of Trustees. . . ." The Peace Tax Fund board would "be responsible for distributing the funds." The tax monies would help finance projects such as: retraining of workers displaced by conversion from military production, or military production–related activities; selected projects of the United States Institute of Peace; disarmament efforts; and improvements of international health, education, and welfare.

· · ·

THE PEACE TAX FUND

. . . Today the Senate has voted to spend $15 billion of the taxpayers money to pay for our war in the Persian Gulf. There are some taxpayers who cannot in good conscience contribute to this effort. Citizens will risk fines and jail sentences to withhold taxes that support war or who will even impoverish themselves and their families rather than be legally bound to pay such taxes. These are people deeply driven by values, born of conscience, and although conscientious objectors to war have not been forced to serve in active combat for 45 years, they are still required to support the military through taxation. Mr. President, if it has ever been clear in the history of our democracy, it is clear now that we need to protect the preeminent rise of conscience of all our citizens . . . This bill would protect the right of conscience by allowing those who object to war to pay their fraction of these taxes to an organized peace tax fund . . . Freedom of conscience is a constitutional right. Establishment of a U.S. Peace Tax Fund would protect that right.

Sen. Mark Hatfield (R-OR)

Voting Green means transcending local and national boundaries and identifying with our fellow human beings and the other creatures that make up the larger biosphere community. Some legislators are beginning to think in biosphere terms, redefining international security to include the shared interests of all of humanity. **Rep. Robert Mrazek (D-NY)** and seventy-one cosponsors have introduced the International Security and Satellite Monitoring Act. The bill would establish a commission to "study areas in which the sharing of information collected by civilian remote sensing satellites could increase international security and stability, including environmental monitoring, disaster preparedness, drug trafficking, and weapons monitoring." This is a far cry from traditional military use of satellites to secure sensitive intelligence information about potential or real adversaries. The idea of shifting our notion of security from one of military might to one of shared participation in a global community is truly revolutionary, and a harbinger of the new Green politics emerging in this decade.

DISARMING THE MILITARY-INDUSTRIAL COMPLEX

In his farewell speech to the nation in 1961, President Dwight David Eisenhower warned of a new and potentially ominous threat to the peace and security of the United States:

"The conjunction of an immense military establishment and a large arms industry is new in the American experience. The total influence—economic, political, even spiritual—is felt in every city, every statehouse, every office of the federal government. In the councils of government we must guard against the acquisition of unwarranted influence, whether sought or not by the military-industrial complex. The potential for the disastrous rise of misplaced power exists and will persist."

Today, American citizens contribute a large amount of their tax dollars to prop up the military-industrial complex. More than 25 percent of federal spending goes to the military. By contrast, housing gets 1.3 percent and education 1.8 percent.

The extraordinary dependence of the American economy on military spending has led many to fear that a peace dividend or Green dividend might cause a recession. Indeed, advocates of a larger defense budget have long argued that increased military spending means more jobs and a healthier economy. This simply isn't the case. According to the Bureau of Labor Statistics, a billion dollars spent on guided missiles in space vehicle production creates 20,175 jobs. The same billion dollars spent on education creates 71,550 jobs. If the billion dollars were spent on mass transit it would support 32,000 jobs.

Swords into Plowshares

Sensing the public's shifting priorities, some voices inside the defense industry are beginning to call for change. According to Kosta Tsipis, Director of the Program in Science and Technology for International Security at the Massachusetts Institute of Technology, "the defense industry is extremely eager to address energy and the environment . . . but there is no market incentive. So they're trying to convince the government that some resources that went into weapons systems should go into civilian things."

Many defense contracting firms are ideally suited to convert to sustainable production technologies. For example, workers at the General Dynamics shipyard in Massachusetts proposed converting their plant from building warships to the construction of "floating plants to convert ocean thermal energy into electricity." Similar plant ships are already being built in Japan. Workers at a McDonnell Douglas aerospace plant in Southern California have proposed retooling their operations to build mass transit vehicles and energy equipment.

The advantages of converting from a military to a Green economy are obvious. Still, the process of conversion is likely to be costly in the short run and will create economic problems for the companies, workers, and communities most intimately affected.

Making the Transition

Several bills have been introduced into Congress to address the issue of national conversion of the military-industrial complex to a sustainable peacetime economy. In the House, bills have been written by Reps. **Ted Weiss (D-NY), Sam Gejdenson (D-CT), Nicholas Mavroules (D-MA),** and **Mary Rose Oakar (D-OH).** All of these bills are designed to ease the transition of companies, workers, and communities in the wake of expected cutbacks in military spending over the coming decade.

© 1990, BOSTON GLOBE. DISTRIBUTED BY LOS ANGELES TIMES SYNDICATE.
REPRINTED WITH PERMISSION.

The Weiss bill, in some ways the most comprehensive piece of legislation that has thus far been introduced, includes the following provisions: (1) All defense contracting firms would be required by law to establish conversion planning committees as "a prerequisite for eligibility for military contracts." (2) The Department of Defense would be required to provide a one-year notice of changes in procurement of contracts that might result in layoffs, to allow contracting firms time to consider alternative production possibilities. (3) The bill also provides for community economic assistance and worker retraining. (4) Workers displaced by Defense Department cutbacks could be eligible for adjustment benefits for up to two years while they retrained for other employment.

In September 1990, Rep. Nicholas Mavroules' amendment to authorize $200 million to create a Defense Economic Adjustment

Program was attached to the Defense Authorization Bill and adopted by the House by 288 to 128.

Rep. Barbara Boxer (D-CA) introduced tough legislation in 1991 that would require defense-contracting companies that close down or severely curtail their plant operations to pay the local county in which the company operates "ten percent of the value of all Department of Defense contracts held by it" as compensation for leaving the community. The bill also directs the Secretary of Labor "to make community economic adjustment grants to counties adversely affected by terminations or layoffs of employees at military bases or facilities of defense contractors as a result of reductions in DOD spending, base closings or realignments, cancellation or termination of a contract, or the failure to proceed with a previously approved major defense acquisition program."

It is becoming increasingly obvious that the nations of the world will need to choose between guns and the environment in the coming decade. The real test of the new Green consciousness will be the willingness of the United States and other major powers to convert their military-industrial complexes to sustainable Green economies. Building a new Green infrastructure—based on effective energy conservation, alternative energy fuels, and use of renewable resources—is an essential undertaking if we are to hope to address our long-term environmental threats.

Turning Arms into a Green Dividend: The Green Vote

☑ Impose sanctions against any company violating the Missile Technology Control Regime Pact. Any company found guilty of selling equipment or technology that could contribute to the acquisition of nuclear-capable missiles would be denied U.S. export licenses and U.S. government contracts. Violators would also be prohibited from importing their products into the United States.

☑ Impose economic sanctions against any foreign person or government that knowingly attempts to acquire or use chemical and biological weapons.

☑ Impose criminal penalties on anyone who knowingly develops, produces, stockpiles, acquires, or possesses biological agents, toxins, or delivery systems designed for use as a weapon.

☑ Outlaw the use of outer space for military purposes.

☑ Terminate the Strategic Defense Initiative Program within the Department of Defense.

☑ Require the President to provide a war impact statement before seeking a declaration of war from Congress. The statement should include an assessment of the expected number of U.S. and foreign casualties, an estimate of the cost and duration of the war, and a plan for how the funds to wage the war will be raised.

☑ Reduce U.S. military assistance and arms sales to developing nations and work toward a worldwide reduction in military spending of 50 percent by the year 2000.

☑ Allow those conscientiously opposed to war to place that portion of their taxable income that would go to the military into a Peace Tax Fund. The tax monies collected by the fund would be used to help finance peace and disarmament activities and improvements in international health, education, welfare, and environmental protection programs.

☑ Require all defense contracting firms to establish a conversion planning committee as a prerequisite for eligibility for military contracts.

☑ Earmark federal government funds to assist communities affected by a reduction or elimination of military production contracts. Provide financial assistance to help convert existing defense-contracting companies to nonmilitary production.

☑ Provide up to two years of adjustment benefits, including benefits for education and retraining for all workers displaced by the scaling down or elimination of defense contracts.

Sustainable International Development

One out of every five of the world's 5 billion people does not have enough to eat or have adequate shelter, clothing, or medical care. Each day is a struggle merely to stay alive. The poor cut down the last of the forest for one more day's firewood; they farm or graze the land until it is exhausted. They overwhelm sources of drinking water by their sheer numbers; they kill endangered elephants for the ivory that will bring a year's earnings in just one day.

Deforestation, desertification, species extinction—as the world's impoverished people struggle to subsist, the global environment is degraded and destroyed. Until the poor meet their needs—and the rich moderate theirs—the global environment will continue on its crash course.

As the link between the plight of the poor and the global environmental crisis has become more apparent, some members of Congress are taking a more critical look at the U.S. development aid program.

Americans have poured billions of dollars into foreign aid for more than three decades, but the results have been discouraging. In fact, poverty, inequality, injustice, and environmental destruction in the third world have intensified because much of the aid that the United States provides to poor countries, directly or indirectly, attempts to foster economic growth without regard for social, political, or environmental realities.

For the most part, foreign aid has been directed to the elites of developing countries in the hope that economic benefits would "trickle down" to the poorest of the poor. This has not occurred.

Most U.S.-funded development projects have promoted economic policies that encourage the production of goods for export to the United States and other developed countries. The net result of third world production for first world consumption has been a steady transfer of economic and biological wealth from the South to the North, as well as a reduction in the amount of food available to the poor in developing countries. (The best land is used to produce crops for export, thus forcing the poor to sustain themselves on marginal lands.)

In other words, the rich have been getting richer, and the poor have been getting poorer—and all at the expense of the environment.

A GREEN APPROACH

Fortunately, a new way of thinking about international development has quietly entered the halls of Congress and promises to revolutionize the way Americans help the world's poor in the years ahead. A number of federal legislators have proposed radical new forms of development aid inspired by several highly committed progressive nongovernmental organizations such as Bread for the World, the Center of Concern, Church World Service/Lutheran World Relief, The Development Group for Alternative Policies (The Development GAP), Friends Committee on National Legislation, RESULTS, and several national environmental organizations including Friends of the Earth, the Environmental Defense Fund, the Sierra Club, the National Wildlife Federation, and the Natural Resources Defense Council.

The new Green approach to foreign aid turns upside down virtually all of our past thinking and practices.

Green development aid is based on a commitment to third world self-determination, self-reliance, and environmental sustainability. It involves filtering smaller, more manageable amounts of government financing through indigenous and U.S. nongovernmental organizations that work closely with the poor. The goal is to build self-reliant, sustainable economic systems from the grass roots up while directly including and involving as many people as possible—particularly the poorest of the poor.

> **Sustainable Development: "Development that meets the needs and aspirations of the present without compromising the ability of future generations to meet their own needs."**
>
> **—The World Commission on Environment and Development**

Thus far, most U.S. development aid has been based on short-term military, political, and security interests. Indeed, two thirds of the U.S. foreign aid budget is security aid to U.S. allies. However, as environmental health, rather than military might, comes to be viewed increasingly as the basis for global security, Green voters look to the day when aid will be given on a needs basis—completely apart from self-serving political objectives.

MOVING FROM BAND-AIDS TO SUSTAINABILITY

Among the crop of proposals for a new kind of development aid are a handful that deal with famine relief and economic development in the Horn of Africa—Ethiopia, Sudan, and Somalia—where some 20 million people are now threatened with hunger.

The sub-Saharan region has been plagued by decades of persistent famine, drought, poverty, and devasting civil wars. Some 2 million Ethiopians and Sudanese have died as a result of war or famine during the past five years. Another 8 million have become refugees or displaced persons. Current estimates are that 9 million people need emergency food in Sudan alone. Northern Ethiopia required some 1 million tons of food aid in 1991.

To date, American aid to famine-stricken Africa has come mostly in the form of emergency "Band-Aid" relief and little in the way of cost-effective long-term development aid to help Africans build their own sustainable agricultural and economic systems.

The Africa Famine Recovery and Development Act, introduced in the 101st Congress by **Rep. Howard Wolpe (D-MI)** and **Sen. Paul Simon (D-IL)**, was designed to amend the Foreign Assistance Act of 1961 to provide not only emergency food assistance to sub-Saharan Africa, but also long-term development aid that is "equitable, participatory, environmentally sustainable, and self-reliant." The bill was passed into law in 1990 as part of the foreign aid package.

Among the key features of the Wolpe legislation were: "close cooperation with the poor majority through African and other private and voluntary organizations in the planning of U.S. development assistance; [the] incorporation of active participation by women in development activities, [and the] establishment of criteria for economic policy reforms to increase incentives for productivity while protecting the vulnerable poor and long-term environmental interests."

> **"Too often our aid programs in Africa have been poorly planned and ineffective because they failed to involve local people—particularly women, who produce 80 percent of Africa's food—and ignored the potential of indigenous African private and voluntary organizations to foster self-reliant development."**
>
> **—Rep. Howard Wolpe (D-MI)**

The bill also delineated required spending levels for five critical components of long-term development: productive and sustainable agricultural development and restoration and maintenance of the environment; improved health conditions; voluntary family-planning services; improved relevance and efficiency of education; and the development of jobs for the unemployed and underemployed.

The bill was the result of extensive consultation and cooperation with private voluntary and nongovernmental environmental, development, and religious organizations in the United States and Africa over a period of several months. Such consultation was unprecedented in the history of foreign aid legislation. Some 114 private nongovernmental relief organizations in the United States supported Rep. Wolpe's legislation.

In the 102nd Congress, **Rep. Byron Dorgan (D-ND)** and **Sen. Paul Simon (D-IL)** introduced the Horn of Africa Recovery and Food Security Act which would "assure the people of the Horn of Africa the right to food and the other basic necessities of life and promote peace and development in the region through grassroots participation." It would also "reformulate U.S. policy toward the region and set forth a comprehensive program to prevent widespread famine and chart a course for long-term recovery and food security."

> "It is time to move away from a preoccupation with {military} security and toward an approach that pays attention to basic human needs and a strategy for recovery and food security. Part of that effort entails solving problems from the bottom up, rather than from the top down."
>
> —Rep. Byron Dorgan (D-ND)

The Dorgan/Simon legislation specifically bans government-to-government nonhumanitarian aid until lasting peace settlements and commitments to human rights and democracy are negotiated in the area, but promotes a "targeted, grassroots, human-needs-based approach that can be undertaken while conflicts persist."

The legislation would "assure noncombatants in the region equal access to food and other emergency relief assistance, particularly those that promote self-reliance (e.g., seeds, fertilizers, pesticides, water projects)."

Emergency relief would be financed by unobligated balances from military and Economic Support Fund accounts.

The language of the Horn of Africa Recovery and Food Security Act was included in the FY 1992–93 foreign aid authorization in both the House and the Senate and was in conference at the time of this writing.

REFLECTING GREEN VALUES

Rep. George Crockett (D-MI) introduced a Green development bill, the Caribbean Regional Development Act, which is among the most progressive pieces of legislation ever presented to Congress.

According to Crockett's proposed legislation, U.S. aid to the Caribbean should, among other things, "help the poor to participate in the development of their societies; support development that is environmentally sustainable; promote Caribbean self-reliance; increase food security; support employment generation while avoiding the displacement of traditional lines of small-scale production; and preserve and reinforce traditional Caribbean culture and social values."

Consultation with the intended beneficiaries of U.S. economic assistance would be required. "Priority . . . [should] be given to supporting indigenous Caribbean institutions including farmers' unions, cooperatives, trade unions and other labor organizations, women's groups, and community organizations that represent, work with, and benefit the poor."

The legislation specifically requires the U.S. Agency for International Development (AID) to "ensure the active participation of Caribbean women in the development process, consult with Caribbean organizations that work with the poor in all stages of the design and implementation of assistance policies, and monitor the effect of economic assistance programs on socioeconomic conditions in the Caribbean."

Immediate goals would include "food sufficiency, integrated rural development, the creation of community-based agro-industries, the development of financial resources for small and medium-sized farms and manufacturing enterprises, expansion of tourism, and enhancing the natural resource base."

Last but not least, the bill would also prevent the dumping of pesticides and toxic waste in the Caribbean by prohibiting AID from providing any assistance for the use of any chemical or substance in the Caribbean if such use is not permitted under the public health laws of a Caribbean nation or the United States.

It would be difficult to conceive of legislation that better reflects Green values. It was written with the help of The Development GAP and nongovernmental organizations in the Caribbean and was the first foreign aid legislation developed by Congress in which the people to be affected by the legislation were actively consulted in its development. Indeed, several planning meetings, involving representatives from a broad range of social and economic sectors, were held in the Caribbean and the bill was, in effect, marked-up there.

The language of Rep. Crockett's bill passed in both the House and Senate in 1991 as part of the foreign aid authorization for 1992–93. At this writing, the measure was before House and Senate conferees.

THE RESOURCEFUL POOR

The U.S. foreign aid bureaucracy has long assumed that the poor lack the capacity to pull themselves out of poverty. Consequently, U.S. development aid has traditionally been designed for, and imposed upon, developing countries in a patronizing, paternalistic manner.

By contrast, Green legislators view the poor as creative, resourceful, and energetic, with high levels of endurance and motivation, but who are caught up in life circumstances that force them to live only in the present, subsisting from one day to the next. People do take the initiative to help themselves out of poverty when presented with opportunities to break out of the daily subsistence cycle and do something concrete for their future.

A new form of aid called micro-enterprise lending has proven to be dramatically successful in providing such opportunities. Micro-enterprise programs foster the development of self-employment and small businesses in poverty-stricken areas by lending tiny amounts of money to poor individuals. The loans, which range from $50 to $300, allow the poor to purchase the materials they need—a loom, a cow, or tools—to get a small business going. Street beggars, landless peasants, and desperately poor women with families are transformed into entrepreneurs who set up banana stalls, raise poultry, weave mats, make clothing, create bakeries, keep bees, make shoes, and sell milk. Some enterprises become so successful that their owners are able to hire employees.

The Grameen Bank of Bangladesh, Indonesia's Badan Kredit Kecamatan, and ADEMI in the Dominican Republic, have been lending tiny sums to some of the world's poorest people for several years. Repayment rates of 95 percent and higher attest to the loan programs' dramatic success, as do studies that indicate that borrowers from these banks have increased their incomes an average of 30 percent over a two-year period. As of October 1990, the Grameen Bank alone had turned an astounding 800,000 landless villagers into owners of small businesses.

SUCCEEDING THE "AMERICAN WAY"

The micro-enterprise concept was first incorporated into U.S. foreign aid strategy by the 100th Congress. Millions of dollars were earmarked for micro-enterprise credit and assistance in foreign assistance bills for fiscal years 1989, 1990, and 1991. A significant percentage of the funding was to be loaned to the poorest of the poor, including women, through loans not larger than $300. AID, however, has failed for the most part to carry out that mandate.

A February 1991 report by the General Accounting Office found that none of the three AID missions it visited targeted their micro-enterprise projects specifically to the poorest 20 percent of the population or to women. Less than 10 percent of spending for the 1988 program, and less than 7 percent of the 1989 program was for loans under $300.

Rep. Benjamin Gilman (R-NY), in the 101st Congress, and Rep. Edward Feighan (D-OH) and Sen. Dennis DeConcini

(D-AZ) in the 102nd Congress, have all introduced bills to get AID back on the micro-enterprise track.

Gilman's Micro-enterprise Loans for the Poor Act, and Feighan's and DeConcini's Micro-enterprise Development Act, expand AID's micro-enterprise lending program and increase the amount of credit assistance to the poorest of the poor and to women. Remaining funds would be used to set up financial intermediaries in developing countries to make the loans, and to finance middle-level business enterprises.

The World Bank estimates that there are more than 400 million self-employed poor in the developing world, and projects that, by the year 2020, the vast majority of African workers will be employed in the informal sector. Increasingly, micro-enterprise loans will be needed to help the poorest of the poor step onto the track of self-sufficiency. By making resources available to the poor and then getting out of their way, we can help them help themselves through their own initiative—"the American way."

ELIMINATING THE WORST ASPECTS OF POVERTY

U.S. law for several years has required the President to do all he can to ensure that the "worst aspects of absolute poverty" are eliminated by the year 2000. But a report by the United Nations Children's Fund indicates that for most of the countries of Africa, Latin America, and the Caribbean "almost every economic signal points to the fact that development has been derailed."

"Even in countries with increasing per capita GNP, the poorest 40 percent of the population often receives a smaller share of the total, resulting in little or no improvement in the standard of living for those on the bottom rungs of the economic ladder," **Rep. Mel Levine (D-CA)** told his colleagues in the House.

Legislation introduced by Rep. Levine and **Sen. Rudy Boschwitz (R-MN)** directs the President to put U.S. development aid back on track by improving the lives of the poorest 40 percent of the world's population. The Global Poverty Reduction Act sets three goals by which the relative success or failure of the U.S. aid program should be measured.

The first goal is to reduce the mortality rate of children under five years old to 70 per 1,000 live births. Currently, the mortality rate in seventy-two countries is above 70; in the poorest of these countries, the mortality rate is above 170 per 1,000.

The second goal is to increase the female literacy rate to 80 percent. Currently, the literacy rate among women in the thirty-three poorest countries is about 22 percent. Studies show that as female literacy increases, child survival rates improve while population rates decline.

The third goal is to "achieve an absolute poverty level of not more than 20 percent of the population." The absolute poverty level is defined as that income level below which minimum nutritional needs and essential nonfood requirements are not affordable. In the thirty-three poorest countries, the percentage of those in rural areas living below this level is 65 percent, and in urban areas, 35 percent.

The legislation requires the President to host a conference of international heads of state and nongovernmental aid organizations to develop a plan and an international agreement on eliminating the worst aspects of poverty by the year 2000. The bills require that such a plan "include target dates for reaching specific measurable goals." Additionally, the legislation "recognizes the importance of environmental problems in the poverty cycle and emphasizes the utilization of development activities which are consistent with maintaining and restoring the renewable natural resource base."

The bills garnered 219 cosponsors in the House and 38 in the Senate in the 101st Congress. The legislation was developed with RESULTS, a grass-roots organization committed to ending hunger, and is supported by more than seventy private aid and development groups.

BENEFITING THE WORLD'S POOREST PEOPLE

"Mr. President, in his 1949 inaugural address, President Harry Truman observed that: 'More than half the people of the world are living in conditions approaching misery. Their food is inadequate. They are victims of disease. Their economic life is primitive and stagnant. Their poverty is a handicap and a threat to them and more prosperous areas.'

"That was nearly 40 years ago, but the message is just as true today as it was then.

"Despite the billions in foreign aid we spend every year, over the past 40 years since Truman's address, the problems humanitarian aid is supposed to address persist. Of the foreign aid allocated in 1988, not all was targeted to help people in developing countries overcome hunger, poverty, illness, and ignorance. . . .

"In fact, of that $14 billion, $5.3 billion is going to military aid and $3.2 billion in cash payments to strategically valuable countries. Less than $3 billion—$2.7 billion to be exact—is spent on bilateral development assistance. Some of these funds help achieve the four [humanitarian aid] goals set forth in the 1961 Foreign Assistance Act. However, much is spent without specific goals in mind. . . .

"Too often, Americans have seen their tax dollars end up in the pockets of dictators like Marcos and Duvalier. Others consider U.S. aid mismanaged, improperly disbursed, wasteful, and ineffective. . . .

"Domestic support would grow if American taxpayers saw measurable results from our foreign aid programs, and if those programs benefited the world's poorest people, not the world's generals, bureaucrats, and despots."

—Sen. Tom Harkin (D-IA)

SAVE THE CHILDREN

> "Children have neither power, representation, nor influence. They simply represent our future and our legacy. It is indeed true that our national character can be measured by how we care for our children. This legislation is a test of our character which we must not fail."
>
> —Sen. Christopher Dodd (D-CT)

Children everywhere, in poor nations and rich ones as well, are under assault. Each year, 14 million children—40,000 every day—die from largely preventable causes. Dehydration, for example, claims 8,000 lives daily in the developing world. In the United States, lack of prenatal care is associated with 46,000 deaths every year.

In 1990, the World Summit for Children, an unprecedented meeting of representatives from 159 countries—including 71 heads of state—developed a blueprint to meet specified goals to benefit the world's children by the year 2000. Those goals include reducing child mortality rates by at least one third, increasing the number of children who complete primary school to 80 percent, and cutting maternal mortality rates and preschool malnutrition rates by 50 percent.

As part of the international coalition, the United States agreed to work toward these goals. Two legislators, **Rep. Matthew Mc-Hugh (D-NY)** and **Sen. Christopher Dodd (D-CT)** have introduced legislation that would implement the plan of action adopted by the World Summit for Children.

The World Summit for Children Implementation Act is divided into two parts, international and domestic. On the international side, the legislation calls for increased U.S. appropriations to provide the children of developing nations with the following benefits:

- low-cost primary health care including immunizations and oral rehydration therapy

- vitamin A (At current rates, 10 million children will go blind in this decade for lack of 2 cents worth of vitamin A.)

- AIDS prevention (More than 2 million women of childbearing age are now infected with the AIDS virus, and the number is increasing rapidly.)

- universal access to, and completion of, primary education (Currently, in the thirty poorest nations, less than one quarter of all children complete primary school.)

- aid to children in exceptionally difficult circumstances, including street children, AIDS orphans, and children displaced by war and natural disasters

The legislation would also provide increased funding for refugee assistance, since more than 60 percent of the world's 16 million refugees are children.

Domestically, the legislation calls for increased expenditures for the Special Supplemental Food Program for Women, Infants, and Children (WIC); the Head Start program, and the children's vaccine program.

The legislation would require the President to submit an annual report to Congress on progress made toward Summit goals.

According to Rep. McHugh, funds to implement the legislation can be found through the reallocation of U.S. military aid abroad.

WOMEN, THE FORGOTTEN HALF

Women are responsible for 80 to 90 percent of food production in Africa, but even by the late 1980s only 21 percent of the participants in AID-funded training programs in Africa were women. If women are left out of development projects, how can sustainable farming techniques be passed on to the developing world?

Third world women also bear most or all of the responsibility for their children's welfare. But if women and girls are not included in development programs, how can education and health care programs be improved? Research conducted by the U.S. foreign aid program has shown that the greater the involvement of women in any assistance project, the more successful it will be.

In 1973, Congress passed the Percy Amendment to the Foreign Assistance Authorization Act directing AID to help developing nations "integrate women into their national economies." At the urging of Congress, AID, in 1982, provided guidelines for increasing the participation of women both as recipients and aid givers. In actual practice, however, the integration of women in the development process has received low priority and has yet to be fully realized.

The 100th Congress made some progress on this issue, and additional gains were made in the 101st and 102nd Congresses when portions of bills introduced by the late **Rep. Mickey Leland (D-TX), Rep. Olympia Snowe (R-ME)** and **Sen. Barbara Mikulski (D-MD)** were passed in foreign operations appropriations bills.

The Leland/Mikulski legislation, the Women in Development Act, insisted that the percentage of women receiving U.S. assistance be "in proportion to . . . their traditional participation in the targeted activities or to their proportion of the population." AID must include the active participation of local women and local women's organizations in planning, designing, and executing development projects.

The bills also require that AID "increase the number of, and the level of responsibility of, [its] women in Washington and in mission-based professional positions within the Agency" to equal the numbers and status of men. Rep. Snowe's bill additionally requires the director of the Peace Corps to incorporate women in every program and at every level in that agency.

Some of the language in the Mikulski bill was incorporated into the Senate version of the 1992–93 foreign aid authorization which was in conference at this writing.

SUSTAINERS OF THE THIRD WORLD

"Women are the poorest, hardest-working, least educated, and most unhealthy people in the developing world. They perform two-thirds of the world's work, receive one-tenth of its income, and own only one one-hundredth of its property. Studies have shown that rural women work, on average, two to four hours more per day than their male counterparts.

Worldwide, one-third of all households are headed by women; in Latin America the figure is as high as 50 percent. Women are the food producers of the developing world. . . . Women are also major income earners; their earnings provide for the most basic needs of their families: food, schooling, and medicines.

Furthermore, women are vital to the informal economy, the 30 to 60 percent of economic activity and employment which often is not officially recognized. In the Philippines, for example, four-fifths of the street food vendors are women. . . .

Despite [these] realities, women continue to be under-represented in, or excluded from, development programs."

—The late Rep. Mickey Leland (D-Texas)

• • •

INDIGENOUS PEOPLES: THE BEST STEWARDS

"Their survival is important for our own; it is imperative that we prevent their extinction. They perceive us as barbaric and strange, too. Yet, not only do we share a common humanity, but we can benefit from each other's knowledge. Indigenous peoples have rich storehouses of information about nature, man, and the balanced relationship of the two. From their beliefs about the spiritual world to their traditional knowledge of rain forests, healing, and agriculture, these societies provide the opportunity for new interpretations about the world and ourselves."

—Rep. Benjamin Gilman (R-New York)

There are groups of people on every continent who have always lived in a sustainable relationship with the earth. Indigenous peoples—Native Americans, Australian aborigines, the Indians of Latin America—have lived in harmony with their natural surroundings for tens of thousands of years. Tragically, as modern society pushes into and encloses the last of the world's wilderness areas, indigenous cultures, many of which still live sustainably in these last outposts, are being destroyed along with the wilderness itself.

In their fight to preserve and protect their homelands from the incursions of the chain saw and the tractor, industry and commerce, indigenous peoples have been warning us of the inevitable calamity that widespread destruction of the rain forests and other natural areas will bring.

In recent years, there has been renewed interest in helping indigenous peoples to preserve their way of life. Environmentalists regard indigenous peoples as the best stewards of endangered habitats and have become increasingly involved in their political struggles to survive. Wildlife biologists know that destruction of the ancient forests and their human inhabitants would result in the loss of thousands of years of priceless knowledge of the earth and its ecology, including precious pharmacological information unknown to modern civilization.

GETTING ORGANIZED

Indigenous peoples comprise about 10 percent of the world's population. Yet, the world over, they find themselves discriminated against, disenfranchised, and marginalized from the political mainstream—even in countries in which they comprise the majority or a significant minority as in Guatemala, Bolivia, Ecuador, and Peru. In many countries they have been, and continue to be, brutally repressed. In recent years, indigenous peoples around the world have organized politically to defend their right to live on and protect their ancestral lands.

In November 1989, the First Inter-American Indigenous Congress on Natural Resources and the Environment was organized by the Kuna Indians of Panama. The first order of business for this gathering of seventy representatives of indigenous cultures from seventeen countries was the protection of native-held lands from the relentless incursions of ranchers, miners, loggers, the oil industry, and homesteaders.

In 1990, Coordinadora de las Organizaciónes Indígenas de la Cuenca Amazonica, an umbrella organization representing more than 1 million Indians from more than 325 tribes living in the Amazon River Basin, met in Iquitos, Peru, to discuss how indigenous peoples from the region could unite to save Amazonia from destruction. Another meeting of representatives of Latin American indigenous cultures, sponsored by the Center for Democracy, took place in Guatamala City with a similar agenda.

LEGISLATION FOR SURVIVAL

In recognition of the rights of indigenous peoples and their importance as protectors of the global environment, a handful of legislators have stepped forward with proposals to lend support to indigenous groups worldwide as part of U.S. foreign policy.

In the House, **Rep. Benjamin Gilman (R-NY)** introduced the International Indigenous Peoples Protection Act, which "directs the Secretary of State and the administrator of the U.S. Agency for International Development (AID) to ensure that U.S. foreign policy and foreign assistance promote the rights of indigenous and tribal people throughout the world; and [that] foreign assistance is not provided for any project or program [that is] detrimental to indigenous peoples' rights or livelihood."

Gilman's bill would require that the Secretary of State and AID consult with nongovernmental organizations with expertise in dealing with the problems of indigenous peoples. They would be required to report on the status of indigenous and tribal cultures around the world, how U.S. development aid affects them, and to delineate any ameliorative steps that could be taken to support such peoples. Further, any report on the status of human rights in any country must include a section on the status of indigenous populations.

A bill introduced by **Sen. Alan Cranston (D-CA)**, the Pan-American Cultural Survival Act, includes all the provisions of Gilman's bill but would restrict the purview of such legislation to indigenous and tribal peoples of the western hemisphere. However, Cranston's bill has an additional proviso that requires the administrator of AID to create the position of Cultural Survival Officer. AID must place such a cultural survival officer at each of its foreign missions "in any country in which the indigenous peoples are under-represented in the country's political life, or could benefit from the development of measures to preserve areas of ecological or environmental significance."

Cranston's bill also urges the President, "in determining whether to conduct an activity of environmental protection assistance for a Latin American country, to consider the value of such activity in promoting the cultural survival of indigenous peoples."

GONE BY THE END OF THE DECADE

A resolution introduced by **Sen. Albert Gore (D-TN)** calls on the government of Malaysia to "preserve the tropical rain forests and the indigenous tribal culture of Sarawak," a region of Borneo and home of the Penan people. Members of this ancient tribe have been killed in clashes with soldiers as they have placed their bodies between loggers and the rain forest they need to maintain their livelihood and way of life.

In recent years, more than half of the forest in Sarawak has been felled for export by Japanese timber companies. It is estimated that, at the current rate of deforestation, the entire forest, and the culture of the Penan, will be gone by the end of the decade. The government of Malaysia has turned a deaf ear to international protest and the pleas of the Penan.

Gore's resolution declares that it should be U.S. policy to call upon the governments of Malaysia and Japan to immediately stop the uncontrolled exploitation of the forest and to formally recognize and uphold the human rights of Malaysia's indigenous people.

A SHAMEFUL RECORD

While current legislation spotlights the troubles of indigenous peoples around the world, Native Americans continue to struggle for their ancestral and political rights here in the United States. Native American tribes have lived sustainably on the North American continent for tens of thousands of years. However, with the arrival of European colonists, these people lost both their human rights and the land they so carefully stewarded over the millennia.

American history is marred by the shameful record of mistreatment of indigenous cultures; a story that is still being written. U.S. citizenship was not conferred on Native Americans until 1924. By law, Indians could not vote in Arizona and New Mexico until 1948. In 1978, a bill introduced in the New Mexico legislature to disenfranchise all Indians living on reservations failed to pass by just one vote. Many informal barriers to the full participation of Native Americans in American political life exist today.

BICYCLING TOWARD SUSTAINABILITY

The lack of affordable and sustainable modes of transportation in the third world has seriously hindered development in many countries. Yet this need has been virtually ignored by development planners.

For the majority of the world's population, the third world poor, daily reality involves hand-carrying water and firewood from faraway sources and carrying goods to and from the marketplace.

Private aid organizations have also found that lack of transportation often blocks or delays the delivery of health care services.

"Unfortunately, development programs, funded in part by the United States, currently promote policies favoring capital-intensive highways and motorized vehicles," **Rep. Claudine Schneider (R-RI)** told her colleagues in the House. "All too frequently, the low-cost, non-polluting, more broadly affordable, human-powered vehicles are marginalized or destroyed."

In Jakarta, Indonesia, for example, 75,000 tricycles were thrown into the sea, supposedly to relieve traffic congestion. El Salvador has spent more than half of its export earnings on petroleum, yet, only a tiny minority in that country can afford to own cars.

The global environment, however, could not possibly sustain the energy requirements and pollution output of Western-style transportation in developing countries. To help remedy the situation, Rep. Schneider introduced into Congress a resolution requiring that "U.S. foreign development assistance encourage access to sustainable means of transportation in developing countries that help meet basic human needs, protect the global environment, and provide affordable, low-cost mobility."

The resolution directs the administrator of AID to encourage the use of a variety of low-cost and nonmotorized transport and to direct funds into a sustainable transportation program. The Peace Corps and the U.S. executive directors of multilateral development banks have a similar mandate.

SUSTAINABLE INTERNATIONAL DEVELOPMENT: THE GREEN VOTE

☑ Increase emergency food assistance and long-term development assistance, to sub-Saharan Africa.

☑ Ensure that U.S. assistance to Africa, the Caribbean, Latin America, and other regions of the world, promotes development that is equitable, participatory, self-reliant, and environmentally sustainable. Ensure that local populations that are supposed to benefit from development aid be consulted and involved in designing and implementing aid programs.

☑ Expand the U.S. Agency for International Development's micro-enterprise lending program; and increase the number of micro-enterprise loans to women and the poorest of the poor.

☑ Direct U.S. foreign development aid to work toward the elimination of the worst aspects of poverty by the year 2000, and set specific goals by which the success of such aid can be measured.

☑ Implement the plan of action adopted by the 1990 Summit for Children to meet specific goals to help the world's poor and disadvantaged children by the year 2000.

☑ Increase the percentage of women receiving U.S. development aid in proportion to their traditional participation in targeted activities, or to their proportion of the population. Increase the numbers, and level of responsibility, of women aid providers within the U.S. Agency for International Development and the Peace Corps.

☑ Ensure that U.S. foreign policy and development assistance promotes and defends the rights of indigenous and tribal peoples throughout the world. Require the U.S. Agency for International Development to employ a cultural survival officer at each of its missions in countries in which indigenous peoples are politically underrepresented or would benefit from measures to preserve areas of environmental significance.

☑ Require U.S. foreign development assistance to encourage increased use of modes of transportation that are affordable, meet basic human needs, and protect the global environment.

A Biosphere Foreign Policy

"Last year we all experienced 'global warming' which scientists believe was partly due to destruction of forests in Latin America. Less than five percent of the tropical forests in South America receive any protection. As the worsening economic conditions and mounting debt pressures in developing countries persist, planners are forced out of necessity to ignore environmental planning and conservation when planning both industrial and rural development projects. Clearly, reforms are needed at the international level to deal simultaneously with the economic and ecological aspects of the problems of developing countries. . . ."

—Rep. Jim Bates (D-CA)

Commercial and military concerns continue to dominate the foreign policy initiatives of the United States and most other nations. Nonetheless, a growing number of Green-oriented elected officials in various nations are shifting their foreign policy orientation from geopolitics to biosphere politics and from national military security to global environmental security. They realize that traditional threats to security pale in contrast to the new genre of global environmental crises that now threaten the very survival of nature and human civilization. They also understand, however, that environmental, economic, and social problems are intimately connected, and that no one problem can be solved in isolation.

BANKRUPTING THE ENVIRONMENT

The wholesale transfer of wealth from the South to the North has devastated economic systems and ecosystems throughout the third world. U.S. foreign assistance programs have played a major role in this transfer of wealth by encouraging the development of cash crops for export and the abandonment of subsistence-based agriculture. Often, the poor are removed from their ancestral lands to make way for corporate agriculture serving the needs of the international commodities market. Even then, fluctuations in world prices for agricultural commodities have forced many third world nations deeply into debt. Their debts are compounded by heavy expenditures for arms and the increasing cost of purchasing oil.

As developing nations hurry to convert ever more of their natural resources into exportable products in order to pay their debts, they are bankrupting not only their economies but their environments as well.

Several ideas for reversing this trend have been proposed by various groups. Among them is the idea of allowing debtor countries to exchange their debt for protection of natural resources. Environmentalists and progressive development organizations caution, however, that not all debt-for-nature swaps are the same. Those that are conditional on economic policy restructuring are usually detrimental. President Bush's Enterprise for the Americas Initiative, part of which was adopted by Congress and was signed into law as part of the Food and Agriculture Act of 1990, is controversial because debt-for-nature swaps allowed under the Initiative will be conditional on the adoption of economic restructuring by debtor nations in Latin America and the Caribbean.

Such conditional economic reform more often than not involves the deregulation of industry and the cutting of environmental oversight budgets, increased austerity measures—which push ever more poor people to use marginal resources, and the promotion of an export-based economy in debtor countries—all of which reinforce current debt-associated problems and negatively affect the environment. It is important to recognize this point because today, the immediate priority of developing nations is the debt crisis—not the environment.

Debt for Nature

Sen. Joseph Lieberman (D-CT) has introduced the Debt for Environment Act, which would allow certain third world debtor nations, already selected for debt rescheduling by the President, to repay 20 percent of their loans in local currency if the debtor nation agrees to use that local currency to improve its environment. The remaining 80 percent would be repaid in dollars. Participating debtor nations would be required to design an environmental improvement plan in consort with the appropriate development bank and in consultation with indigenous nongovernmental environmental organizations and representatives of the U.S. government.

"The Debt for Environment Act goes beyond previous debt relief proposals because it lays the foundation for participation in these swaps by other developed nations through the regional development banks or the United Nations," Lieberman told his colleagues in the Senate. "These institutions can act as a conduit for not only the reduction of U.S. official debt but for the reduction of government debt of other developed nations. If this process is successful in both reducing the debt burden of developing nations, and at the same time helping them clean up their environment, then it can serve as a prototype for . . . other industrialized nations holding substantial third world debt."

Rep. Peter Kostmayer (D-PA) introduced his own debt-for-nature bill for countries in the western hemisphere. The Western Hemisphere Debt-for-Nature Conversion Act "authorizes the President, under debt-for-nature agreements, to release eligible Latin American and Caribbean countries from obligations to repay economic assistance loans."

The bill directs the President, in determining eligibility, to take into account "the need for financial resources for protecting or restoring environmentally critical areas and resources in such country; and the commitment of the country's government to such protection and restoration."

Rep. John Porter (R-IL) introduced the Tropical Forest Protection Act "to enable and encourage developing nations with external debt and tropical forests to preserve, restore, enhance, and manage such forests by reducing their debt to private lenders if such nations demonstrate actions to protect tropical forests or other endangered ecosystems or species."

The bill requires the Secretary of the Treasury to instruct the U.S. executive directors of multilateral development banks to promote programs in which such countries, through debt reduction, could buy back private debt at discount rates in the secondary market if they (1) "convert an agreed-upon amount of debt to local currency for use in 'debt-for-nature swap' programs for the protection of forests, ecosystems, or species; or (2) demonstrate a commitment to the protection of forests in the form of swaps for set-asides or conservation easements."

Porter's bill was incorporated into other legislation that was passed by the 101st Congress and signed into law as the International Development and Finance Act.

Rep. Jim Bates (D-CA) introduced a resolution "calling on the International Bank for Reconstruction and Development to . . . reduce the debt service burden of debtor nations in exchange for steps taken by such nations to protect tropical rain forests and other natural resources." The resolution further urges the Comptroller of the Currency, the Chairman for the Board of Governors of the Federal Reserve System, and the Federal Deposit Insurance Corporation to encourage each bank under their jurisdictions to do the same.

BANKING ON ENVIRONMENTAL PROTECTION

The World Bank and other multilateral development banks, in cooperation with private lending institutions in the United States, Japan, and Europe, together provide nearly 90 percent of the developing world's capital. When the projects for which these banks lend money are developed without environmental protection in mind, massive ecological and economic damage often results.

While the World Bank, which is looked to around the globe for leadership on lending issues, has recently developed some environmental standards for its lending programs, environmentalists and private development organizations feel that such internal voluntary measures need to be supported and strengthened by the application of external pressure. The United States contributes more resources to international lending institutions than any other nation and therefore plays a significant role in determining their projects, policies, and lending practices.

The late **Sen. John Heinz (R-PA)** introduced the Environmental Sector Lending Act, which requires the Secretary of the Treasury to instruct the U.S. executive director of the International

Bank for Reconstruction and Development to "initiate discussions with bank officials and propose the establishment of a three-year pilot environmental sector lending program to be made available to any and all interested countries with a demonstrated commitment to national resource conservation."

The executive director would be required to "support, through program loans and projects based on long-term economic return, the sustainable use and protection of tropical forests, soil erosion control, maintenance and improvement of fisheries, water supply regulation, and indigenous knowledge of the management and use of natural resources."

Sen. Heinz reasoned that this kind of farsighted lending would reduce the need for future lending to reforest and otherwise restore environmentally degraded areas.

Rep. John Porter's Tropical Forest Protection Act which, as noted earlier, was passed into law, contained a similar provision for a three-year environmental sector lending program for "the refores-

• • •

"Examples abound of projects financed by the international community that have gone seriously awry because of bad planning and implementation. A beef export project in Botswana has resulted in widespread desertification and destruction of wildlife populations. The cruelest irony is that despite large exports of beef, 65 percent of that country is now dependent on foreign food aid where once it was self-sufficient.

"In Brazil, the Polonoreste project has been an economic and social debacle. Thousands of people were encouraged to relocate as part of a multi-faceted development project. The result has been the destruction of rain forests; a failed attempt to farm land that was unsuited to agriculture; and a displaced and impoverished population.

"In light of these and other failures it is time that the United States take the initiative to constructively influence reforms as a member of the World Bank and the three regional development banks."

—*Sen. Max Baucus (D-MT)*

Threatening the Global Environment

". . . The environmental record of the multi-lateral development bank investments has been dismal. Poorly engineered dams have unintentionally flooded thousands of acres of tropical forest, while others have been rendered useless by siltation. Large-scale export agricultural projects have displaced small farmers, driving them into the rain forest where the soil cannot support them.

"This has happened because these loans require such massive interest payments. For example, they have had to put in big mechanized farms to grow soybeans to sell on the world market to get the money to pay the interest payments. Then they move the farmers off those fields, as they go to bigger mechanized operations, and push them into the rain forest. The way they get in there, of course, is because the World Bank loans have helped them with infrastructure programs.

"Of these, perhaps the most detrimental ones have been the relocation and infrastructure programs intended to address political pressures, but ill conceived from an environmental standpoint. These projects entice migration into forested areas, only to result in rampant disease, deforestation, and, in the end, greater poverty.

"Mr. President, there is a growing consensus that the United States should be more conscientious about where it invests U.S. tax dollars. . . .

"When development proves to be unsustainable, we waste taxpayer dollars, destroy natural resources, depress underdeveloped peoples, and threaten the very global environment in which we live."

—*Sen. Steve Symms (R-Idaho)*

• • •

tation and restoration of environmentally degraded areas based on the estimated long-term economic return expected from the sustainable use and protection of tropical forests, and the benefits from maintenance of biological diversity and climate stabilization." The environmental lending portion of Porter's bill also encouraged greater international collaboration between development banks and environmental protection organizations.

Taking another tack on the problem, **Rep. James Scheuer (D-NY)** and **Sen. Steven Symms (R-ID)** introduced the National Environmental Policy on International Financing Act.

The Scheuer/Symms legislation would amend the National Environmental Policy Act to require that "before casting the U.S. vote on a proposed action by an international financial institution significantly affecting the quality of the environment, the appropriate federal official request [from the bank] an environmental impact statement."

Rep. Nancy Pelosi (D-CA) introduced the International Banking Environmental Protection Act which amends the International Financial Institutions Act "to prevent the U.S. executive director of a multilateral development bank from voting in favor of any proposed action by such bank unless a comprehensive environmental impact assessment has been furnished." The Secretary of the Treasury would later be required to report to Congress on "the efficacy of U.S. efforts to encourage consistent and timely environmental impact assessments of proposed multi-lateral development bank actions."

Pelosi's bill passed and became law during the 101st Congress.

BALANCING TRADE WITH ENVIRONMENTAL PROTECTION

"We can no longer stand idly by while some U.S. manufacturers, such as the U.S. carbon and steel alloy industry, spend as much as 250 percent more on environmental controls as a percentage of gross domestic product than do other countries. The steel industry has made a commitment to meeting new standards in controlling toxic air pollutants, among others, but these new standards are adding $15 per ton to the cost of steel. . . .

"[We need to] send a clear signal to companies around the world that avoidance of public health responsibilities will not lead to economic gain and that American companies will not be penalized because they are meeting their environmental obligations."

—Sen. David Boren (D-OK)

As presidential administrations and Congress attempt to reconcile the interests of the global environment with thorny national policy questions such as trade and competitiveness in the global marketplace, more often than not the environment emerges the loser. However, in his new bill, the International Pollution Deterrence Act, **Sen. David Boren (D-OK)** trys to create a win/win equation for both the environment and international trade.

Sen. Boren has noted that U.S. manufacturers, constrained by environmental protection laws and costly pollution controls, are at a competitive disadvantage against manufacturers in countries that do not impose such environmental controls. By failing to enact and enforce adequate environmental and public health standards, the governments of such countries allow their manufacturers to enjoy this economic advantage at the cost of global environmental destruction and damage to human health.

With the dual goal of balancing the competitive scales and protecting the global environment, Boren's proposed legislation would impose a duty on goods exported to the United States from countries that fail to impose and enforce meaningful pollution controls. The duty to be levied on such imported goods "shall consist of the cost which would have to be incurred by the manufacturer or producer of the foreign articles of merchandise to comply with environmental standards imposed on U.S. producers of the same class or kind of merchandise."

Under Boren's bill, 50 percent of the duties collected would be placed in a special Pollution Control Export Fund administered by the U.S. Agency for International Development (AID) and used to help developing countries purchase U.S. pollution-control equipment. The remaining 50 percent would be placed in a Pollution Control Research and Development Fund administered by the Environmental Protection Agency (EPA) and used to help U.S. companies research and develop new pollution-control equipment and technology.

Boren's bill also requires the administrator of the EPA to produce an annual report on the level of pollution control reached by the top fifty trading partners of the United States in the areas of air, water, hazardous waste, and solid waste.

ENCOMPASSING THE GLOBAL ENVIRONMENT

The National Environmental Policy Act (NEPA), now more than two decades old, is considered by many to be the most important environmental protection law in the world. The law requires that all federal agencies take a "hard look" at the environmental effects of the actions they propose to take, and that they consider alternatives that avoid or minimize environmental harm.

Under the law, all federal agencies must prepare environmental assessments or environmental impact statements—analyses that outline potential environmental problems and detail ameliorative steps or alternatives for every proposed action.

While Rep. Scheuer and Sen. Symms proposed amending this law to encompass U.S. involvement in multilateral banks, **Rep. Gerry Studds (D-MA)** introduced legislation to broaden the NEPA requirements. He proposed that the Council on Environmental Quality—an advisory panel to the President whose primary responsibility is enforcement of the law—issue regulations that require federal agencies to consider the effects of their proposed actions on the *global* environment, not just the U.S. environment. Studds's bill pertains to both atmospheric and water pollution, which know no national boundaries, as well as U.S. actions overseas.

Although a requirement to consider the global environment has always been implicit in the NEPA law, federal agencies, in actuality, have not completed environmental impact statements pertaining to the global environment or when planning U.S. activities overseas. Had an environmental impact statement been com-

"We are concerned now, as we were when NEPA [the National Environment Policy Act] was enacted, about polluted rivers, dirty air, and unplanned development. But we did not worry then that the earth might someday suffer an even greater loss—the loss of the very features that distinguish it from its interplanetary neighbors: a healthy ozone layer, a proper balance between oxygen and carbon dioxide in the atmosphere, and the ability to sustain human life.

"That is why the time has come to apply the principles of NEPA not just to our national environment, but to the global environment as well.

"[My] amendment eliminates any doubt that NEPA applies—as I believe it always has—to major federal actions having a significant environmental impact on the atmosphere, the oceans, Antarctica, and other areas that make up what is commonly referred to as the global commons.

"Second, it requires the Council on Environmental Quality (CEQ), consistent with the national security and foreign policy of our country, to issue regulations requiring federal agencies to consider the impact of their actions, including extra-territorial actions, on global climate change, depletion of the ozone layer, the loss of biological diversity, trans-boundary pollution and other matters of international environmental concern.

"That sounds like common sense. But the fact is that federal agencies currently make long-range decisions about agriculture, forestry, water resources, coastal zone resources, and energy policy with little or no regard for the cumulative impacts of those actions on the global climate.

"We seek, if the president is to be believed, to take the lead on international environmental issues. But today it is we who are the world's largest generator of the emissions that cause global warming. We are the largest user of the CFCs that deplete the ozone layer. We are by far the world's largest consumer of fossil fuels. And yet, a recent survey by CEQ indicated that not one federal action was systematically reviewed for its impact on the international environment—as required by NEPA—during the last decade."

—*Rep. Gerry Studds (D-MA)*

pleted before the start of Operation Desert Storm, the United States might have extended economic sanctions against Iraq rather than risk the environmental devastation that, in fact, did result from an all-out war.

The Studds legislation passed the House in the 101st Congress.

AN UNFINISHED AGENDA

Despite the number of progressive bills introduced in the 101st Congress and the first quarter of the 102nd Congress, not much in the way of Green foreign aid or foreign policy legislation was passed.

There were attempts to include Green ideas in House efforts to rewrite the Foreign Assistance Act of 1961. In 1989, the House passed a two-year foreign aid authorization that included environmentally sustainable development as one of the four pillars of U.S. foreign assistance.

The 101st Congress passed freestanding foreign aid appropriations bills for 1990 and 1991 that contain some provisos for protecting the global environment. Among them were provisions that urge the multilateral development banks to address global warming, forest protection, energy conservation, and renewable energy when deciding whether to fund development projects. The legislation also requires that 25 percent of the U.S. contribution to the World Bank be withheld until the bank submits a report detailing environmental protection activities undertaken during the previous fiscal year. Another provision prohibits the use of foreign assistance funds for any activities that would result in the loss of tropical rain forests.

In 1991, both the House and the Senate passed 1992–93 foreign aid authorization bills that include provisions relating to global environmental protection. At this writing, conferees from the House and Senate were meeting to iron out the details of the legislation. Both the House and the Senate bills include environmentally sustainable development among the primary objectives of

U.S. foreign aid programs. Both bills provide funding for population control programs and the United Nations Environmental Program. Both bills authorize environmental assistance for Eastern Europe. They also authorize the President to expand his program to set up environmental trust funds for Latin American countries under the Enterprise for the Americas Initiative—a plan, which as previously noted, has both good and bad implications for the environment and the poor.

The Senate bill contains additional provisions promoting energy efficiency in developing countries and placing restrictions on funding of foreign aid programs that would threaten tropical forests.

A BIOSPHERE FOREIGN POLICY: THE GREEN VOTE

☑ Encourage and allow developing nations with external debt to reduce or eliminate their debt by taking actions to preserve and maintain their tropical rain forests and other environmentally significant areas. Promote only those U.S. initiatives that do not force developing nations to adopt economic policies and programs that will have a negative effect on the environment and the poor.

☑ Require U.S. representatives of multilateral development banks to insist that environmental impact statements accompany all development proposals, promote only environmentally sustainable development projects, and veto any projects that do not have an accompanying environmental impact statement or that are not environmentally sustainable. Require U.S. multilateral bank representatives to work closely with U.S. and indigenous environmental protection organizations.

☑ Impose a duty—an environmental protection tax—on manufactured goods exported to the United States from countries that do not impose and enforce pollution controls on their industries. Require that the funds collected be funneled into programs to help such nations adopt pollution controls.

☑ Require all federal agencies to consider the effects of their proposed actions in the United States and overseas on the *global* environment—not just the environment of the United States.

Opening The Global Commons

As we noted in Section I, the modern era has been characterized by a relentless and systematic effort to enclose and commercialize the global commons.

Now, however, a new generation of Green-oriented elected officials are challenging many of the assumptions underlying the conventional approach to foreign policy with its emphasis on geopolitics and enclosure. Nowhere is this new thinking more in evidence than in recent legislative initiatives to protect the world's oceans and the Antarctic continent—the two remaining global commons on the planet. For the first time, elected officials are talking openly about our collective responsibility to preserve and protect these unenclosed regions, a shift in foreign policy thinking that could have a profound impact on the conduct of international relations in the years ahead.

Oceans: A Public Trust

For nearly two centuries, the great oceanic commons have served as dumping grounds for industrial and residential waste. Today 89 million Americans live within 50 miles of the Atlantic and Pacific oceans. Garbage from cities, industrial parks, and residential communities is seeping into the sea at an alarming rate, threatening marine life and the stability of ocean ecosystems. Seals in the Gulf of Mexico are reported to have the highest level of pesticide contamination of any mammal. Fishermen along the Atlantic coast stretching from New England to the Chesapeake Bay report catches of lobsters and crabs with holes in their shells and fish with rotted tails and ulcerous lesions. In Louisiana, 35 percent of the state's oyster bed was closed in 1988 because of sewage contamination. San Francisco Bay is contaminated with high levels of mercury, nickel, copper, and other heavy metals that have been discharged in industrial waste.

Plastic waste is now so prevalent in the world's oceans, that it can be seen floating on the surface on any given day anywhere on the planet. Nearly 2 million seabirds and 100,000 marine animals die every year from consuming plastic debris or from becoming entangled in it. Sea turtles have been found choked to death by plastic bags. Sea lions have been found strangled by plastic mesh.

Ocean pollution has now reached such crisis proportions that it is threatening the future of the commercial fishing industry around the world. Already commercial fishing is on the decline in most of the world's oceans as a result of increased pollution and overfishing. In some regions clam and oyster catches have decreased by as much as 50 percent over the past decade.

Fish are often so contaminated from pollution that state health authorities are imposing bans or issuing public warnings not to consume certain fish during certain times of the year. Contaminated fish are the cause of a range of human illnesses including cholera and hepatitis A. The New York State health authorities have warned women of childbearing age to avoid eating most fish caught in New York coastal waters.

Rep. Claudine Schneider (R-RI) introduced the Ocean Dumping Enforcement Improvement Act "to prohibit unauthorized ocean dumping in the exclusive economic zone"—the exclusive economic zone extends 200 miles from the coastline. Congress passed a law in 1988 outlawing ocean dumping of sewage and industrial waste, including medical waste, toxic chemicals, sludge, and other garbage. Unfortunately, as Schneider points out, the Ocean Dumping Ban Act lacked tough enforcement provisions. The new bill "prescribes fines pursuant to the Federal Criminal Code and up to one year of imprisonment or both for negligent violations" of the ocean dumping ban and doubles the maximum punishment for subsequent violations. Schneider's act also establishes civil penalties of up to $250,000 for violations of the dumping ban. The bill even contains a provision authorizing the Administrator of the EPA or the Secretary of the Treasury "to pay awards of up to $10,000 for information leading to findings of liability, civil judgment, criminal convictions, or forfeitures of property" of any parties guilty of ocean dumping.

Public concern over ocean pollution came to a head in 1989 when the *Exxon Valdez* oil tanker struck a reef in Prince William Sound in Alaska, dumping more than 11 million gallons of oil into coastal waters. The oil spill, the worst in U.S. history, devastated the region, killing off much of the wildlife and seriously undermining the commercial fishing and tourist industries. Nightly television coverage of the catastrophe, showing seabirds and sea otters smothered in oil, unable to move and gasping for breath, enraged the American public. After years of congressional inaction on the issue of ocean dumping, Green legislators began to mobilize their forces on the Hill to address the question of oil spills on the high seas.

Rep. Walter Jones (D-NC) and **Senator George Mitchell (D-ME)** introduced similar oil spill legislation in the House and Senate. The bills, which were subsequently combined and passed into law, established new liability requirements for oil spills as well as new structural requirements for oil tankers. The Oil Pollution Act of 1990 makes the owner and operator of a vessel liable for any discharge of oil into the ocean. Liability includes the cost of containing and cleaning up a spill, loss of profits or earnings as a result of damage inflicted by a spill, natural resource damage, loss of income by those who rely on those resources for their livelihood, loss of tax revenues by local and state governments, and costs incurred by federal, state, and local governments, including additional public services required during cleanup activities.

The act also sets up a $1 billion oil liability trust fund to cover any additional costs of cleanup and compensation beyond the financial capability of the owner/operator of any vessels charged with ocean dumping. The fund is financed by a 5-cents-per-barrel tax on oil.

To help minimize the possibility of oil spills in the future, the act requires double-hull containment systems on all tankers and barges operating in U.S. waters or subject to U.S. jurisdiction. All existing tankers without double hulls are to be phased out beginning in 1995. Unfortunately, the act grants an exemption for certain tankers. Vessels unloading at deep-water ports and ships used to transfer oil to other ships will not have to be equipped with double-hull containment until 2015, seriously compromising the spirit of the act and making potential oil spills a continued threat well into the twenty-first century.

Finally, the act requires the President to intervene and coordinate all federal, state, local, and private cleanup efforts if an oil spill poses "a substantial threat to public health and welfare." This provision was considered particularly important because valuable time was lost in the days following the *Exxon Valdez* spill as the company and local officials fought with each other over how to proceed. In the eleven days of indecision following the spill, the oil slick spread to an area covering 850 square miles.

ANTARCTICA: THE LAST LAND COMMONS

Today, the Antarctic continent remains the only sizeable land commons left on earth. Antarctica covers 10 percent of the world's surface, extending over some 5.41 million square miles. An ice sheet covers 98 percent of the continent and comprises nearly 70 percent of the world's freshwater reserves. The Antarctic is home to more than 700 species of plants, 200 invertebrate animals, 50 species of birds, several species of whales and squid, a large number of penguins, and vast amounts of krill. It is the most pristine ecosystem left on earth. The Antarctic also contains vast amounts of mineral deposits, making it a choice target for commercial exploitation.

In 1961 twelve nations signed the historic Antarctica Treaty which prohibits military bases on the continent as well as nuclear and other weapons tests. The treaty also called for joint scientific exploration of the continent. Twenty-six nations, including the United States, are now signatories to the treaty.

Over the past few years, increasing pressure has been applied by commercial concerns interested in exploiting the mineral potential of the last untouched continent. The prospect of partially enclosing the Antarctic land mass for commercial gain has touched off a heated battle between global corporations and environmentalists.

Parliaments around the world have begun to take up the question of whether or not to partially enclose the Antarctic. In our own Congress several legislators have led the opposition to commercial enclosure, arguing that Antarctica ought to be preserved as a global commons.

Congressman **Bruce Vento (D-MN)** and thirteen cosponsors introduced the Antarctic World Park and Protection Act. The act would direct the Secretary of the Interior "to establish a plan for the management of Antarctica as a world park." The bill would also "prohibit mineral exploration or development in Antarctica." The legislation identified specific areas in Antarctica that would be open to tourists and carefully prescribed the number of visitors allowed and the conditions of their stay. The bill also contained provisions for scientific studies, environmental monitoring, and restoration of damaged environments. Finally the act directed the President to enter into negotiations with other nations to establish an international agreement on making Antarctica into a world park.

While the Vento bill was the most ambitious effort to date to protect the Antarctic and preserve it as a global commons, other bills along similar lines were introduced.

Rep. Wayne Owens (D-UT), Rep. Walter Jones (D-NC) and **Sen. Albert Gore (D-TN)** all introduced legislation that would protect the Antarctic. Owens' bill (in the form of a resolution), would like Vento's, maintain Antarctica as a global commons "closed to commercial mineral development and related activities for an indefinite period." Seventy-seven cosponsors joined Rep. Owens in support of his bill. Rep. Jones introduced two different pieces of legislation. His first bill would require the director of the National Science Foundation to prepare and implement "a waste management plan for waste produced or disposed of in the Antarctic by U.S. citizens." The second bill would make it unlawful "for any person or vessel subject to U.S. jurisdiction to discharge oil in the Antarctic Treaty area." The bill authorized civil penalties and required the violators "to remove the oil, restore the effected environment, and compensate persons for the removal and restoration costs and damages." (Sen. Gore's bill in the Senate included many similar provisions for waste disposal and oil-spill liability.)

Two pieces of legislation to protect the Antarctic passed into law in the 101st Congress. **Rep. Silvio Conte (R-MA)** and **Sen. John Kerry (D-MA)** sponsored the Antarctic Protection Act of 1990, which "prohibits prospecting, exploration and development of the Antarctic mineral resources by United States citizens and other persons subject to the jurisdiction of the United States." The second bill, in the form of a joint resolution of Congress, called on the United States to "encourage immediate negotiations toward a new agreement among Antarctic Treaty consultive parties for the full protection of Antarctica as a global ecological commons." This bill was sponsored by **Rep. Wayne Owens (D-UT), Rep. Stephen Neal (D-NC),** and **Sen. Albert Gore (D-TN).**

In June 1991, the twenty-six signatory nations of the Antarctic Treaty met to ratify a new agreement that would protect the Antarctic from commercial mineral exploration and exploitation for fifty years. Only the United States delegation opposed the ban. Curtis Bohlen, the chief American delegate to the conference, stated for the public record that "the Bush administration has been consistently opposed to a permanent mineral activity ban." A month later, President Bush bowed to public pressure and announced that the United States would agree to the ban on commercial mining activities on the Antarctic continent.

Oceans and Antarctica: The Green Vote

☑ Impose heavy fines and up to one year of imprisonment, or both, for negligent violations of the Ocean Dumping Act.

☑ Increase liability limits for oil spills, making owners and operators of oil tankers liable for the cost of containment and cleanup, property loss or damage, damage to the environment, loss of earnings, loss of tax revenue to local and state governments, and the increased cost of public services during the cleanup activities.

☑ Support a $1 billion oil spill liability trust fund to cover any additional costs of cleanup, and compensation beyond the liability limits imposed on the owner/operator of responsible vessels.

☑ Require double-hull construction on all oil tankers and barges operating in U.S. waters or subject to U.S. jurisdiction, by the year 2000.

☑ Require the President to intervene and coordinate containment and cleanup efforts for oil spills that pose a substantial threat to public health or the environment.

☑ Preserve the continent of Antarctica as a global commons. Prohibit all commercial mining and oil exploration.

☑ Establish regulations to control tourism and minimize waste disposal on the Antarctic Continent.

TOWARD AN ECOLOGICAL AGRICULTURE

American agriculture, long touted as the most productive agricultural system in history, is also the most polluting and environmentally destructive form of farming ever practiced. Modern agricultural practices are ruining the nation's soil base, poisoning agricultural produce, contaminating the groundwater, and contributing to the increase in global warming.

Squeezed by overproduction and falling prices, American farmers have been forced to overuse existing cultivated land and exploit ever more marginal land just to make ends meet. The result has been widespread and massive soil erosion. Over 4.8 billion tons of topsoil are blown or washed away every year. The U.S. is now losing one inch of topsoil on its agricultural lands every nineteen years. Overall, 100 million acres of U.S. agricultural land has been abandoned because of soil erosion. The National Academy of Sciences estimates that over one third of the agricultural topsoil in the United States is already gone, much of it lost in the last four decades. The loss of topsoil costs American farmers and the economy over $44 billion a year.

To compensate for the loss of topsoil, American farmers are spreading massive amounts of costly fertilizers on the land. As mentioned earlier, the use of fertilizers has increased dramatically since 1960 when 7 million tons were applied to soil in the United States. By 1989, nearly 20 million tons were being applied to the land in a futile attempt to maintain production on depleted and eroded soils. Today farmers apply 119 pounds of fertilizer per acre of cropland—that's 157 pounds of fertilizer for every man, woman, and child in the United States.

We are growing our food on a fossil fuel energy base, using up vast amounts of the remaining fuel reserves on the planet. American mechanized agriculture now accounts for 3 percent of the total energy consumed in the United States each year. In addition, petrochemical fertilizers emit nitrous oxide, one of the global warming gases. Nitrous oxide emissions account for over 6 percent of the global warming effect.

While fertilizers are increasingly used to bolster the productivity of a thinning soil base, massive amounts of chemical pesticides are being sprayed on crops to prevent insect infestation. Crop monoculturing, has so weakened the resistance of crops to infestation, that farmers have applied more and more pesticides in an effort to minimize their losses. The worldwide use of chemical pesticides has increased to over 4 billion pounds today. In the United States, alone, over 800 million pounds of pesticides are applied to crops each year at a cost exceeding $7 billion. Ironically, the farmers still lose over 37 percent of their crop to pests, in part because much of the pesticides never reach the plants. Most of the pesticides disperse into the surrounding ecosystem, seeping into the groundwater, contaminating freshwater wells and reservoirs.

Pesticide contamination from agricultural runoff now threatens the nation's water supply. In Kansas, water in 72 to 78 percent of the wells tested in the 1980s was contaminated with pesticides. In Nebraska, 70 percent of the wells have been tainted. In Iowa, 55 percent of the wells are contaminated. According to the U.S. Geological Survey's Pesticide Monitoring Network, one quarter of all the water-sampling stations contain residue from the pesticide atrazine, while DDT, chlordane and dieldrin were found in one third of the sediment tested in a nationwide survey.

The pesticides that find their way onto crops pose a serious public health threat. Today over 50,000 pesticides containing 700 ingredients are registered for commercial use in the United States. Some 496 of those ingredients are commonly found in tomatoes, apples, lettuce, beans, grapes, and other produce. In 1987 the National Academy of Sciences warned American consumers that

REPRINTED BY PERMISSION. TRIBUNE MEDIA SERVICES.

"90% of all fungicides, 60% of all herbicides, and 30% of all insecticides may cause cancer."

Detoxifying the Farm

A new Green awareness is emerging among some farm organizations and their supporters in the halls of Congress. In the past, farmers and environmentalists have often been at odds over agricultural policies. Today, there are signs that a growing number of farmers—especially among the younger generation—are beginning to question recent agricultural practices that degrade and poison the land, leaving it less productive and manageable. The new Green vision emphasizes partnership with the ecosystem and a sustainable relationship with the environment. This kind of Green thinking is a far cry from modern agricultural policy, with its emphasis on control over nature and the substitution of an artificially imposed environment awash in synthetic chemicals.

A series of bills were introduced into the 101st Congress to ease the transition from high-input petrochemical agriculture to low-input sustainable agriculture. **Sen. Wyche Fowler (D-GA)** and five cosponsors introduced the Farm Conservation and Water Protection Act. The bill contains several key provisions to help farmers introduce low-input sustainable agriculture methods. One of the provisions would provide incentives to the farmers to employ new low-input rotation of legumes as an alternative means of adding nitrogen to the soil. Many farmers are reluctant to grow resource-conserving crops because "it would reduce the base acreage on which federal payments are determined." Under the Fowler bill the planting of legumes would be considered as part of the program crop acreage, just like wheat, feed grains, cotton, rice, and other crops. In addition, the Secretary of Agriculture would be authorized to pay 50 percent of the cost of planting the legumes. Another provision "makes the conversion to and maintenance of low-input agricultural production systems eligible for operating loans." The bill also amends the Federal Crop Insurance Act "to prohibit crop insurance discrimination against producers utilizing low-input agricultural production systems."

The Fowler legislation directs the Secretary of Agriculture to "establish a program to assist producers in adopting low-input agricultural production systems," including technical assistance and grants. The bill would establish a Farmer's Conservation Service within the USDA extension service to assist producers to implement low-input agricultural production systems. This last provision is designed to open up the USDA to the new Green way of thinking about agriculture. Many of the agricultural universities and extension service centers are so mired in traditional high-input petrochemical agricultural practices, they lack the expertise to advise farmers about more ecologically sustainable approaches. For example, **Sen. Alan Cranston (D-CA)**, a cosponsor of the bill, pointed out in remarks on the Senate floor that Monterey, California, a county that generates over $2 billion in fruits and vegetables, "had only one entomologist to advise farmers on integrated pest management programs." The proposed Farmer's Conservation

Service would provide the kind of scientific and technological expertise needed to make the transition to low-input farming practices.

Other bills have also been introduced to encourage low-input sustainable agriculture. **Sen. Patrick Leahy's (D-VT)** bill directs the Secretary of Agriculture to "establish a federal-state matching grant program to create or enhance state sustainable agricultural research, extension, and education programs."

THINK GLOBALLY, ACT LOCALLY

- The Nebraska Department of Agriculture has awarded the University of Nebraska Institute of Agriculture and Natural Resources a grant of $836,000 for a twelve-state research survey on sustainable agriculture.

- The State of Iowa imposes a tax on fertilizers and pesticides. The revenues are used to support research and development of sustainable agriculture.

- Minnesota provides below market loans of up to $15,000 to farmers engaged in low-input sustainable agriculture programs.

• • •

To ensure that USDA personnel and others are knowledgeable about the new farming practices, Leahy's bill calls for the establishment of a national training program on sustainable agriculture. The bill requires that "at least 20 percent of all federal extension [service] staff participate in such training."

Rep. Jim Jontz (D-IN) and nineteen cosponsors introduced the Sustainable Agriculture Adjustment Act in the House to encourage low-input sustainable agricultural practices.

Many of the provisions and suggestions contained in the above bills were incorporated into the Food, Agriculture, Conservation, and Trade Act of 1990.

SuperGreen Farming

The Land Institute in Salina, Kansas, is experimenting with permaculture, an approach to agriculture based on planting a variety of perennial grasses, sunflowers, legumes, and grain crops together in the same field rather than planting a single species. The goal, according to Dr. Wes Jackson, founder of the institute, is to mimic the natural conditions of the prairie. In a wild prairie environment a range of plants flourish under extreme fluctuations: drought, floods, intense heat, and cold. Prairie soils are also very effective at storing water and sustaining nutrients. At the Land Institute, scientists are planting together native species like Illinois bundle flower, Maximillian sunflower, Eastern gamma grass, wild senna, sorghum, and legumes.

These innovative approaches to agriculture combine age-old agricultural practices with new, highly sophisticated ecological experimentation. By combining traditional wisdom with the latest developments in the ecological sciences, it is possible to envision a regenerative agricultural development program that can gradually wean the world away from its addiction to petrochemical-based agricultural practices. Greater reliance on nitrogen-fixing plants, natural manuring, integrated plant rotation and pest management, are essential features of a sustainable agricultural program that works with—rather than against—the environment.

• • •

ORGANIC LABELING

In recent years, American consumers have become increasingly concerned over the use of pesticides, synthetic chemicals, antibiotics, and hormones in their food. In 1989 a Harris Poll found that 84 percent of the public favor organically grown fruits and vegetables and nearly half of all consumers say they are willing to pay more to supermarkets for organic produce. Some twenty-two states have passed laws governing organic certification and labeling. Unfortunately, these laws differ substantially on the meaning of organic, giving rise to a confusing array of definitions. Then too, because there has been no single national standard, many food-processing companies have mislabeled products, claiming they are "organic" or "natural" even though they are not.

Rep. Peter DeFazio (D-OR) and **Sen. Patrick Leahy (D-VT)** introduced companion bills in the House and Senate to establish organic labeling standards and promote organically grown foods. The Organic Foods Production Act garnered twenty-two cosponsors in the House and twenty-two cosponsors in the Senate. Under the provisions of these bills, organically produced means "food grown by farmers without using substances known to be harmful to health—such as synthetic pesticides, hormones or antibiotics—or to cause environmental pollution." To qualify for organic certification, a farmer would have to refrain from using synthetic chemicals for three years. The bill also establishes a monitoring service. Produce would be periodically tested for any chemical residue, and unannounced on-site inspection of organic farms would be made by government agencies. A National Organic Promotion Board would also be established to promote the cause of organic agriculture among farmers and consumers.

• • •

GREEN FARMING IS GOOD BUSINESS

Organic farming uses no petrochemical fertilizers or pesticides but, rather, relies on natural organic manuring, nitrogen-fixing crop rotation, and natural pest management practices. Studies over the past decade have shown that once established, organic-based agricultural and chemical-based agriculture provide roughly the same yield per acre. Organic farming, however, uses two-thirds less energy to produce the same output, giving it a cost-competitive advantage over higher input chemical farming. Organic farms use 6,800 BTUs of energy to produce a dollar of output, whereas chemical farms use over 18,000 BTUs. One study found that highly mechanized chemical farming costs approximately $47 per acre, while low-input farming costs only $31 per acre, giving it a decisive edge.

© 1989, BOSTON GLOBE. DISTRIBUTED BY LOS ANGELES TIMES SYNDICATE.
REPRINTED BY PERMISSION.

Many of the provisions in the DeFazio and Leahy bills were incorporated into the Food, Agriculture, Conservation, and Trade Act of 1990 and made into public law. The growing public clamor for organically produced food is reflective of the new Green consciousness emerging in the country. A decade ago, the issue of pesticide, chemical, and antibiotic use in American agriculture would have been of interest only to environmentalists and public health organizations. Today many farmers and consumers have joined the Green ranks, broadening and deepening the Green constituency. Increasingly, the public is beginning to view personal health and the health of the environment as inseparably linked, marking a fundamental change in perspective.

THE CIRCLE OF POISON

While some efforts are being made to reduce the use of pesticides in American agriculture, a loophole in federal laws makes it possible for American chemical companies to export dangerous pesticides abroad that are prohibited from being used in the United States. The pesticides then find their way back to the United States in produce entering the country destined for grocery store shelves and public consumption. The process has come to be known as "the circle of poison."

Rep. Mike Synar (D-OK) and **Sen. Patrick Leahy (D-VT)** have introduced companion bills entitled the Circle of Poison Prevention Act, with 52 cosponsors in the House and 23 cosponsors in the Senate. The bills would prohibit the export and sale of unregistered pesticides abroad. The bills also prohibit the importation of food into the United States "unless the commodity importer files with the Secretary of Health and Human Services and the Secretary of the Treasury a document identifying each pesticide chemical used in connection with the commodity."

The bill also includes a provision to assist other countries in making a transition from use of chemical pesticides to sustainable organic farming practices.

The Circle of Poison legislation acknowledges the need to think globally on issues of public health and the environment. With multinational companies now operating in a single world market, governments will increasingly have to take into consideration the impacts new technologies and products have on the biosphere and the well-being of other peoples. Taking responsibility, in a Green context, means caring for the well-being of the entire planet.

Protecting Farm Animals

Until recently, farm animals lived relatively natural lives before they were sent to slaughter. Cows with their calves and sheep with their lambs grazed placidly on acres of pasture. Pigs, who are highly social creatures, were kept outdoors where they could wallow in the mud with their fellows. Chickens had nests and yards where they could perform their entire repertoire of natural behaviors: scratch in the dust, spread their wings, and engage in ritual mating activities.

Unfortunately, these conditions no longer exist except in children's storybooks and on some of America's few remaining family farms. Since the end of the Second World War, with the rise of multinational corporations and the widespread mechanization of agriculture, most farm animals in this country have been caught up in the cold, grinding gears of a terrible machine—the intensive-confinement farm. This farming system is the equivalent of the contemporary industrial plant, except that its raw materials and products are not iron ore and steel girders, but warm-blooded, sentient beings: cattle, pigs, sheep, chickens, turkeys, and their young. Virtually all of the 6 billion animals that Americans eat every year pass through its gates.

The miserable life of a milk-fed veal calf is typical of the suffering imposed by the intensive-confinement system. Calves intended for veal production are taken from their mothers at birth to spend their entire lives isolated and chained at the neck in wooden crates so small that they cannot turn around or lie down with their legs outstretched. Housed indoors, they see the sun and socialize with their fellows only once—the day they are loaded into the slaughterhouse truck.

Lack of exercise and a purely liquid diet of milk replacer low in iron, slows muscle development to ensure that their meat will be pale and tender. As a consequence, veal calves frequently become anemic and suffer from chronic diarrhea and weakness. To keep the animals alive until slaughter and to ensure speedy growth, veal calves (and virtually all intensively reared animals) are given large amounts of antibiotics and growth hormones that have devastating impacts on the animals and unknown health effects on consumers.

It is worth noting that if a person were to treat a dog in the same manner that agribusiness routinely treats veal calves, that person could be arrested, fined and/or imprisoned. State anticruelty laws routinely exempt livestock from protection, however, and there is no U.S. law to protect farm animals from outright cruelty, brutal handling, or inhumane living conditions.

Only two federal laws pertain to farm animals, and neither regulates living conditions. The Twenty-eight Hour Law, which pertains only to the approximately 5 per cent of animals who are transported by rail and over water, requires that animals must be given rest, food, and water if they are in transit more than twenty-eight hours. The Humane Slaughter Act, adopted in 1958 and put into effect in 1960, requires that some animals be rendered unconscious before slaughter unless they are ritually slaughtered for religious reasons.

ROOM TO TURN AROUND

The first attempt to regulate the living conditions of any farm animals in the United States was made in the 100th Congress by **Rep. Charles Bennett (D-FL)** in the form of a proposed bill to impose standards of humane care for veal calves. **Sen. Harry Reid (D-NV)** later introduced similar legislation in the Senate.

This historic piece of legislation, the Veal Calf Protection Act, would require veal producers to meet the following two requirements: (1) that a "calf is free to turn around without difficulty, lie with its legs outstretched, and groom itself, without any impediment such as too small an enclosure or chaining or tethering." (2) that a "calf is fed a daily diet containing sufficient iron and, if the calf is more than 14 days old, sufficient digestible fiber to prevent anemia and to sustain full health."

Although this legislation would provide only the simplest and most minimal of protections, it was vehemently opposed at hearings on the bill by the agribusiness industry and members of the so-called Animal Welfare Caucus in Congress.

Rep. Bennett also tried to get the veal calf bill passed as an amendment of the 1990 Omnibus Farm Bill, but it was defeated by a voice vote. Fortunately, the bill had enough support in the 101st Congress (ninety-two cosponsors in the House and five in the Senate) to encourage its reintroduction in the current session of Congress.

So far, the introduction of the Veal Calf Protection Act remains Congress' sole foray into the question of whether farm animals have the right to be provided with humane care. Although Congress, as a whole, has not done well on this issue, a few bright lights are leading the way. And if what has been occurring in other developed countries is any indication, it is only a matter of time before legislation to protect all farm animals is enacted in the United States.

* * *

"Mr Chairman, about a year ago . . . I watched on TV . . . a program about how veal is being raised . . . in the United States. It was an excruciatingly painful thing to see.

"I had no previous interest in the matter at all, but when I saw what was being done with regard to these veal calves, I concluded something ought to be done about it. When I looked into it I found it is not only very cruel raising these calves, but also very injurious to the consumer because these calves have to be sick to make white meat. That is what white veal is; it is sick meat . . . (People have found) out that white veal is bad for you because it often has medicine in it, put in the calves in order for the calves to even survive.

"But if you saw the cruelty involved, you would be very touched. I was very touched by it myself. I am not a fanatic on any subject . . . but I was touched in my heart when I saw these calves that could not lie down, could not move at all. They are bigger than the stalls they are in, and they are kept there for their entire lifetimes."

—*Rep. Charles Bennett (D-FL)*

"Mr. Chairman, I think that most Americans think its all right to kill animals and eat them. I do not. But most Americans do, the overwhelming majority. I think hardly any Americans would want animals tortured, though, before they are slaughtered. . . . I believe it would ease the conscience of the nation to accept this amendment. I am proud to support it."

—Rep. Andrew Jacobs (D-IN), speaking in support of Rep. Charles Bennett's proposed Veal Calf Protection Amendment to the 1990 Omnibus Farm Bill

Some legislation that will indirectly help farm animals was passed by the 101st Congress in those portions of the 1990 Omnibus Farm Bill that deal with the U.S. Department of Agriculture's sustainable agriculture program. One of the stated purposes of the program is "to encourage research designed to increase our knowledge concerning agricultural production systems that . . . promote the well-being of animals." This portion of the Farm Bill was introduced into Congress by Sen. Thomas Daschle (D-SD) as the National Agricultural Research, Extension, and Teaching Policy Act of 1990.

The 1990 Farm Bill also included an organic-food certification program that sets forth national standards for organically raised food, including livestock and poultry. The Organic Foods Production Act of 1990, which was introduced by Sen. Patrick Leahy (and already mentioned earlier in this section), is important to farm animals because organically raised farm animals generally lead more natural lives, under more humane conditions, than those raised under factory conditions. Uniform standards for organic produce will spur the growth of the fledgling organic-livestock industry. However, such legislation, although helpful, can never take the place of badly needed humane legislation that respects the inherent rights of farm animals.

TOWARD AN ECOLOGICAL AGRICULTURE: THE GREEN VOTE

☑ Promote incentives to farmers to plant legumes as part of an integrated crop rotation system. Legumes offer an alternative means of adding nitrogen to the soil, reducing or eliminating the need to use petrochemical fertilizers. Allow farmers to count legumes as part of their program crop acreage when determining federal payments.

☑ Establish a Farmer's Conservation Service within the USDA to assist farmers in implementing a low-input sustainable agricultural production system. Provide scientific and technical expertise to farmers making the transition from chemical to organic farming practices.

☑ Make the conversion to and maintenance of low-input agricultural production eligible for operating loans.

☑ Establish a federal matching grant program to assist state efforts at promoting low-input sustainable agriculture programs.

☑ Establish a national training program in sustainable agriculture. Require at least 20 percent of all federal extension service staff to participate in the training.

☑ Establish uniform national standards governing the labeling of organically produced food to allow consumers to make informed choices in their purchases and to encourage farmers to begin producing organically grown crops.

☑ Prohibit the export and sale abroad of any pesticide banned from use in the United States.

☑ Prohibit the importation of food into the United States if banned chemical pesticides were used during its production.

☑ Assist other countries in making the transition away from

chemical pesticides to nontoxic sustainable pest management practices.

☑ Adopt laws to ensure that veal calves and all other farm animals are provided with an environment that satisfies their basic physical and psychological needs.

STEWARDING PUBLIC LANDS

The Arctic National Wildlife Refuge has been called the "crown jewel of America's wild lands" by the National Audubon Society. Together with Canada's Northern Yukon National Park, it forms "the single most important haven for Arctic life in the world."

The 19-million-acre refuge in northeastern Alaska supports such an abundance of wildlife—polar and grizzly bears, wolves, musk-oxen, and thundering herds of caribou—that it is frequently referred to as the "American Serengeti." It is also the source of sustenance for an Indian nation, the Gwich'in people of Canada, who depend upon the caribou herds for their survival.

Unfortunately, the refuge also may contain what could be the last significant, but as yet untapped, oil fields on the continent.

In the aftermath of the war in the Persian Gulf, President Bush has made increased domestic oil production, including drilling in the Arctic National Wildlife Refuge, a critical priority in his new plan to make the United States more energy independent. Only Congress can authorize oil drilling in the refuge; but the "environmental President" has stated that he will veto any energy legislation that does not include drilling there.

The battle over the refuge's fate is now raging on Capitol Hill; but it is more than just another spat between conservationists and supporters of development. It is a fight over the nation's energy policy.

Oil as "National Security"

At the center of the controversy is the Arctic National Wildlife Refuge's 1.5-million-acre plain along the Arctic Ocean, an area that biologists believe is the biological heart, the most ecologically sensitive part, of the refuge. In 1980, the year the refuge was created, Congress, in a compromise measure, designated the coastal plain a "special study area" so that its potential for oil and gas might be explored.

As pressure has steadily mounted to locate new sources of domestic oil, the reported potential of the coastal plain to produce oil has also risen. Geologic studies conducted by the U.S. Bureau of Land Management (BLM) in 1987 predicted that there was only a 19 percent chance of recovering a large quantity of oil from the refuge.

But in 1991, after the Bush administration's energy plans were announced, the BLM suddenly revised its estimate and issued a memo boosting the chances of recovering oil to 46 percent. The BLM has refused to share the data on which this latest estimate was based; environmentalists have bitterly condemned the memo as a politically timed announcement of questionable veracity. In July 1991, a federal judge ruled that the BLM's revised figure was unsubstantiated.

Oil companies and other proponents of drilling in the refuge argue that the United States is too dependent on foreign oil and that it is a matter of "national security" to open up the refuge and increase domestic oil production in order to meet the nation's growing energy needs. In the aftermath of the Persian Gulf war, Rep. Don Young (R-AK) and Sen. Ted Stevens (R-AK) introduced bills in the 102nd Congress to open the refuge for development. Sen. Bennett Johnston (D-LA), chairman of the Senate Energy Committee, and Sen. Malcolm Wallop (R-WY) also introduced a comprehensive energy package into Congress that would include drilling in the refuge.

Johnston's committee passed the Johnston/Wallop energy

SAVE THE ARTIC REFUGE!

"I believe the vision of our nation has to exceed our grasp. We have to look to the future well-being of our fragile environs. We have to understand that our responsibility to protect the environment for the health and well-being of generations to come greatly outweighs the need for convenient short-term solutions to energy needs. We have to understand that the short-term gains are overshadowed by long-term consequences. . . .

"To illustrate how short-term these gains are, the mean recoverable estimates—if oil is found—would provide an average of two percent of the nation's annual oil consumption over the life of the field. "Would we want to dam the spectacular geological phenomenon of the Grand Canyon for electricity or drill Yellowstone for geothermal energy? The answer is 'No.' We want to save these natural resources and protect them for enjoyment by future generations. There is no difference (between) these decisions and the ones we have to make concerning the coastal plain, an area of such beauty and wildlife that it should remain pristine wilderness. . . .

"We are buying rain forests to stem the tide of deforestation; we are spending millions of dollars to restore swamps and protect wetlands and wildlife, and we now have a chance to save the only entire Arctic ecosystem that is left and that has not been exploited in one way or another. It is an opportunity of a lifetime that we must not let slip away."

—Sen. William Roth (R-DE)

• • •

package in May 1991, and defeated, by a margin of 11 to 8, a motion by **Sen. Timothy Wirth (D-CO)** to strike the section of the bill that permits drilling in the refuge. The Johnston/Wallop package closely resembles the National Energy Strategy proposed by President Bush. In addition to drilling in the refuge, it includes restrictions on public input regarding nuclear power facilities, a loosening of federal controls over major electric power producers, and no provisions to improve auto efficiency standards.

Fortunately, a bipartisan group of Senators strongly opposed to Bush's energy strategy filibustered in November 1991 and Johnston withdrew his bill—at least for the time being. The filibuster was led by Sens. **Richard Bryan (D-NV), Max Baucus (D-MT), Howard Metzenbaum (D-OH), William Roth (D-DE), Timothy Wirth (D-CO), Joseph Lieberman (D-CT), and Paul Wellstone (D-MN).**

Similar legislation to permit drilling in the refuge had passed the Senate energy committee in 1989. Eight days later, however, the *Exxon Valdez* oil tanker hit a reef and poured 11 million gallons of crude oil into Alaska's pristine Prince William Sound. The nation's worst oil spill convinced many in Congress that oil and wilderness don't mix, and the legislation died.

• • •

OIL AND WILDERNESS DON'T MIX

Myth: "There's plenty of wilderness for everybody. We don't need this small piece [of the Arctic National Wildlife Refuge.]"

Fact: Less then 4 percent of the original U.S. wilderness remains. The Arctic refuge's coastal plain is virtually the last stretch of the Arctic coastline of Alaska not open for development.

Myth: "The oil industry has an excellent environmental record at Prudhoe Bay, the Endicott field, and other Alaskan oil fields."

Fact: In 1986 alone, 64 million gallons of toxic drilling waste were discharged directly onto the tundra by north slope oil operations. In contrast, the *Exxon Valdez* spilled 11 million gallons of Alaskan oil.

Myth: "The impacts of development on coastal plain wildlife will be minimal."

Fact: According to the U.S. Department of the Interior, oil production and support activities are likely to result in a population decrease or change in distribution of 20 to 40 percent in the region's caribou population; 50 percent in the numbers of snow geese; and 25 to 50 percent in musk-ox populations.

—*The National Audubon Society*

WANTED: SUSTAINABLE ENERGY PLAN

Opponents of the Bush National Energy Strategy argue that destroying America's last pristine wilderness is not the way to respond to America's energy "crisis" and note that oil from the refuge would not be needed if a national plan for energy conservation were adopted.

Increasing the average fuel-economy standard for new cars from 27.5 to 34 miles per gallon by the year 2001, for example, would save more oil than could ever be recovered from the refuge. What's more, ten times the estimated potential of the Arctic refuge could be saved by the year 2020 if the fuel efficiency standards of cars were raised to 44 miles per gallon by the year 2000, and 60 miles per gallon by 2010.

Additional enormous savings could be realized by reducing the amount of energy wasted in homes, appliances, and elsewhere. Currently, more energy is wasted through the leaky windows of America's homes than flows through the Alaska pipeline.

"Drilling in the Arctic can at best only provide a temporary respite to our energy policy—it is only a delay," Sen. Timothy Wirth (D-CO) told the National Audubon Society. "Yet it would extract a high cost in sacrifice of other important values. . . ."

Even the most optimistic forecasts concede that the oil from the refuge would meet the nation's entire energy needs for only seven months. The country would soon find itself right back where it started from. In the meantime, the country will have imposed a huge industrial complex on the fragile coastal plain, destroying the last pristine Arctic wilderness in North America.

OPPORTUNITY OF A LIFETIME

Rep. Morris Udall (D-AZ) and **Sen. William Roth (R-DE)** introduced legislation in the 101st and 102nd Congresses to designate the coastal plain of the Arctic National Wildlife Refuge as wilderness, thereby rendering it off limits to oil development.

Because Sen. Udall resigned from Congress in April 1991 due to poor health, **Rep. Robert Mrazek (D-NY)** has assumed House leadership for protecting the refuge. Rep. Mrazek introduced a joint resolution, the Morris K. Udall Wilderness Act, which incorporates all of Rep. Udall's bill to protect the coastal plain. The resolution so far has seventy cosponsors.

Sen. Roth also introduced the Northern Yukon Arctic International Wildlife Refuge Act, which would establish, with the government of Canada, an international wildlife refuge composed of the Arctic National Wildlife Refuge and contiguous protected Canadian wilderness to permanently conserve "the last complete Arctic ecosystem in North America."

WILDLIFE REFUGES NEED REFUGE

When the National Wildlife Refuge System was first set up in 1903 by President Theodore Roosevelt, its purpose was clear and indisputable. Wildlife refuges were to be "inviolate sanctuaries" for wildlife, oases of relative peace, places where wild animals could escape human harassment and pursuit, and regenerate their numbers. During the past four decades, however, this intent has been subverted to an extraordinary degree.

The Arctic National Wildlife Refuge is not the only refuge in trouble. Today many national wildlife refuges are havens and wonderlands not for animals, but for hunters and trappers; ranchers; the oil, gas, timber and mining industries; power-boaters; and off-road vehicle enthusiasts.

Currently, 259 of the nation's 452 wildlife "refuges" permit sport hunting of more than 133 species of animals including deer, bears, mountain goats, antelope, elk, swans, geese, and ducks. Last year, hunters killed or crippled hundreds of thousands of these animals with bullets and arrows.

Sport and commercial trapping takes place in 91 "refuges"; many others permit trapping as a wildlife management tool. Last

HUNTING BLINDS?!.. THIS ONE FOOLS 'EM EVERY TIME!

© 1984, ERIC SAKACH, HSUS NEWS.

year, tens of thousands of refuge animals including foxes, wolves, bobcats, coyotes, raccoons, otters, beavers, and lynx died excruciating deaths in leghold, and other, traps.

In a scathing report prepared for Congress in 1990, the U.S. General Accounting Office found that activities considered harmful to wildlife occur in nearly 60 percent of the nation's refuges. For example, mining operations are permitted in 26 refuges; logging is conducted in more than 60 refuges; airboating is allowed in 36, off-road vehicles in 37, water-skiing in 53, large power boating in 114; and airborne military maneuvers (including practice bombing!) are permitted to take place in more than 55 refuges. Oil and gas drilling and cattle grazing are also permitted in refuges.

The U.S. Fish and Wildlife Service (FWS) began to open the refuges to these and other kinds of inappropriate activities in the 1950s. Vague legislation passed in the 1960s allows the Secretary of the Interior to permit any activity he finds "compatible" with a refuge's "primary purpose." What is deemed "compatible" is left up to each refuge manager to decide. Under the Reagan and Bush administrations, more refuges were opened to exploitive activities than ever before.

ECOLOGICAL HAVOC

Perhaps the ultimate violation of wildlife refuges, however, is the government's practice of killing predator species—often to provide more waterfowl and other "game" animals for hunters to kill. FWS calls this practice "wildlife management" or "predator control."

On at least two dozen "refuges," FWS kills predator species and other species that "interfere" with waterfowl production, including foxes, skunks, raccoons, badgers, certain birds, coypu, beavers, turtles, snakes, weasels, mink, rats, squirrels, muskrats, and rabbits in order to produce more waterfowl for hunters to shoot.

In addition to humane concerns, such abuses within the nation's wildlife refuges also wreak havoc with the natural balance of refuge ecology. The nation's refuges are home to more than 750 species of birds, 230 mammals, and 100 endangered species. These animals are disrupted, displaced, or killed by hunting, trapping, and invasive industrial and recreational activities, not to mention the government's wildlife "management" programs.

That such activities occur regularly in forests and woodlands across the country is bad enough; that they should also occur on the only lands this nation has set aside for wildlife is unconscionable.

REFUGE REFORM ON THE HORIZON?

At least two legislators have stepped forward with proposed remedies—**Rep. Gerry Studds (D-MA)** and **Rep. Bill Green (R-NY)**

Studds' bill, the National Wildlife Refuge System Act, would amend the National Wildlife Refuge System Administration Act of 1966 by requiring the Secretary of the Interior, acting through the director of the FWS, to issue regulations that detail a standard process for determining whether a proposed use is compatible or incompatible with a wildlife refuge. The bill "directs the Secretary to prepare and revise at least once every ten years a comprehensive

THE CASE AGAINST HUNTING AND TRAPPING IN REFUGES

What's wrong with hunting and trapping in wildlife refuges? For starters, hunting and trapping in themselves are antiecological. In a natural environment, species remain strong because weak and sick animals are killed off by disease, predators, and competition for limited food. Given a choice, however, hunters target vital, healthy animals and leave the sick ones to weaken a species' gene pool.

Trapping is also a devastating practice because traps do not discriminate between species and because they also tend to catch active, healthy animals.

Refuge hunts are not always the "fair game" and "clean kill" that hunters claim. A hunt supervisor and biologist for the Fish and Wildlife Service, for example, described a hunt in the Sand Lake National Wildlife Refuge in South Dakota in which 50,000 snow geese and blue geese were blasted out of the sky. Of the birds that were killed, half of them—25,000 geese—were not even taken for food; they were left to rot on the ground.

"Most of the hunters I saw or talked to had no respect or compassion for the birds or concern for what they were doing to them," the FWS supervisor said. "Hunters repeatedly shot over the line at incoming flights where there was no possible chance of retrieving. Time and time again I was shocked at the behavior of the hunters. I heard them laugh at . . . dazed cripples that stumbled about. I saw them striking the heads of retrieved cripples against fence posts."

Today many duck populations are in drastic decline. Yet hunters are regularly permitted to kill ducks in refuges.

The fact that hunting and trapping are permitted in refuges is all the more troubling when one considers that the National Wildlife Refuge System comprises only about 90 million acres, a tiny percentage of all lands available to sportsmen. If a ban on hunting in refuges were enacted tomorrow, hunters would still have more than 200 million acres of state land, 600 million acres of federal land, and more than 1 billion acres of private land on which to hunt. To add insult to injury, at least 97 percent of all refuge visitors come only to enjoy nature and view wildlife, not to hunt or trap. Yet visitors find that, during hunting season, public access to refuges is often severely restricted.

—The Humane Society of the U.S.

BLOOM COUNTY

by Berke Breathed

plan governing the administration" of the refuge system, and to "identify and discontinue incompatible and harmful uses of refuges that do not meet established refuge purposes."

Green's bill, the Refuge Wildlife Protection Act, would end recreational and commerical hunting and trapping in national wildlife refuges. Green's proposed legislation garnered seventy-two cosponsors in the 101st Congress and is supported by the Wildlife Refuge Reform Coalition, a group of more than thirty animal protection and environmental organizations.

The bill "amends the National Wildlife Refuge System Administration Act to require that any wildlife management or other activity which affects wildlife in any area of the system be conducted in the most humane manner possible."

In addition, it "permits the Secretary of the Interior to authorize any killing of a member of a wildlife species within any area of the system based upon evidence that such killing is necessary for the health and habitat of wildlife species within the area or to protect public health and safety, and that non-lethal management alternatives are not available." The Secretary is also required "to provide the scientific information upon which the authorization is based as well as details such as the numbers [of animals] to be killed," and "authorizes public hearings on such decisions unless an emergency exists."

CATTLE: NEMESIS OF THE WEST

Americans own in common one third of the land surface of the United States, primarily in the West. But that doesn't mean the public controls it. Powerful ranchers and livestock producers have effectively ruled over public lands in the West for more than a century, and they still do—to the detriment of the environment and the taxpayer.

Livestock grazing is currently the predominant use of the Western public lands. Some 89 percent of rangeland managed by the Bureau of Land Management (BLM), 69 percent of rangeland managed by the U.S. Forest Service, and other public lands, a total of nearly 300 million acres, is open for grazing. Grazing is also permitted on most of the larger wildlife refuges in the West—including 103 of 109 refuges in the Rocky Mountain region alone. And although national parks and monuments, like national wild-life refuges, were specifically designated to preserve natural biolog-ical communities, grazing is allowed in many, including Grand Teton, Great Basin, and Capitol Reef national parks, and Black Canyon of the Gunnison National Monument.

But at what cost? According to a new study prepared for the United Nations Environment Program, as much as 85 percent of all rangeland—public and private—in the Western United States is being degraded, primarily by overgrazing. BLM figures from 1989 indicate that more than 68 percent of the land under its jurisdiction is in "fair" or "poor" condition and less than 3 percent is in "excellent" or "good" condition.

Millions of acres of publicly owned land have been so denuded by decades of grazing, that the soil, water, and native plants and animals may never recover. Millions of head of cattle strip the land of vegetation (each animal eats, on the average, 900 pounds of herbage per month), destroy the ecology of the soil by compacting the earth with their hooves, and trample and pollute streams and surrounding riparian zones with their hooves and their waste. A 1990 report by the Environmental Protection Agency found that, "riparian areas throughout the West are in the worst condition in history."

Despite this, the BLM, along with the Forest Service, has for years allowed ranchers to graze their animals on these lands for a fraction of what it costs to graze livestock on private lands. Cur-rently, about 8 percent of Western ranchers, or about 31,000 per-mit holders, graze millions of head of cattle on Western public lands.

RAISE THE FEES, RECLAIM THE LAND

Rep. Michael Synar (D-OK) and **Rep. George Darden (D-GA)** introduced legislation in the 101st and 102nd Congresses that would dramatically raise fees for livestock grazing on public lands to reflect their fair market value. Synar's Fair Market Grazing for Public Rangelands Act and Darden's nearly identical Public Rangelands Fee Act, remove the current incentive to overgraze publicly owned land, the first step toward reclaiming public lands in the West.

Rep. Synar also submitted his bill as an amendment to the 1992 Interior Department spending bill and it was passed by the House in June of 1991 by a vote of 232 to 192. Powerful western senators, however, saw to it that the measure failed to pass the Senate.

The legislation would have raised the grazing fee over a four-year period to reflect the fair market value of the forage. Currently, the BLM and the Forest Service charge $1.97 per month to graze a cow and a calf while private landowners charge an average of $9.22. Synar's legislation would have raised the fee to $8.70 per month by 1995.

Federal agencies currently spend several times more to administer the grazing program than they collect in fees from ranchers. Because of this, taxpayers have lost $650 million over the past six years, according to Synar, who is a rancher himself. Synar has called the current situation "an ecological and fiscal disaster."

ANIMAL CONTROL OUT OF CONTROL

"We have seriously misread our relationship with the earth and the earth's other species. It is a misreading that is proving costly to life itself. . . . We are discovering, however painfully, that this is more than a mechanistic world that we can shape to our own ends. We are learning that costs are paid when human hands tip the scales of ecological balance.

"Among the many areas where our desires for dominion have exceeded nature's bounds is in wildlife management. . . . We are beginning, through studies in ecology and evolutionary biology, to understand just how important predators are in the ecosystem. We are learning to see predators not just as obstacles to the flourishing of life, but as vital components in the chain of life that includes man. In fact, in this chain, predators have a niche every bit as important to the survival of the earth's species as any other part of that chain. . . . The wholesale slaughter of predator species carries with it the long-range threat of impeding the survival-by-adaptation of significant animal species. By implication, we impede human progress. Animal species, of which man is one, are interdependent."

—Sen. Alan Cranston (D-CA)

Wild animals, too, have suffered from the tyranny of the ranchers. An extermination program, the Animal Damage Control Program, run by the U.S. Department of Agriculture at taxpayer expense, kills millions of wild predators and "nuisance" animals on public lands every year at the behest of cattle ranchers and other livestock producers.

In 1989, American taxpayers paid $38 million to kill predators which ranchers claim caused them to lose cattle and sheep worth $27.4 million. In that year, the government's army of four hundred hunters killed 86,502 coyotes, 1,220 bobcats, 7,158 foxes, 237 mountain lions, 236 black bears, and 80 gray timber wolves, just to list a few species. In 1988, Animal Damage Control killed approximately 4.6 million birds, 9,000 beavers, 76,000 coyotes, 5,000 raccoons, 300 black bears, 200 mountain lions, and many others. These animals were shot from helicopters and planes, poisoned, burned in their burrows and dens, run down by dogs, drowned, gassed, or sprayed with toxic substances.

The federal government got into the business of killing predators in 1915 when Western ranchers convinced Congress to appropriate $125,000 to exterminate wolves and coyotes. Indeed, the program was nearly successful. Wolves were hunted to near extinction in the lower forty-eight states. Coyotes, fortunately, proved to be more resilient. The program was expanded in 1931 to include other predators and nuisance animals.

Administrators of the program claim that its hunters kill only those individual animals who are suspected of killing livestock. However, a 1989 study by the General Accounting Office found that there was no evidence to support that claim and that large numbers of wild animals were indiscriminately exterminated.

Environmental scientists have often stated that predator "control" programs create ecological havoc and even worsen the predator "problem" as species naturally adjust to new conditions. Guard dogs and fencing, as well as herding and corralling livestock at night are all more effective, less costly, and more ecologically sound ways of protecting livestock from predators.

Putting the Brakes On

Sen. Alan Cranston (D-CA) has recognized the ethical and ecological damage caused by predator control. He introduced a joint resolution "to establish a national policy for the taking of predatory or scavenging mammals and birds on public lands."

Cranston's proposed national policy would "prohibit the taking of predators or scavengers naturally occurring on public lands without the written approval of the applicable Secretary." The killing of such animals would be permitted "only after an opportunity for public comment, and only if such taking will maintain the species at a level consistent with its role in the ecosystem, and is in the public interest."

Unfortunately, despite the vast importance of establishing such a policy, Cranston's resolution did not attract any cosponsors.

Killing Horses on the Range

Predators are not the only animals to suffer from the government's management of publicly owned rangelands for the benefit of ranchers. Hated by livestock producers, wild horses and burros, too, are being managed by the government for the ranchers' benefit.

In the mid nineteenth century, millions of wild horses roamed the Western range; but by 1967, after years of killings by ranchers who claimed the horses competed with cattle and sheep for forage, less than 10,000 remained. Alarmed that the wild horse would go the way of the buffalo, Congress, in 1971, adopted the Wild, Free-Roaming Horse and Burro Act and ordered the Bureau of Land Management (BLM) to adminster it.

The act prohibits the removal or killing of wild horses or burros from the range without government permission. However, the law also states that any "excess" horses and burros can be rounded up by the BLM and relocated, humanely destroyed, or placed in private hands. Unfortunately, Congress never defined the meaning of "excess" and so it is up to the BLM to decide how many horses and burros are too many. From the start, the BLM sided with the ranchers.

Each year, the BLM rounds up and removes thousands of "excess" wild horses and burros from the range. Many are warehoused and neglected in corrals and "sanctuaries" at the cost of millions of taxpayer dollars each year. Some of the animals end up in unsuitable homes, including prison yards where they are broken in by prisoners. Large numbers of wild horses have also ended up at slaughterhouses.

Although the BLM caters to ranching interests, ranchers nonetheless feel that the BLM is not doing enough to control "the destruction of the rangelands by horses and burros." In recent years, thousands of horses and burros have been killed, often quite cruelly, at the hands of outlaw rancher "vigilantes."

Sen. Harry Reid (D-NV), who has expressed outrage at such killings, introduced a bill that would increase penalties for those convicted of maliciously killing or harassing wild horses or burros. The legislation would amend the Wild, Free-Roaming Horse and Burro Act by making violation of the law a felony rather than a misdeamenor, and punishable by as much as a two-year jail term and a large fine.

THERE FOR THE TAKING

In the late 1800s, the government sponsored great land giveaways to encourage pioneers to pack up and move out West. There was so much land that all one had to do was stake a claim in order to receive ownership. Free land to build a homestead on, free grass for one's cattle to graze on, gold and other minerals that could be had just for the taking—to our predecessors, the West was a vast grab bag of resources that would never be exhausted.

While shopping malls and parking lots have replaced much of what was once the old Wild West, some things have never changed. The ranchers' belief that they can have their way with public rangelands is one of them. Another is the General Mining Law of 1872, often referred to as "the last of the great land give-aways." Now, 120 years after its enactment, the law still gives miners free access to public lands without having to pay royalties or restore the land to its original state.

The mining law, which was adopted during the presidency of Ulysses S. Grant, regulates hardrock mining, including the mining of gold, silver, lead, copper, uranium, and zinc. Because the law was enacted to encourage rapid development of the Western frontier, it was meant to be a giveaway. But today the law remains wide open for abuse by unscrupulous mining companies as well as land speculators and others with no interest in mining.

PUBLIC GIVEAWAYS

As unbelievable as it sounds, the law permits any person or corporation to mine any public land that has not been classified as wilderness or park by simply declaring their belief that the land contains valuable minerals. What's more, the law allows any person or entity to assume legal ownership of public land by "patenting" it. This is accomplished by simply paying the federal government $2.50 to $5.00 per acre, a price that has not changed since the law was enacted. Even more stupifying, because the law does not require a patented property to be mined, such properties frequently have been purchased by land speculators at 1872 prices and immediately resold at market value at great profit.

Since the law was adopted, the government has sold more than 3.2 million acres of public land under the patent provision of the mining law—an area the size of Connecticut. In the ten years between 1980 and 1990, the BLM issued 657 patents for a total of 4,752 claims, comprising nearly 180,000 acres—all for $5.00 per acre or less. Many of these properties were immediately turned around by their new owners for windfall profits. Some of the most notorious of these land giveaways occurred not in the old Wild West, but in recent times—during the Reagan and Bush administrations.

In 1986, for example, patent holders sold 17,000 acres of oil shale land to major oil companies for $437 million just weeks after they had patented the land by paying the government a paltry $42,500.

Patent claims have not only been resold at great profit, they have also become sites for vacation-home developments, casinos, junkyards, and homes. In one case, a claimant who had no intention of mining his claim opened up a methamphetamine drug factory on the claim site in the Klamath National Forest in California. Chemicals capable of producing 1.5 million doses of the dangerous illicit drug were seized by authorities.

As if this weren't bad enough, in a significant number of cases in which patent holders inherited claims from their forebears, the claims were made for lands that are now inside national parks or wilderness areas. Such claims place some of the nation's natural treasures at great risk.

In 1989, a mining company patented 700 acres of beautiful land in the heart of the Dunes National Recreation Area on the southwestern coast of Oregon. Having paid $5.00 per acre for the publicly owned land, the company intended to open up a sand quarry there. When a huge public uproar ensued, the company offered to sell the land back to the government at market value— as much as $12 million. Currently, there are more than 700 patented, and nearly 1,500 unpatented, mining claims in national parks.

In addition to allowing the sale of public lands for far less than market value, the 1872 mining law allows companies to mine valuable minerals on publicly owned land without compensating the American people. While royalties are paid to the government by oil, gas, and coal companies, and by hardrock miners on state and private land, hardrock miners mining on federal lands pay nothing to ransack and destroy some of our natural treasures—even when the mining companies are foreign owned.

For example, the American people own the land and the gold in the Goldstrike mine in Nevada, which is estimated to be worth $6 billion. Yet, according to *The Wall Street Journal,* not one cent is paid back to the government by the mining company, American Barrick Resources, which is Canadian controlled.

At another mine in Nevada, the Amax Company has extracted $100 million in gold, and netted $64 million, according to the *Journal,* but didn't pay a penny in royalties to the government.

The mining of minerals on public lands is estimated to be worth between $3.9 billion (BLM estimate) and $6.1 billion (Wilderness Society estimate) per year. If only a 5 percent royalty were imposed, hundreds of millions of dollars could be returned annually to to the U.S. Treasury—a small price to pay for pillaging public lands.

THE RAPE OF THE LAND

The 1872 mining law does not require that other land uses and values be taken into consideration when a mining claim is staked. Mines can be situated in or next to areas that are environmentally sensitive, or on the edge of a densely populated town. Nor does the law provide for mine reclamation. The General Accounting Office estimates that some 424,000 acres of federal land are currently unreclaimed as a result of hardrock mining.

Frequently, miners will abandon their mines or give their patented land back to the government when a mine has been exhausted, leaving behind tremendous environmental damage, hazardous waste, and a huge cleanup bill for the American people. In fact, more than a hundred sites on the Environmental Protection Agency's priority cleanup list are mining related and will cost billions of dollars to clean up; half of these are located on public lands in the West.

In recent years, a new mining technology has taken hold in the West that has devastating implications for the environment. The "heap-leach" method of mining uses extremely poisonous chemicals and heavy metals such as cyanide, mercury, and arsenic to extract tiny amounts of gold from tons of iron ore. It is an extremely wasteful method. Miners will crush a ton of iron ore and treat it with the poisonous solution only to end up with particles of gold that, when combined, may yield a lump no larger than a tooth filling.

It takes little imagination to see that a mining company can destroy entire mountainsides looking for specks of gold. To make matters worse, the poisons used to remove the gold are normally stored in outdoor holding ponds which attract and then kill birds and other wildlife; the poisons also leach into groundwater, causing irreparable harm.

WILL CONGRESS ACT?

Since 1872 we have learned that our resources are not infinite and that destruction of the environment has its costs. Now we can no longer afford those costs. Accordingly, moves are being made to update this outdated law. **Sen. Dale Bumpers (D-AR)** and **Rep. Nick Rahall (D-WV)** introduced reform legislation in both the current and last sessions of Congress. However, the 101st Congress was overwhelmed by pressure applied by mining industry lobbyists, and the legislation was defeated.

Although Bumpers' bill does not provide a comprehensive solution to the nation's mining problems, it is clearly the stronger of the two. Bumpers' Mining Law Reform Act would eliminate the practice of patenting, and thereby permanently stop the sale of public lands for firesale prices. Miners would be required to pay the government a 5 percent royalty on gross income from mineral production on public lands. The bill would also empower the BLM and Forest Service to regulate mining to minimize adverse impacts on the environment, and would require reclamation and bonding for most mining activities. The BLM and Forest Service would have authority to condition, restrict, or prohibit mining activities in areas in which they would conflict with more important land values; such determinations could be made only after public hearings are held.

Rep. Rahall's Mineral Exploration and Development Act would also do away with patenting and require reclamation. However, it would not require royalty payments, opting for a surface leasing plan instead. The proposed legislation also would not empower the BLM and Forest Service to prohibit mining in sensitive areas.

This Land Is Your Land

"It is not just the big crown jewels, the Grand Canyons, the Yellowstones and the Grand Tetons that I am worried about. I'm just as concerned about the little places that help make life meaningful in every community across America. It's that quiet spot along the banks of the river just outside of town where a couple of kids can sit and watch and dream. It's the park on the other side of town where a family can go on a weekend to relax, be together, and enjoy themselves.

"It's the field houses and basketball courts of an inner city where a kid can compete and maybe pick up a little guidance along the way. It's the historic old building in an industrial neighborhood that not only houses invaluable stories about the past but promises economic revitalization in the future.

Where will we be, what kind of life will our children
have, if we don't provide for these places?"

—Rep. Morris Udall (D-AZ)

Public lands are not just great expanses of Western plains, and
they are not all as spectacular as the Grand Canyon. Public lands
come in many different varieties—a wildlife refuge in New England, a recreational lake in Minnesota, a basketball court and
urban park in Newark, New Jersey—all are part of the public
domain.

In recent years, federal funding to acquire new open space on
the national, state, and local levels has declined dramatically in the
face of huge military expenditures and the soaring federal deficit.
Congress has been loath to purchase new properties when social
programs are being cut. Consequently, many lands and historical
properties that should be preserved and saved for the community
are being developed. A new boom in urban and rural development
is currently underway, consuming hundreds of thousands of acres
of wetlands and farm- and forestland each year.

For more than a quarter of a century, the Land and Water
Conservation Fund (LWCF) and the Historic Preservation Fund
(HPF) have provided for the purchase of open space and historic
preservation both nationally and at the local level. Funded by oil
and gas leasing revenues, and from sales of surplus federal real
estate, the LWCF receives up to $900 million each year, and the
HPF receives $150 million annually. While the funds accrue auto-
matically each year, it is up to Congress to decide how much
money to spend and for what purpose during the appropriations
process. Under both the LWCF and HPF funding programs, state
and local awards are made on a matching grant basis.

LWCF monies have helped to acquire 5.5 million acres of critical habitat for endangered and threatened species, national parks,
wildlife refuges, scenic rivers and trails, seashores, lakeshores, and
recreational lands, as well as 20,000 local and urban park facilities.
HPF grants have helped states to identify and protect historic and
archeological treasures and to restore more than 6,000 historic
sites.

Although Congress long has been committed to these conservation and preservation programs, in recent years it has not appropriated all of the available funds. Since 1980, LWCF appropriations for land acquisitions have declined precipitously from an annual peak of $805 million to an average of less than $20 million per year. HPF grant appropriations have averaged under $30 million per year. Consequently, there is now an authorized but unappropriated balance of approximately $6.1 billion in the combined funds.

Congress' reluctance to spend has resulted in an enormous backlog of lands that should be preserved but which may soon be lost to development. The National Park Service alone has reported a current backlog of $2 billion in authorized land purchases within park boundaries. For the last five years, states have submitted LWCF applications averaging $400 million per year.

THE AMERICAN HERITAGE TRUST

To get the program back on track, **Rep. Morris Udall (D-AZ)**, a key sponsor of the original LWCF and HPF legislation, and **Sen. John Chafee (R-RI)**, introduced the American Heritage Trust Act. The act would not increase funding for the LWCF and HPF; rather, it would create a self-perpetuating trust fund and new funding mechanism that, after a period of years, would require no more oil and gas revenues. It also would ensure that all available monies in the fund are spent.

Udall and Chafee have proposed that the American Heritage Trust, a real trust fund, be created to fund both the LWCF and HPF. Under this plan, the Secretary of the Treasury would take the current authorized but unappropriated balance of funds ($6.1 billion) together with the existing annual flow of revenues ($900 million per year for the LCWF and $150 million per year for the HPF) and invest the total in interest-generating government securities. The usual annual deposits from oil and gas revenues and accumulated interest for both funds would be available for appropriation the following fiscal year. Any amounts not appropriated in a given year would automatically become a permanent part of the interest-bearing trust principal. Once the corpus of the trust is large enough to yield $1 billion per year in interest for LWCF purposes, and $250 million per year in interest for HPF purposes, the flow of revenues to the trust would stop, and the trust would be self-financing with no new oil and gas revenues needed ever again.

In the meantime, and in perpetuity, the interest from the trust would be automatically appropriated. Congress would still have control over which projects receive funding, but would have to spend, at the minimum, a certain percentage of the total available funding each year, and would have to grant funding in accordance with a formula that would ensure state and local needs are not neglected. (State and local funding would still be made on a matching grant basis.)

The American Heritage Trust is certainly an idea whose time has come. Currently, LWCF and HPF monies sit idly in a Treasury envelope collecting no interest. Rep. Udall and Sen. Chafee have calculated that the American Heritage Trust would take only ten years from the date of enactment to become self-perpetuating.

This legislation has been presented to Congress twice before; but each time opponents have succeeded in blocking it. Many Republican members of Congress and members from Western states believe that the government already owns too much land. Others have stated that the country cannot afford to spend money on land acquisition while the national deficit remains so large. However, the Congressional Budget Office has informed members of Congress that the program would have absolutely no effect on the deficit since, by law, the funds in the trust cannot be used for any purpose other than land acquisition and historic preservation.

STEWARDING PUBLIC LANDS:
THE GREEN VOTE

☑ Designate the coastal plain of the Alaska National Wildlife Refuge as wilderness thus rendering it off limits to oil and gas development.

☑ Join with Canada to create an international Arctic refuge composed of the Alaska National Wildlife Refuge and contiguous protected Canadian lands.

☑ Stop inappropriate and harmful uses of wildlife refuges, including hunting and trapping, commercial and industrial uses, and invasive recreational uses. Turn the refuges back into the inviolate sanctuaries for wildlife they were intended to be.

☑ Raise the fees for grazing on public rangelands as a first step in reducing the number of cattle and other livestock grazing on and destroying public lands.

☑ Stop the wholesale slaughter of predators and "nuisance" animals on public lands, and promote the participation of the public in decisions affecting wildlife.

☑ Make the killing or harassing of wild horses and burros a felony offense and promote biodiversity on public lands.

☑ Repeal or reform the General Mining Law of 1872 to eliminate the practice of patenting, require miners to pay royalties, empower regulatory agencies to deny mining claims and to control environmental impacts, require bonding and reclamation of mines, and promote the participation of the public in land-use decisions.

☑ Create the American Heritage Trust to provide a self-perpetuating trust fund for land acquisition and historic preservation at the national, state, and local levels, and to ensure that all monies available for such purposes are spent.

PROTECTING FORESTS AND WETLANDS

The multiple threats of soil erosion, species extinction and global warming have focused greater public attention on forest preservation in the United States and abroad. Forests are being cut down at an unprecedented rate around the world in commercial logging operations and to provide land for cultivation and cattle grazing. The forest cover that anchors the soil and whose canopy provides habitat for most of the animal species of the planet is being systematically razed. Some 2000 years ago the tropical rain forest alone extended over 5 billion acres and covered over 12 percent of the land mass of the earth. In just the past century over half of the tropical forests have been cut down. The U.N. Food and Agricultural Organization estimates that at the current rate of destruction, nearly 30 percent of the remaining tropical forest will be eliminated by the end of the decade. The destruction of the world's forests is leading to widespread desertification of the earth's soil and the mass extinction of species. It is estimated that more than 15 percent of all the remaining species of plants and animals may face extinction by the year 2000.

Closer to home, 95 percent of America's virgin forests have been cut down in this century. Only about 3 million acres of ancient forests remain out of 50 million acres of federally owned forest.

The clearing and burning of trees also contributes to global warming. Trees take in and absorb carbon dioxide. When they die or are burned they release the stored carbon into the atmosphere. More than 1.2 billion tons of carbon dioxide were released into the atmosphere from clearing and burning the forests of Amazonia in the peak year of 1987. In that year, deforestation of Amazonia contributed 9 percent of the total worldwide additions to global warming from all sources.

THE UTILITARIANS VS. THE STEWARDS

No other issue so divides the Green members of Congress from their colleagues as national forest policy. The traditionalists favor the commercial exploitation of national forests, even if it means irreversible harm to the soil, the extinction of species, and the deterioration of the earth's biosphere. Many in Congress have close ties to the timber industry, the cattle industry, and others who benefit from the clear-cutting and burning of the national forests. They perceive environmentalists as obstructionists who care more about nature than about economic productivity. By contrast, the Green members of Congress argue that a healthy environment is essential to a healthy economy and that preserving our national forests is essential in maintaining a sustainable economy for present as well as future generations.

The battle over forest policy has been fought on several fronts in the Congress. Perhaps the most bitterly contested campaign has centered on the old-growth forests of the Pacific Northwest and the question of commercial logging vs. species preservation.

In June 1990, the U.S. Fish and Wildlife Service concluded that commercial logging in the old-growth forests was driving the threatened northern spotted owl toward extinction. To protect the spotted owl, new logging restrictions in federally owned forests would have to be implemented. Timber companies have complained that doing so would throw thousands of loggers out of work and imperil rural communities throughout the Pacific Northwest. Environmentalists, on the other hand, note that with only six percent of the ancient forest still standing, anyone whose job depends on liquidating the publics remaining old-growth forests is going to be out of work in five to six years at the current

rate of logging. If the ancient forest is lost, the spotted owl and several other threatened species—including marbled murrelets, the Pacific yew tree, Townsend's warbler, Vaux's swift, the red tree vole, the dusky-footed wood rat and the Pacific giant salamander—would also be extinguished.

In an attempt to save the ancient forest, **Rep. Jim Jontz (D-IN)** and ninety cosponsors have introduced the Ancient Forest Protection Act. The bill would establish the National Ancient Forest Reserve System and designates certain ancient forest ecosystems in the states of California, Oregon, and Washington to be "components" of the system.

Very recently, **Sen. Brock Adams (D-WA)** introduced a similar ancient forest protection bill that also provides economic relief for any workers who lose their jobs as a result of forest conservation legislation.

While Representative Jontz and others are attempting to keep commercial logging companies out of the old-growth forests of the

Pacific Northwest, **Rep. James Scheuer (D-NY)** has introduced a bill calling for a new national policy of "no net loss of forests within the United States and its territories." The Global Forests Emergency Act "directs the President to declare a national forest emergency and work with other nations . . . for no net loss policies." The bill also calls for "U.S. participation in a global survey of forests and forest resources" and the creation of "an Endangered Forest Research Initiative to study forest ecology, sustainable yield forestry, and forest restoration."

Many American consumers are unknowingly participating in the destruction of tropical rain forests in their purchase of wood products. **Sen. Albert Gore (D-TN)** and **Rep. Peter Kostmayer (D-PA)** have introduced the Tropical Forest Consumer Information Protection Act. The bill "calls on the Secretary of Commerce to make available to the public information on tropical forest logging practices and would require tropical wood products to bear a label indicating the country of origin and the wood used to produce them." In introducing the legislation, Sen. Gore pointed out that "the United States imports a significant amount of tropical wood, about one third of the world's trade. We therefore have a tremendous opportunity to encourage sustainable forest practices. To do so, however, we need to provide consumers with the information they need to make sound purchasing decisions. This legislation is an important first step."

URBAN FORESTS

Mounting public concern over global warming, increased energy costs and urban pollution has spurred an interest in urban forestry legislation in Congress as well as in state and local legislatures. Aside from absorbing carbon dioxide and filtering a variety of air pollutants from the atmosphere, trees also provide shade in the summer months, reducing the need for air-conditioning. Less reliance on air-conditioning means a reduction in the release of ozone-depleting chemicals from refrigerants as well as a reduction in the amount of oil and coal burned at power plants to generate electricity to run the air conditioners. The energy savings, in turn, reduces the emission of additional carbon dioxide into the atmosphere.

Rep. Jim Jontz (D-IN) and **Sen. Paul Sarbanes (D-MD)** have introduced companion bills to promote urban forestry programs in the United States. The legislation would "establish an urban and community forestry competitive grants program of which the federal share would not be more than 50%, and authorizes $20 million to carry out the program." The bills also provide for educational and technical assistance to state and local authorities "in inventorying urban forest resources and identifying opportunities for expanding tree cover in urban areas."

A WETLANDS POLICY

The nation's wetlands—the Florida everglades, tidal salt marshes, bogs, swamps, and ponds—have been dramatically reduced in recent decades to make room for commercial and residential real estate development, farming, oil drilling, and other activities.

Wetlands are essential wildlife habitats, providing a home for diverse species including migratory birds. The coastal wetlands serve as a breeding ground for many fish and shellfish. Wetlands also aid in flood control and perform a critical function in filtering and purifying water as it flows from land surfaces into rivers and bays.

A few members of Congress have begun to turn their attention to the protection of the nation's 100 million acres of wetlands. **Rep. Charles Bennett (D-FL)** has introduced legislation in the House that would guarantee a "no net loss" of the nation's remaining wetlands. The bill, which enlisted forty-four cosponsors, would establish a Wetlands Preservation Trust for the purpose of acquiring "wetlands and former wetland areas for the purpose of restoring, creating, or preserving these areas." The bill also establishes The Wetlands Preservation Account and requires the Secretary of the Treasury to deposit $300 million annually into the fund from the Land and Water Conservation Fund. Additional funds would be collected from fines imposed for violations of the Federal Water

Pollution Control Act. The account would be used to make grants to states to implement wetlands preservation programs. The bill even contains a provision that would allow a tax deduction for contributions of land to a wetlands trust. Finally, the Bennett bill would establish an office of Wetlands Identification and Preservation within the U.S. Fish and Wildlife Service whose responsibilities would include identifying wetland areas "suitable for preservation and acquisition by states, by the federal government, or by the Wetland Preservation Trust."

In August of 1990, President Bush effectively undermined congressional efforts to ensure a "no net loss" of wetlands by announcing that he would narrow the definition of "wetland" and thereby remove nearly half of the nation's wetlands from protected status. Bush said that his decision was motivated by the need to "balance two important objectives—the protection, restoration and creation of wetlands, and the need for sustainable economic growth and development."

In November 1991, Bush revised his proposal to remove "only" 30 percent—rather than half—of the wetlands from federal protection.

PROTECTING FORESTS AND WETLANDS: THE GREEN VOTE

☑ Prohibit commercial logging in the old-growth forests of the Pacific Northwest.

☑ Establish a national policy of no net loss of forests.

☑ Require all tropical wood products to be labeled indicating their country of origin and the type of wood used to produce them so that consumers can make informed choices in their purchases.

☑ Promote urban forestry programs and provide technical and financial assistance to states and localities to plant trees in and around urban areas.

☑ Establish a no net loss of wetlands policy.

CHAMPIONING THE RIGHTS OF ANIMALS

"I believe in animal rights as well as human rights, that is the way of a whole human being."

—Abraham Lincoln

Many people have strong personal feelings about animals. In some ways, we see them as being profoundly like us. Many have eyes and ears, feet and legs. They breathe just as we breathe; they feel pain as we do, and they also feel joy. They are clever; they plan things and solve problems. Many have close family ties and are sometimes altruistic in their behavior. We are awed by their self-sufficiency, their independence, their completeness.

Over the past two decades science has confirmed what some people have known intuitively for centuries—that animals are smarter, more emotional, more like us than most of us have ever imagined. At the same time, however, animals are deeply different. They express themselves in ways that we do not understand. They are like an ancient and mysterious tribe whose language and ways are sophisticated, yet unfathomable to outsiders.

It was naturalist Henry Beston who perhaps said it best: "They are not brethren; they are not underlings; they are other nations, caught with ourselves in the net of life and time. . . ."

As fellow travelers upon the earth, animals have inherent value and intrinsic rights that need to be respected.

RESPECTING ALL OF NATURE

Acknowledging the inherent value and rights of animals, indeed, respecting all of nature, is the essence of Green-mindedness. From the Green point of view, all forms of life have intrinsic value—apart from any usefulness they may have to humankind and apart from their importance in ecology.

In Green philosophy the rights of animals flow from the same principles of fairness and justice that are the foundation of human rights; they are manifest simply because, like humans, animals exist. Implicit in the inherent right to exist is the right not to be harmed unavoidably.

Other inherent rights flow from the intrinsic needs or attributes of animals. For example, animals are sentient beings who can feel pain and suffer; therefore, to be protected from human cruelty is their right. Animals also have the need and the right to live in unpolluted natural habitats and to express the full range of their natural behaviors.

The need to respect the intrinsic rights of animals and inherent value of nature becomes all the more meaningful when considered within the larger context of the biosphere. The biosphere is an interdependent biotic community composed of the atmosphere, rivers, lakes and oceans, soil and rocks, and plants and animals, including human beings.

Because all life is interdependent, to be healthy, to remain whole, each part of the biotic community deserves equal consideration since decisions that affect one part of the community affect the viability of other parts and the community as a whole.

INHERENT RIGHTS VS. LEGAL RIGHTS

While increasing numbers of people believe that animals have inherent rights, nowhere in the world do animals have legal rights.

THE ANIMAL BILL OF RIGHTS

A petition to the 102nd United States Congress:

I, the undersigned American citizen, believe that animals, like all sentient beings, are entitled to basic legal rights in our society. Deprived of legal protection, animals are defenseless against exploitation and abuse by humans. As no such rights now exist, I urge you to pass legislation in support of the following basic rights for animals:

- THE RIGHT of animals to be free from exploitation, cruelty, neglect, and abuse

- THE RIGHT of laboratory animals not to be used in cruel or unnecessary experiments

- THE RIGHT of farm animals to an environment that satisfies their basic physical and psychological needs

- THE RIGHT of companion animals to a healthy diet, protective shelter, and adequate medical care

- THE RIGHT of wildlife to a natural habitat [that is] ecologically sufficient to a normal existence and a self-sustaining species population

- THE RIGHT of animals to have their interests represented in court and safeguarded by the law of the land.

Signature of petitioner _____

Petition prepared and distributed by the Animal Legal Defense Fund

For all intents and purposes, under our legal systems, domestic animals are considered to be property whose only worth is their monetary value in the marketplace. Wild animals have no status whatsoever.

In some countries, including the United States, some laws exist to protect animals from certain kinds of human cruelty. However, under these laws, injured animals are viewed as damaged goods, not as entities with rights.

It is a cruel irony of our system of justice that purely artificial entities such as corporations, trusts, and even ships under maritime law, have legal personalities with legally recognizable interests and access to the courts. Natural beings, such as animals, and natural "things," such as rivers and trees, however, have no such status, nor do they have access to the courts. What's more, organizations that represent the interests of animals and nature, such as The Humane Society of the United States and the Sierra Club, routinely encounter legal barriers in their attempts to protect those interests.

Animal protection organizations, in particular, have enormous difficulty in proving to the courts that they have "standing," the right to represent an injured animal, in court. As U.S. law is currently written, a plaintiff must claim an injury to himself in order to have legal standing and stay in court.

It is for such reasons that a growing number of people believe that animals should be granted certain legal rights—rights that could be tailored to the characteristics and needs of animals in the same way that legal rights have been tailored to meet the needs of human beings who are viewed under the law as being incompetent: minor children, the mentally retarded, the seriously mentally disturbed, and the comatose. Just as parents can sue on behalf of their minor children and conservators can sue on behalf of incompetent wards, human representatives should be able to legally fight to protect the interests of animals.

So far, however, the courts and the legislature have been reluctant to grant such powers because, according to the general counsel of The Humane Society of the U.S., "they perceive that animal protection litigation might be a revolutionary instrument that has the potential to threaten, or at least challenge, significant, entrenched economic interests that prosper and depend upon the use and exploitation of animals."

BEHIND LOCKED DOORS

Animals are systematically exploited and abused in practically every societal context. In developed countries like the United States, cruelty to animals is so ubiquitous that it is virtually institutionalized. Because it is built into our society, animal cruelty often goes unrecognized; in fact, it is virtually invisible.

Few Americans, for example, have ever witnessed the process by which meat gets to their table, or how a leather sofa comes to be. Not many people have seen a fur coat being made from beginning to end. And few are aware of the extent to which cheap animal body parts and fluids have found their way into nearly any commercial product one could name, from shampoo and lipstick, to photographic film and plastics.

The most hidden, the most secret, kind of animal exploitation, however, takes place in the research laboratory.

The U.S. government has conservatively estimated that some 20 million animals are used in laboratory experiments each year; but animal protection groups say the actual number may be as high as 50 million. While rats and mice compose the majority of this number, experimental subjects also include hundreds of thousands of other highly sentient creatures including dogs, cats, chimpanzees, monkeys, rabbits, birds, various wild animals, and farm animals such as cows, sheep, and pigs.

The institutions using such animals include major chemical and pharmaceutical corporations, universities, the U.S. Department of Defense, and other government agencies. In one recent year, for example, American Cyanamid, the giant chemical company, used 55,460 animals (including 4,244 in unrelieved painful experiments), not including rats or mice. The Bayer Corporation used 39,984 animals in one recent year (including 25,550 in unrelieved painful experiments) not including rats or mice. The Uni-

THE GREATNESS OF A NATION . . .

"The greatness of a nation and its moral progress can be judged by the way its animals are treated."

—*Mohandas Gandhi*

Each year in the United States:

- 6 *billion* animals are inhumanely raised and brutally slaughtered for their meat and hides
- 20 to 50 million animals suffer and die during laboratory experiments and testing
- 14 million animals suffer and die in product tests conducted by cosmetics companies and household-products manufacturers
- 17 million animals are brutally trapped and killed to make fur coats
- 5 million nontarget or "trash" animals, including pet dogs and cats and endangered species, are accidentally caught in traps intended for commercially useful fur-bearers
- 5 million animals are inhumanely raised and slaughtered on fur "ranches" for fur coats
- 365 million animals are hit and killed by motor vehicles
- 200 million animals are hunted and killed for fun by sportsmen
- 7.5 million unwanted dogs and cats are euthanized at shelters and pounds

versity of California used 76,698 animals, not including rats or mice, in just one recent year.

More than one third of animals used in research experience pain, and one out of five of those animals is denied painkilling drugs because their use would interfere with test results.

Animal protection groups such as The Humane Society of the U.S., the American Society for the Prevention of Cruelty to Animals (ASPCA), the Animal Welfare Institute, People for the Ethical Treatment of Animals, United Action for Animals, Veterinarians for Animal Rights, the Physicians Committee for Responsible Medicine, the Medical Research Modernization Committee, and many other respected organizations have documented thousands of brutal, repetitive, and unnecessary animal experiments.

Dogs have been placed in pools of water from which they cannot escape to see how long it will take them to swim to exhaustion and drown. Fully conscious pigs have been blowtorched in burn studies. Kittens have had their eyes sewn shut to see how this affects their mating behavior. Baby monkeys have been permanently separated from their mothers at birth to see how the babies will react. (The babies become severely disturbed and often die.)

In 1985, a videotape, which showed highly respected researchers at the University of Pennsylvania laughing and joking as they crushed the skulls of fully conscious baboons used in head-injury research, was made public by an animal protection group. The experiments were finally stopped by the university and the laboratory was closed as a result of months of public protest and the cancellation of federal research funding.

In 1988, after touring a Maryland laboratory where hundreds of chimpanzees used in experiments are forced to spend their lives isolated in 52 × 30 × 39-inch glass compartments, chimpanzee expert Dr. Jane Goodall, shocked and enraged, lobbied Congress for a year to pass better animal protection laws.

THE GUTTING OF THE ANIMAL WELFARE ACT

The Animal Welfare Act was signed into law in 1966 after six years of battle with research and pharmaceutical interests. Amended again in 1970, 1976, and 1985, the law currently provides only minimum standards of care for certain animals (excluding rats, mice, and birds) used in laboratories. The act does not address the nature of experiments; instead, it deals almost exclusively with minimal standards for housing, maintenance, and veterinary care.

The latest amendment to the act requires that anesthesia or painkillers be used during and after painful procedures—except when a researcher decides that the administration of painkillers would interfere with the goals of an experiment. This loophole results in tens of thousands of unrelieved painful experiments each year.

The act also provides minimum care standards for animals in zoos, circuses, and those held by animal dealers.

The intention of Congress in adopting and amending the act was to ensure that all animals used in laboratories are treated humanely. Yet, in developing regulations to implement the act, the U.S. Department of Agriculture (USDA), which enforces the act, and the Office of Management and Budget (OMB) under the Reagan and Bush administrations have continually subverted the will of Congress and have virtually gutted this important piece of legislation.

The regulations interpret the will of Congress more loosely than Congress had intended, resulting in many large loopholes for researchers. In spite of repeated congressional orders to do so, the USDA and OMB have steadfastly refused to include rats, mice, and birds as protected animals under the act, and, until quite recently, also refused to cover farm animals used in biomedical research. In addition, both the Reagan and Bush administrations have drastically underfunded the federal animal protection program, resulting in extremely poor enforcement of this rather mediocre law.

Newsweek has reported that Congress receives more mail on the subject of animal experimentation than any other topic, with opinion running 100 to 1 against the use of animals in research. Fortunately, several members of Congress have been responsive to their constituencies—both human and animal.

• • •

SUING ON BEHALF OF ANIMALS

"Mr. Speaker, courts have decreed that because citizens or animal protection organizations don't own the animals they want to protect, they can't sue. So, Mr. Speaker, we have to ask this—if the animals can't sue on their behalf, and if people can't sue on their behalf, who can? . . . We are not going to get the enforcement of the Animal Welfare Act we demanded when we adopted toughening amendments in 1985 until we grant standing to sue on behalf of animals.

"As a matter of fact, we should note that here we are, more than three years after those amendments became law, and we have yet to see the first word of them in regulations. That should tell us something about the absence of desire to enforce animal protection decreed by Congress.

"Why? Mr. Speaker, the Agriculture Department knuckles under to the Office of Management and Budget's delaying dictates calling for draft upon draft of proposed regs, but OMB obeys the researchers, and stalls and stalls the approval of a single word of them.

"The constitutional provision that tells us the President 'shall take care that the laws be faithfully executed' is a joke to the pliant plodders in Agriculture and the wheeler-dealers of OMB. We ourselves are not entirely without fault for allowing this to go on year after year without calling the Administration to account on it, but we can do something corrective about it by approving standing to sue."

—*Rep. Charles Rose (D-NC)*

RESPONDING TO ANIMAL SUFFERING

One of the foremost champions of animals over the years has been **Rep. Charles Rose (D-NC)**. Rose has introduced, for several years running, one of the best animal protection bills Congress has ever considered. The bill would amend the Animal Welfare Act to give any concerned person or organization legal standing to sue the USDA on behalf of animals to compel enforcement of the act. If enacted, the legislation would solve the enforcement problems that have plagued the Animal Welfare Act since its adoption.

Rose's bill garnered sixty-eight cosponsors in the 100th Congress, but unfortunately, only twenty-three in the 101st.

EVERYONE'S COVERED

Another proposed amendment to the Animal Welfare Act, introduced by **Rep. Edolphus Towns (D-NY)**, would specifically include mice, rats, and birds within the definition of animals protected by the act.

Although Congress had fully intended that mice, rats, and birds be protected by the act when this legislation was adopted, the USDA has steadfastly refused to enforce the act for these animals. Towns' bill would simply make the congressional mandate explicit and would force the USDA to include these animals in its inspections of laboratories.

STOLEN FOR RESEARCH

An extremely controversial part of the laboratory animal issue has revolved around the use of pets in laboratory experiments.

Research facilities obtain dogs and cats in several ways. They can buy specially bred puppies and kittens from licensed breeding companies; they can buy "secondhand" dogs and cats from USDA-licensed animal dealers; or they can obtain low-cost dogs and cats from municipal pounds and private shelters in states that have not banned this practice, which is called "pound seizure."

Besides the horrors implicit in subjecting any dog or cat to laboratory experiments, this system of acquiring animals has created several problems. For one, the business of supplying research facilities with dogs and cats has come to be an extremely profitable one, so much so that the theft of pets from owners' backyards has become a major problem. Animal protection groups estimate that 1 to 2 million pets are stolen annually for use in laboratories. In addition to stealing animals, several USDA-licensed dealers have been caught obtaining dogs and cats under false pretenses from "Free to Good Home" ads found in the classified section of newspapers.

Many pounds and shelters compound the problem by shipping their charges off to laboratories without giving the owners of lost dogs and cats enough time to find and reclaim their pets.

Concerned about the trade in stolen pets, **Sen. Patrick Leahy (D-VT)** and **Sen. Wendell Ford (D-KY)** sponsored legislation that would reduce the numbers of these animals ending up in laboratories. Fortunately, the legislation was incorporated into the 1990 Omnibus Farm Bill and became law as part of the Food and Agriculture Act.

Although animal protection groups would have preferred an outright ban on pound seizure, or, even better, a ban on the use of all dogs and cats in research, the new law will cut down on the number of these animals who are obtained under false pretenses.

Rep. Toby Roth's (R-WI) bill, the Animal Welfare Protection Act, was also incorporated into the 1990 Farm Bill and made law. The legislation amends the Animal Welfare Act to grant the Secretary of Agriculture much-needed authority to seek temporary restraining orders and injunctions against those who commit serious violations of the Animal Welfare Act. Animal dealers and exhibitors who deal in stolen animals or who knowingly endanger animals covered by the act may lose their licenses until such problems are resolved. Violators will no longer be able to appeal and delay decisions while continuing to break the law.

Before this amendment was enacted, it often took the USDA one to two years to process violations of the act, during which time

MAN'S BEST FRIENDS

Approximately 200,000 dogs and 60,000 cats are used as experimental subjects each year in the United States. Of this total, a substantial number come from pounds and shelters and are, or were, someone's trusting companion.

Dogs and cats are used in some of the most painful and distressing research imaginable. Countless numbers are used each year by researchers studying everything from the effects of burns and radiation poisoning to germ- and chemical-warfare agents and other weapons. Thousands more find themselves the subjects of nervous-system and pain studies, toxicology and pharmacology studies, addiction studies, and cruel behavioral experiments.

A review of biomedical experiments conducted between December 1985 and April 1987 on mongrel dogs (most of whom were former pets obtained from animal shelters) revealed shocking results: more than 65 percent of the experiments inflicted significant pain or discomfort, while 12.9 percent of the experiments involved procedures that caused severe, unrelieved pain to conscious, unanesthetized dogs. The median duration of the two most painful categories of experiments was three weeks.

Many dogs and cats used in long-term experiments suffer severe stress—especially those who were raised as trusting pets and are accustomed to loving human attention and gentle treatment. It is not uncommon to find, in a laboratory, dogs who shake paws and do tricks, or cats who are extremely social with people. In fact, it is the most friendly dogs and cats who are selected from animal shelters for use as experimental subjects.

Many of these animals are forced to undergo such cruelties as having their vocal cords cut so that researchers will not be annoyed by their barks and cries. As highly social, active animals, dogs in laboratories also suffer greatly from being caged in isolation and from lack of exercise.

—*The Humane Society of the U.S.*

"THIS ONE WE GOT FROM THE COUNTY POUND IS HOUSEBROKEN AND EVERYTHING. AND LOOK... HE EVEN KNOWS HOW TO BEG!"

© 1986, WAYNE STAYSKAL, TAMPA TRIBUNE.

an offender could continue to break the law by harming animals. In addition, even if an animal dealer was eventually found guilty of serious offenses, revocation of the offender's USDA license has been very rare.

TARGETING ANIMAL TESTING

In addition to the 20 to 50 million animals used in experiments annually, another 14 million are subjected each year to crude and cruel toxicity tests of chemicals and products ranging from oven cleaners to paint removers to pesticides.

Two of these tests, the Lethal-Dose 50 test and the Draize test, are particularly brutal.

In the Lethal-Dose 50 (LD50) test, chemicals are administered to a group of animals until half of them die. In the most common variation of the test, large numbers of animals are forced to eat the test substance. In others, they are forced to inhale a substance, or the substance is applied to shaved skin or injected into their bodies. These tests produce signs of poisoning that include bleeding from the eyes, nose, or mouth; labored breathing, convulsions, tremors, paralysis, and coma. If the animals do not die from poisoning, they are killed at the end of the testing period, which normally lasts two weeks.

The LD50 has been characterized as "an anachronism" by the director of the National Toxicology Program and as "a ritual mass execution of animals" by a chief toxicologist at the World Health Organization. Fortunately its use is in decline.

In the most common version of the Draize test, the test substance is placed in the eyes of live, restrained rabbits, causing reactions ranging from mild redness to severe, painful ulceration, hemorrhage of the eyeball, and blindness. In a variation of this test, substances are placed on the shaved, abraded skin of an animal, causing swelling, overheating, abcesses, and severe pain.

These tests, which have been criticized by scientists as unreliable, have little relevance to human safety. In 1987, 47,000 people were rushed to emergency rooms after being injured by household products that had been tested on animals.

Such tests become all the more unacceptable when one considers that in recent years, scores of scientifically sophisticated "in vitro" (test-tube), tissue culture, and computer-modeling tests have been developed that not only spare animal lives, but are actually more reliable and less expensive to conduct.

No laws require animal tests of cosmetics and household products, but many companies routinely conduct such tests, regarding them as both their ultimate defense in case of lawsuit and their best chance of getting new products past federal safety regulators. While some major companies—under pressure from animal protection groups—have made the switch to the new technologies, many continue in their old ways. (The LD50 test was developed in the 1920s; the Draize test, in the early 1940s.)

Several members of Congress have been very concerned about the continued use of these unnecessary and unethical tests.

The Consumer Products Safe Testing Act was introduced by

HE DIED SO
THE WORLD
MIGHT HAVE SAFE
EYE SHADOW

Rep. Barbara Boxer (D-CA) and Sen. Harry Reid (D-NV) to "provide for the modernization of testing of consumer products which contain hazardous or toxic substances." Their companion bills "prohibit federal department or agency heads from considering LD50 test results when determining product safety, labeling, or transportation requirements" under federal regulations, and "require them to specify non-animal test alternatives for product testing."

The bills also require "federal department and agency heads to review and evaluate directives that call for the use of an animal toxicity test, and promulgate regulations specifying the use of non-animal alternatives." In addition, the bills "require that animal toxicity testing regulations be subject to periodic agency review and to public comment."

The rationale behind the proposed legislation is that if federal regulatory agencies, such as the U.S. Food and Drug Administration, by law can no longer accept results from certain animal tests, there will be no incentive for companies to conduct such tests. And specifying which nonanimal tests would be acceptable would make it easier for companies to comply with the government's demand that their products be safe.

Unfortunately, this bill has languished in Congress even though it secured one hundred thirty-three cosponsors in the House and seven in the Senate in the 101st Congress.

Sen. Reid offered his bill as an amendment to the 1990 Omnibus Farm Bill. However, it failed in the Senate by a margin of 62 to 29.

Rep. Andrew Jacobs (D-IN) also introduced legislation in the form of a resolution on the matter of animal testing. The resolution expresses the sense of Congress "that any federal agency that utilizes the Draize rabbit eye irritancy test should develop and validate alternative opthalmic testing procedures that do not require the use of animal test subjects."

REDUCING THE NUMBERS

One of the most innovative bills to reduce the numbers of animals killed in laboratories is the proposed Information Dissemination and Research Accountability Act introduced by **Rep. Robert Torricelli (D-NJ)** which garnered an impressive ninety-three cosponsors in the 101st Congress. The bill is designed to improve communications between scientists and the government to prevent the duplication of experiments on live animals.

The bill establishes a computerized National Center for Research Accountability at the National Library of Medicine "to assist in eliminating duplication of effort in federal research proposals involving live animals" by requiring all federal research proposals to be approved by the center before funding is granted. The bill "prohibits federal funding of any proposal the Center determines would duplicate other [animal] research completed or in process."

The legislation also requires that the center and the library report to the President and Congress on progress made in reducing the numbers of laboratory animals used annually.

EATING WITH CONSCIENCE

"It's my own metaphysical view . . . that nature strikes back at violence to itself. And I think there may also be locked in nature some sort of reward if you rise above the predatory animals on earth. . . .

"Nature created the predatory animals, but there's a lot of evidence that we're not one of them. First of all, the predatory animals—carnivores—generally have very short intestines. Humans do not. Humans have intestines that match the victims of the predators. . . . So if you want a hint from nature whether we're supposed to head toward civilization or the jungle, my guess is that we're supposed to head toward civilization.

—Rep. Andrew Jacobs (D-IN)

One member of Congress who believes that it is immoral to eat animals when it is not necessary to do so is **Rep. Andrew Jacobs (D-IN)**. An ethical vegetarian, Jacobs has introduced a resolution into Congress that "expresses the sense of the Congress that federally funded school lunch programs should provide nutritious meatless meals for students who conscientiously believe such meals to be best for themselves."

Jacobs, who is currently serving his twenty-sixth year in the House, became a vegetarian during the years when he voiced his

Respect vs. Utility—Legislators Choose Sides

Traditional political labels fall away when the issue is animal welfare. Democrat vs. Republican, left vs. right—these distinctions are becoming irrelevant in a world that is increasingly being shaped by the opposing ideas of "respect for life" and "life as utility."

A history-making bipartisan caucus, the Congressional Friends of Animals, was formed in the 101st Congress by legislators who lean toward the Green politics of reverence for life. The caucus provides a base of support for pro-animal legislation in Congress.

Unfortunately, the animals also have detractors in Congress. Soon after Congressional Friends of Animals formed in 1989, an anti–animal protection caucus, the Congressional Animal Welfare Caucus (a purposeful misnomer) was formed. Members of this group lean very much toward the "life as utility" end of the new political spectrum and have opposed legislation that would protect animals.

Congressional Friends of Animals, 102nd Congress

Rep. Tom Lantos (D-CA), cochair	Rep. Charles Rose (D-NC), cochair
Rep. Charles Bennett (D-FL)	Rep. Robert Mrazek (D-NY)
Rep. Robert Borski (D-PA)	Rep. Major Owens (D-NY)
Rep. William Broomfield (R-MI)	Rep. Frank Pallone (D-NJ)
Rep. Tom Campbell (R-CA)	Rep. Matthew Rinaldo (R-NJ)
Rep. Ronald Dellums (D-CA)	Rep. Robert Roe (D-NJ)
Rep. Robert Dornan (R-CA)	Rep. Ileana Ros-Lehtinen (R-FL)
Rep. Peter Kostmayer (D-PA)	Rep. Steven Schiff (R-NM)
Rep. Jerry Lewis (R-CA)	Rep. Lawrence Smith (D-FL)
Rep. John Lewis (D-GA)	Rep. Robert Torricelli (D-NJ)
Rep. Edward Markey (D-MA)	Rep. Edolphus Towns (D-NY)

Rep. Charles Wilson (D-TX)

In the 101st Congress, this caucus also included:

Rep. Robert Smith (R-NH)*, former cochair	Rep. Walter Fauntroy (D-DL-DC)**
Rep. Jim Bates (D-CA)**	Rep. Harley Staggers (D-WV)

*Currently Sen. Robert Smith (R-NH)
**Currently out of office

Congressional [Anti-]Animal Welfare Caucus, 102nd Congress

Rep. Vin Weber (R-MN), chairman

Rep. Byron Dorgan (D-ND)	Rep. Greg Laughlin (D-TX)
Rep. Joseph Early (D-MA)	Rep. Timothy Penny (D-MN)
Rep. Fred Grandy (R-IA)	Rep. Joe Skeen (R-NM)
Rep. Steven Gunderson (R-WI)	Rep. Charles Stenholm (D-TX)

In the 101st Congress, this caucus also included:

Rep. Virginia Smith (R-NB)**	Rep. Thomas Tauke (R-IA)**

**Currently out of office

opposition to the Vietnam War. A veteran of the Marine Corps who served in Korea, Jacobs experienced firsthand the horrors of war and was injured in combat. After witnessing the carnage, Jacobs began to ponder cruelty in all its aspects. He came to the conclusion that there is but one ethic of compassion and that it must be extended to all members of the earth community—not just to humankind.

During a House debate on the Vietnam War, Jacobs referred to the ease with which the President and Congress were sending young men to war by saying, "Many eat meat, but few go to the slaughterhouse." Jacobs' own remark led him to investigate conditions for animals in slaughterhouses. What he learned caused him to stop eating meat in February 1970. He has been outspoken on the issue ever since.

Clearly, meat eating is an animal rights issue. More than 6 *billion* animals in the United States are brutally killed for their meat and hide each year. In has been estimated that the average meat-eating American eats 12 cattle, 1 calf, 2 lambs, 29 pigs, 984 chickens, and 37 turkeys in his or her lifetime. Most of these animals are forced to live their entire lives indoors under appalling intensive-confinement "factory farm" conditions; they also suffer cruel transportation conditions and handling before slaughter.*

But meat eating is also more than a question of animal rights; it has dire implications for human and environmental health as well.

Cattle and other livestock consume more than 70 percent of all the grain produced in the United States. One third of the world's total grain harvest is fed to livestock. Yet, as many as 1 billion people worldwide suffer from chronic hunger and malnutrition. As hundreds of millions go hungry for lack of grain, millions more in the developed world are crippled and die from diseases—among them heart attacks and cancer—caused by an excess of animal fat in their diets.

Livestock production is also wreaking havoc on the environment, destroying ecosystems on every continent. Millions of acres of tropical forest are being felled and cleared to make way for pastureland to graze livestock. Livestock herding and overgrazing are responsible for much of the spreading desertification in the American West, Africa, and Australia.

Livestock is responsible for the depletion of much of the reserves of fresh water on the planet. (Most water is used to grow animal feed crops). Organic runoff from factory-farm feedlots is now a major source of organic pollution in U.S. groundwater. Live-

---

* For more information on what legislators are doing to help farm animals, see "Toward an Ecological Agriculture," pp. 149–63.

stock is also a major contributor to global warming. A vast amount of methane, the most potent of the greenhouse gasses, is emitted by the billions of domestic animals on the planet.

Kicking the meat habit is the single most important, most effective, action individuals can take to reduce animal suffering and environmental devastation. Requiring that the vegetarian option be offered in all federally funded school lunch programs won't save the world—but it would be a great start.

THE CRY OF THE WILD

In an increasingly enclosed biosphere—one in which virtually every life form is now prey to genetic engineering and patenting—the term "wild animal" may soon become an oxymoron. But even as we witness their habitats shrinking and their genes being manipulated, many people persist in believing that wild animals are free—free from human abuse, free to roam where they like, free to exercise their inherent right to be wild.

In fact, however, wild animals are frequently abused; and in many places they are not free to roam or express their wildness. Wild birds are caught for the pet trade. Millions of dolphins have been purposefully encircled by fishermen's nets and drowned. Many wild animals are managed by the government for "sportsmen" who shoot or trap them for fun—even on wildlife refuges. Others are systematically exterminated by the government for the benefit of ranchers and other livestock producers.

TRAPPED!

The steel-jaw leghold trap should have been outlawed long ago. Although this trapping device is already banned in more than sixty-five countries, trappers in the United States continue to use this torturous trap simply because not enough members of Congress have supported legislation that would ban its use.

Most of the 17 million wild animals—foxes, wolves, coyotes,

raccoons, bobcats, beavers, muskrats, otters, opossums, and mink —trapped for the fur industry each year in the United States are caught with this infamous trap. The tremendous force with which the trap snaps down on the paw or limb of an animal can be likened to having one's hand crushed in a car door—and left there indefinitely.

In frantic attempts to escape, animals frequently bite off their own trapped limbs. State laws regarding the placement and handling of traps vary widely in how often they require traps to be checked, and some states have no checking requirement. Trapped animals left for long periods of time are likely to suffer and die from exhaustion, dehydration, predation, freezing, or starvation. Worse, many animals have been found alive after having been left in traps for as long as two weeks.

There are no laws or regulations regarding how trapped animals may be killed. Consequently, they are killed in whatever way is easiest for the trapper and does not damage the pelt. Popular killing methods include beating an animal with a blunt instrument or holding onto an animal's rear legs while slamming his head against a tree or rock. Another method is to stomp on the animal's chest, thus slowly suffocating the creature or stopping his heart. Animals who are trapped in or near water, such as beavers and muskrats, are drowned.

In addition to commercially valuable fur-bearers, an additional estimated 5 million so-called "trash animals"—domestic animals and unwanted wild species, including endangered species—are accidentally caught in these traps and suffer agonizing deaths each year.

Rep. James Scheuer (D-NY) has, for several years, introduced the Steel-Jaw Leghold Trap Prohibition Act, but to no avail. In the 101st Congress the bill won sixty-nine cosponsors in the House, but no Senate sponsor could be found. In the 102nd Congress, however, one has come forward—**Sen. Daniel Akaka (D-HA)**— and he has introduced a companion bill.

The proposed legislation would "prohibit the shipment, in interstate or foreign commerce, of steel-jaw leghold traps and of articles of fur derived from animals trapped in such traps."

The bills would also "direct the Secretary of the Interior to reward nongovernment informers for information leading to a conviction under the Act; empower enforcement officials to detain, search, and seize suspected merchandise or documents, and to make arrests with and without warrants; and subject seized merchandise to forfeiture."

The legislation may have a better chance of passing in this session of Congress. In the fall of 1991, the European Council of Ministers adopted a proposal banning imports of furs into the European Community (EC) from countries that have not banned the leghold trap. The use of the trap in EC countries was also banned, effective 1995.

Many Green-oriented voters look to the day when not only leghold traps are banned, but fur coats as well.

FLUTTERING AT THE BARS OF A CAGE

"A Robin Red breast in a Cage
Puts all Heaven in a Rage."

—William Blake, "Auguries of Innocence"

Perhaps the most often captured and caged wild animals are birds. Nothing compares to the blend of outrage and despair evoked by the sight of a bird—whose every instinct compels her to stretch her wings and soar in the open air—fluttering at the bars of a cage, or forlornly swaying back and forth on a lonely indoor perch.

In recent years, animal protection and environmental groups and legislators have focused on the problem of exotic wild birds hunted and captured for the pet trade. While the vast majority of birds sold in American pet stores have been bred in captivity, another 8 to 20 million are taken from the wild each year to satisfy collectors in the United States, Europe, and Japan.

As a result of the appalling cruelty and astronomical death rates involved in capturing and transporting these birds, many exotic wild bird species are becoming highly endangered. Habitat destruction—the clearing of rain forests—has also contributed to their demise. Like most endangered species, exotic birds have become caught in a terrible cycle of destruction: the more rare they become, the more collectors want them.

It is estimated that for every exotic bird sold in a pet store, between one and one hundred birds, depending upon their species and country of origin, have died.

About 250,000, or half of the nearly 500,000 exotic birds imported into the United States each year are parrots, and most of these are taken from the wild. Currently, about 25 percent of the world's known parrot species (about seventy-five species), and nearly a third of parrot species from the western hemisphere (about forty species), are endangered. The tragedy is compounded by recent scientific revelations that parrots are as intelligent as chimpanzees and dolphins and form very strong attachments to mate and family when in the wild. In captivity, they must suffer more than we know.

Although it is against U.S. law to import birds from countries that do not permit their export, smugglers easily circumvent this by transporting the birds to a neighboring country from which they can then be exported to the United States. In addition, endangered birds are often smuggled into the country in shipments of other goods.

The methods used to capture these delicate animals are so brutal that it is estimated that half die before leaving their country of origin.

Birds are caught in many ways, all of them cruel. Trees are felled and flegdlings scooped out of their nests. Adhesives are applied to tree limbs to cause birds to become stuck after they land. Large birds are sometimes shot at with the intention of "winging" them. Birdcalls and decoys are used to lure large birds such as parrots to hidden snares and small birds to nets. Frequently, live birds, tied to stakes hammered into the ground, are used to attract other birds, who are then netted.

Transportation takes an additional toll. Of the 461,000 exotic birds imported to the United States in 1989, 17,471 were dead on arrival, and an additional 48,279 died while in quarantine.

While U.S. regulations state that no more than 50 birds may

be packed to a crate, 200 to 800 birds per crate are often unloaded. Birds are also smuggled, their bodies and beaks bound with tape, inside car doors or inside vases that are not much larger than the birds. The animals may go for days without food or water and may suffer from extremes of temperature, especially in the cargo holds of planes.

In response to this tragedy, **Rep. Gerry Studds (D-MA)** and **Sen. Max Baucus (D-MT)** introduced the Wild Bird Protection Act, which would immediately ban the importation into the United States of exotic wild-caught birds for the pet trade. Exceptions would be made for the importation of wild birds by zoos, researchers, and captive-bird breeders only if such importation would not have a detrimental effect on wild bird populations. Importation of species of birds who are extremely delicate and unlikely to survive capture and transportation, however, would be banned, as would the importation of any members of a species that is already available in the United States.

Killing Dolphins to Catch Tuna

Marine mammals received a great deal of attention by the 101st Congress. Dolphins, in particular, benefited from legislation designed to help free them from the nets of the U.S. and foreign tuna fishery. More needs to be done, however, before these animals can be considered safe. Over the past three decades, tuna fishermen have killed 6 to 10 million dolphins.

Legislation introduced by **Rep. Barbara Boxer (D-CA)** and **Sen. Joseph Biden (D-DE)**—the Dolphin Protection Consumer Information Act, passed both houses of Congress just two hours before the 101st Congress adjourned for the last time. The new legislation, adopted in the form of an amendment to the U.S. Marine Mammal Protection Act, enables consumers to identify canned tuna that has been produced without killing or harming dolphins. Companies may now label brands of canned tuna as being "Dolphin Safe" if the tuna was caught by means that do not kill or harm dolphins. Penalties are provided for false labeling.

Passage of the legislation was the culmination of two years of work on behalf of both legislators. The bill garnered 182 House cosponsors and 35 cosponsors in the Senate. Biden introduced his bill at the urging of his then-eight-year-old daughter.

Rep. Mel Levine (D-CA) introduced a similar bill that would have required all tuna products to be labeled as to whether the tuna was caught by methods that endanger dolphins or not. While it was a good bill, it was not as complete as the Boxer/Biden legislation.

Millions of dolphins have drowned in tuna nets since the late 1950s when the purse-seine method of catching tuna became widely used. The slaughter is unique to the Eastern Tropical Pacific, a stretch of ocean extending from California to Chile, where, for unknown reasons, large yellowfin tuna tend to swim under herds of dolphins. Knowing this, tuna-fishing vessels spot dolphin herds by helicopter, then encircle both dolphins and tuna with a mile-long net called a purse seine. The bottom of the net is then pulled closed like a woman's drawstring purse.

The Marine Mammal Protection Act requires American tuna fleets, and fleets from foreign countries from which American canneries buy tuna, to attempt to free netted dolphins. Rescue, however, is a tricky procedure that can easily result in disaster when tides or winds cause the net to fold over and entrap the dolphins. As many as 2,000 of these gentle, air-breathing mammals have been documented to have drowned at one time when a rescue failed.

To make matters worse, the act specifically permits the American tuna fleet to drown 20,500 dolphins each year without penalty, and allows the foreign fleet, from which American canneries import, a comparable kill rate. This exemption from the law has resulted in the deaths of more than 100,000 dolphins each year for the past several years.

Tuna fleets not only kill dolphins, they also chase millions to exhaustion in their search for tuna. No one knows how the constant harassment, stress, and breaking up of dolphin families are affecting their ability to survive as species.

Serendipitously, just before the bill's passage, the two largest tuna-processing companies in the United States, which produce

Starkist and Chicken of the Sea brands, announced that they will no longer buy or sell tuna caught "on dolphins" or with driftnets, and will label their product accordingly. The decision resulted from a widespread boycott of tuna organized by animal protection and environmental groups. Several other tuna companies later changed their policies as well.

Although this breakthrough for dolphins occurred before the tuna-labeling legislation passed, the legislation was still necessary because the companies' change of policy, although exemplary, was only voluntary. In addition, the legislation was needed to provide a definition of "Dolphin Safe" and to provide penalties for false claims. The amendment to the act prevents the use of "Dolphin Safe" labels if the tuna inside a labeled can has been caught "on dolphins" or with driftnets.*

DOLPHIN PROTECTION AND FAIR FISHING

Despite the gains made in 1989 and 1990, however, dolphins are still not completely safe. Rep. Boxer has submitted another bill, the Dolphin Protection and Fair Fishing Act, which would provide further protections for these animals.

The bill would impose a ban on the practice of setting purse-seine nets on dolphins to catch tuna by the end of 1992, and would require the presence of an observer on board every tuna-fishing vessel to ensure that no dolphins are harassed or killed. Although most American tuna companies are voluntarily buying tuna that has not been caught in association with dolphins, this legislation is needed to make such practices mandatory and permanent.

In addition, tuna vessels from foreign countries would be required to comply with all U.S. dolphin protection practices, including the carrying of observers on board, if they wish to export their tuna catch to tuna canners in the United States. This provision may run into trouble, however, in light of an August 1991

* For more on what legislators are doing about driftnets, see "Saving Endangered Species and Preserving Biodiversity," pp. 243–70.

decision by a panel set up by the General Agreement on Tariffs and Trade (GATT), the world's principal international trade treaty. The panel's ruling stated that GATT prohibits its 108 member nations from imposing import restrictions based on environmental concerns. The ruling further stated that current U.S. bans on tuna imports from Mexico and other countries whose tuna-fishing fleets kill dolphins in large numbers violates the treaty. At the time of this writing, the Bush administration was still considering how to respond to the GATT advisory.

Boxer's bill also "authorizes appropriations for research and development of alternative tuna-fishing methods and technologies that do not involve intentional encirclement of dolphins or other intentional takings of marine mammals."

Imprisoned by Love

Many people have had their consciousness raised by the well-publicized tragedy of dolphins drowning in tuna nets and are now avid fans of dolphins. Ironically, it now appears that the nation's love of dolphins is contributing to dolphin deaths.

It is a strange quirk of human nature that once we love something we want to capture and imprison it so that we have access to it at all times. Dolphins, and other marine mammals including whales, are being captured and imprisoned in increasing numbers to satisfy the nation's growing demand to see these animals up close, watch them perform, and even swim with them. Tragically, dolphins are also being captured for the U.S. Navy, which trains them in weapons delivery and other underwater warfare activities.

Marine mammals such as dolphins and whales are extremely intelligent and sensitive social creatures who are accustomed to having free access to their fellows and to the vast oceans of the world. When they are captured and placed in tiny tanks they become highly stressed and vulnerable to disease and often die— their life expectancy dramatically reduced. Unfortunately, our love of these animals has created a big business—the capturing and selling of marine mammals to zoos, aquaria, and even hotels that invite patrons to swim with dolphins who have been placed in small swimming pools.

In response to citizen complaints, the state of Florida has banned the taking of marine mammals in designated state waters. However, the U.S. Marine Mammal Protection Act takes precedence over state law and allows the taking of marine mammals with a permit obtained from the federal government. As a result, dolphin catchers are still capturing dolphins in Florida waters despite the wishes of its citizens.

Rep. Porter Goss (R-FL) has introduced the Marine Mammal Public Display Reform Act, which would grant states authority to override the federal law and ban the taking of marine mammals in state waters.

THROWAWAY COMPANIONS

> "To illustrate the scope of the pet overpopulation problem, I would like to share some statistics with you: One female dog and her offspring can be the source of *67,000* puppies in just six years; one female cat and her offspring can be the source of 420,000 cats in only seven years. There are 70,000 dogs and cats born in the United States every day, compared to 10,000 humans; 12 million dogs and cats are brought to animal shelters each year, and 7.5 million must be destroyed because there are not enough homes for them. Nationwide, animal control and animal shelter programs cost communities almost $800,000 million each year."
>
> —Rep. Dean Gallo (R-NJ)

Dogs and cats are much loved in this country. Yet they are profoundly betrayed. Victims of the animals-are-objects mentality, puppies and kittens are frequently abandoned after being used to show children the "miracle of birth." Adult animals are cast out when old age makes them "no fun anymore," or when the installation of a new carpet makes it inconvenient to have an animal around.

More than 7.5 million unwanted dogs and cats are euthanized at shelters and pounds every year. Countless other homeless animals fend for themselves until they are hit by cars or die from exposure. In fact, in the United States, only two out of every ten dogs and cats who live to adulthood will ever find themselves well cared for in a loving home.

The law should require the mandatory spaying or neutering of the millions of stray and unwanted animals that pass through the pound and shelter system every year. Unfortunately, only a handful of states have enacted such laws.

To help publicize the overpopulation problem, **Sen. Alan Cranston (D-CA)** and **Rep. Dean Gallo (R-NJ)** introduced joint resolutions to designate the month of April as "National Prevent-a-Litter Month." The legislation was signed into law in 1990.

Concerned that, when necessary, euthanasia be administered humanely, **Rep. Andrew Jacobs (D-IN)** introduced a resolution that condemns the use of rapid decompression as a method of euthanasia, and encourages states "to prohibit the manufacture and use of decompression chamber devices." Decompression chambers suck the air out of animals placed inside them. Their use is considered by virtually all animal protection groups to be a cruel method of euthanasia and one that should be outlawed.

ANIMAL RIGHTS COMES OF AGE

Sen. Harry Reid (D-NV) and **Rep. Frank Pallone (D-NJ)** introduced a joint resolution in Congress designating one week in June as "Animal Rights Awareness Week." The resolution may not be earthshaking, but its introduction shows how far the movement for animal rights has come. Less than a decade ago, the animal rights concept was virtually unknown in the United States. But in the 102nd Congress, fifty-two representatives cosponsored legislation promoting the idea that animals have inherent rights.

ANIMAL RIGHTS: THE GREEN VOTE

☑ Amend the Animal Welfare Act to grant any person or organization standing to sue the U.S. Department of Agriculture on behalf of any animal to compel enforcement of the act.

☑ Amend the Animal Welfare Act in order to include mice, rats, and birds under its protections.

☑ Ban toxicity tests on animals.

☑ Reduce the numbers of animals used in experiments by eliminating the duplication of animal experiments.

☑ Require federally funded school lunch programs to provide vegetarian meals to all students and teachers who conscientiously abstain from eating meat.

☑ Outlaw the steel-jaw leghold trap.

☑ Ban the importation of wild-caught birds for the pet trade.

☑ Ban the practice of setting fishing nets on dolphins to catch tuna; require observers aboard all tuna-fishing vessels to ensure compliance; and promote the development of fishing technologies that do not involve the harassment or killing of dolphins and other marine mammals.

☑ Amend the Marine Mammal Protection Act to allow states to ban the taking of marine mammals from state waters for public display.

☑ Require the sterilization of all dogs and cats who pass through the nation's pound and shelter system.

☑ Ban decompression and other inhumane methods of animal euthanasia.

☑ Promote the idea that animals have inherent rights.

A GENETICALLY
ENGINEERED NATURE

"Mr. President, shortly after the United States dropped the first atomic bombs on Hiroshima and Nagasaki, American poet E. B. White observed: 'The quest for a substitute for God ended suddenly. The substitute turned up and who do you suppose it was? It was man himself, stealing God's stuff.' . . .

"More than four decades have passed since the conclusion of World War II and yet we continue in our irresponsible and indeed immoral quest to 'steal God's stuff.' I rise on this floor today to introduce legislation which would suspend animal patenting for five years. . . . Put simply, Mr. President, the patenting of animals blurs the distinction between man's work and God's work in a way I believe is tremendously dangerous. . . . It is becoming increasingly clear that the U.S. Office of Patents and Trademarks has no way of dealing with the various economic, social, governmental, environmental, and ethical issues which arise from its decision to extend patents to animal life. . . .

"Genetic engineering now allows us to take human genetic traits and insert them into the permanent genetic code of animals. We are also gaining the increased ability to mix and match the genetic traits

226

of animals, insects, and plants, creating new and different species. To suddenly and unconditionally grant patents for the development of any and all of these genetic creations is irresponsible and imprudent. . . ."

—Sen. Mark Hatfield (R-OR)

In the short twenty years since its birth, the new technology of genetic engineering has changed our world more profoundly than any of history's discoveries. Yet the world is generally unaware of, and fully unprepared for, the changes this new science has brought.

There are two astonishing and revolutionary aspects to genetic engineering. For the first time, humankind has the capacity to effect changes in individual organisms that will be passed down to future generations through heredity. Equally startling, we now have the ability to join the genes of various animal species that could never mate in nature and to cross the fundamental biological barriers between plants and animals—including human beings.

Since American molecular biologists first perfected methods of incorporating functioning genetic material of one organism into another in 1972, mind-boggling manipulations of nature have taken place. Genes responsible for "lighting up" fireflys, for example, have been inserted into tobacco plants, causing the plants to light up like the insects. Human genes that cause a predisposition to cancer have been implanted into the genetic makeup of animals, causing the animals and all their progeny to also be so predisposed. According to scientists, the grafting of plant genes into animals is imminent.

Certainly, the world of genetic engineering is seductive. But before we get swept up in the rush, we need to stop and think about how this new technology will change us and the rest of the natural world.

Genetic engineering is the application of engineering principles and values—utility, efficiency, expediency—directly onto the code of life; as such, it is the antithesis of all that is Green. In the brave new world of genetic engineering, humankind becomes the architect of life—designer and master—separate from, and above, nature.

If Green represents reverence for life, respect for the integrity of individuals and species, recognition of the right of nature to exist, and stewardship of the community of life on earth, genetic engineering is the negation of all that. A utilitarian, coldly reductionist science, genetic engineering represents the ultimate degradation of life, reducing it all to bits of information—genetic code —that can be arranged and rearranged at human whim.

At a time when Green-oriented activists are opening more minds to the idea that life is sacred and should be respected, the world of science is fighting just as hard for its utilitarian vision. The battle for the future will be waged over these two competing and diametrically opposed ideas: reverence or utility. We are at a crossroads; the world seems poised to go in either direction.

VISIONS OF WEALTH, VISIONS OF POWER

The growth of the biotech industry was spurred by two historic events. In 1980, the U.S. Supreme Court ruled, in a highly controversial 5–4 vote, that "man-made" microorganisms can be patented. The decision was the result of a patent lawsuit brought by a General Electric Company research microbiologist who had developed a genetically modified bacterium capable of breaking down components of crude oil. General Electric hoped the genetically engineered bacterium would be useful in cleaning up oil spills. The U.S. Patent and Trademark Office had originally denied the researcher's request for a patent on the organism, ruling that microorganisms are products of nature and therefore cannot be patented.

The court decision ignited the biotech industry. Seemingly overnight, small biotech companies popped up everywhere. The multinational corporations soon joined in the biotech boom, pouring billions of dollars into the fledgling genetic-engineering industry. The first generation of biotech products to be developed were genetically engineered bacteria "factories" that could, by virtue of their new genetic programming, produce pharmaceuticals and generate new fermentation processes.

To date, the patent office has received more than 19,750 biotech patent applications.

ANIMALS AS HUMAN INVENTIONS

The second catalyst occurred in April 1987 when, independent of any direction from Congress and without public debate, the U.S. Patent and Trademark Office suddenly announced that all forms of life—including animals, but excluding human beings—may be considered "human inventions" qualifying as "patentable subject matter" if they have been genetically engineered with characteristics not attainable through classic breeding techniques. (While the patent office specifically excluded human beings from patenting, human body parts and human fetuses were not exempted.)

The following April, the patent office awarded the first and to date, only, animal patent. It went to Harvard University for mammals genetically engineered to contain a human cancer-causing gene. Exclusive license to use the patent went to E. I. Du Pont de Nemours & Co.

Currently, there are at least 145 patents pending for genetically engineered animals.

CUSTOM-DESIGNED CREATURES

With the legal opportunities for patenting greatly expanded, genetic engineers set their sights on the "improvement" of animals, especially those used for food and those used in laboratory experiments.

Among the first custom-designed creatures to be "invented" were "geeps." Part goat, part sheep, these animals were engineered through the process of cell fusion, the mixing of goat and sheep embryos. Animals created by cell fusion are called "chimeras" and

Whose Body Is It, Anyway?

The genetic engineering of human body parts, now a booming business, began in rather bizarre fashion. In 1976, cancer-patient John Moore had his spleen removed by doctors at a University of California hospital. More than a decade later, Moore discovered that the university doctors who performed the operation had won a patent on a cell-line that they had removed from Moore's body and later altered through genetic engineering to produce a new drug that is potentially worth $3 *billion.*

The university sold the cell-line to a small Boston biotech company, which later sold exclusive monopoly rights to Sandoz, the huge transnational chemical corporation. Along the way, the hospital and Moore's doctor had earned $3 million in royalties on the patent and 75,000 shares of stock.

Claiming that he should be recompensed, Moore sued for property rights and a share of the profits. Moore won in the California Court of Appeals, but subsequently lost in the California Supreme Court. Lawyers for the biotech industry argued that private ownership of body materials would cause biotechnology research costs to skyrocket and thus cripple further research.

The trade in human tissue exploded in the late 1980s and is now well established, earning companies $2.2 billion in 1990 alone. According to a recent congressional investigation, the incidence of medical schools seeking patents on products made from human tissue increased 300 percent in five years.

• • •

are not truly transgenic because alterations are made at the cellular level rather than at the genetic level. Chimeras, however, were the precursors of animals whose very genes would be altered, enabling new characteristics to be passed down to subsequent generations.

The first of these genetically engineered animals were pigs whose genomes were altered through the insertion of a human gene responsible for the production of human growth hormone. Scientists hoped that the experiment would yield bigger, more meaty pigs. Instead, they produced pain-racked creatures who were severely arthritic, nearly blind, and prone to developing ulcers and pneumonia. The animals were also sterile.

In spite of this bad start, and spurred on by visions of enormous wealth, scientists began to dream up new genetic recipes for farm animals who would produce more meat and less fat faster on less food and on new foods such as sawdust, cardboard, and industrial and human waste.

Agricultural experts and trade journals began to speculate on what the future might bring.

A Canadian researcher speaking at a farmers' convention told the group that: "At the Animal Research Institute [Agriculture

Canada] we are trying to breed animals without legs and chickens without feathers."

A university scientists says: "I believe it's completely feasible to specifically design an animal for hamburger."

In a recent article, the U.S. Department of Agriculture predicted that "the face of animal production in the 21st century could well be . . . broilers blooming to market 40 percent quicker, miniature hens cranking out eggs in double time, a computer 'cookbook' of recipes for custom-designed creatures."

Custom-designed creatures have also been "created" to serve in laboratory experiments. Scientists have even developed "medicine factories," mice implanted with human genes for producing human enzymes, proteins, and drugs that can be harvested. Cows, sheep, and other milk-producing animals have been targeted for further experimentation in this area.

Although still in its infancy, biotechnology is already a multibillion-dollar-per-year gold mine. "Imagining the profits," said one biotechnologist, "can unhinge even a sane scientist."

To date, scientists have "created" hundreds of animals nature never could have made.

LACK OF CONGRESSIONAL WILL

The genetic engineering of animals; the mixing and matching of plant, animal, and human genes; and the sudden decision by the patent office to allow the patenting of animals, left many people stunned. Some were deeply disturbed that a federal agency was allowed to issue a ruling with such broad and profound implications without having consulted society at large, or even Congress.

In response to the growing public concern, a history-making coalition of religious, environmental, animal protection, family farm, and other organizations formed in opposition to the patenting of animals. The coalition published a manifesto, listing its objections to the patent office announcement.

Alarmed that the technology was out of control, **Sen. Mark Hatfield (R-OR)** introduced legislation in the Senate that would

"In economic terms, this controversial patent policy transforms the genetic makeup of the biotic community from a common heritage of us all to the private preserve of the major corporations. Major biotechnology and chemical corporations will increasingly compete for control and ownership of the gene pool of animal species, patenting those creatures that they can successfully genetically engineer. . . .

"Additionally, a variety of ethicists and religious denominations have expressed deep concerns about the dissemination of human characteristics throughout the animal kingdom. They have also questioned the wisdom of characterizing the living world as patentable 'manufactures'. . . . In 1989, the World Council of Churches' central committee agreed that: 'Animal life forms should not be patented; (this) calls for further study of the profound moral and social implications of patenting life forms.'

"And in June, 1989, the European Patent Commission (EPC) rejected a patent application by Harvard which was virtually identical to the patent granted in the United States. The EPC cited both legal and ethical grounds for its rejection of the patent application.

"Finally, there is growing concern about the possibility of patenting human forms, especially pre-embryos, since these forms are without constitutional protection."

—*Sen. Mark Hatfield (R-OR)*

• • •

enact a five-year moratorium on the granting of patents on genetically engineered animals "in order to establish a federal regulatory and review process to deal with the economic, environmental, and ethical issues raised by the patenting of such animals." The bill passed the Senate in the 100th Congress, and was reintroduced in the 101st and 102nd Congresses.

In the House, **Rep. Benjamin Cardin (D-MD)** introduced legislation in the 101st and 102nd Congresses that would impose a two-year moratorium on "the patenting of animal life until there is a proper regulatory review and approval process in place that takes into consideration environmental, health, safety, and biomedical ethical standards on the commercialization of an animal."

Aware of the devastating economic consequences the patenting of farm animals would have on farmers, **Rep. Robert Kastenmeier (D-WI)** submitted legislation that would exempt farmers from having to pay royalties each time the offspring of a patented farm animal was sold by the farmer. The Kastenmeier bill also declared that human beings are not patentable subject matter.

The coalition rallied around the Hatfield and Cardin legislation. Although the Kastenmeier bill did not question the fundamental legitimacy of patenting animals or ask for an ethical review, the coalition also supported it because, if passed, the bill would eliminate the financial incentive for the development of genetically engineered farm animals and thus might stop the technology in its tracks.

It remains to be seen whether the 102nd Congress will have the courage to enact the proposed moratorium so that the country will have an opportunity to make educated decisions, in democratic fashion, about the technology's future. In the meantime, the business and scientific community continues to lobby members of Congress to defeat the moratorium bills, arguing that even a short hiatus would seriously compromise their financial prospects and competitive position in the international community.

RISKY RELEASES

To be sure, some of the products of genetic engineering will prove to be beneficial. However, the promised benefits of this new technology are accompanied by serious risks.

The biotech industry is preparing to release scores of genetically engineered viruses, bacteria, plant strains, and transgenic animals into the environment in the next few years. In coming decades, hundreds, even thousands, of genetically engineered life forms may enter the world's ecosystems in massive commercial volumes. Environmental scientists are increasingly concerned

---

THE DEVIL'S DOCTRINE

"What can be done, must be done." Erwin Chargaff, the eminent Austro-American biochemist who is often referred to as the father of modern molecular biology, coined this phrase, which he called "The Devil's Doctrine." Chargaff, who once referred to genetic engineering as a "molecular Auschwitz," would have chosen not to use the technology, even though we have it.

"I have the feeling that science has transgressed a barrier that should have remained inviolate," he wrote in his autobiography, *Heraclitean Fire,* just over a decade ago. Noting the "awesome irreversibility" of genetic engineering, Chargaff warned that "you cannot recall a new form of life . . . it will survive you and your children and your children's children.

"An irreversible attack on the biosphere is something so unheard-of, so unthinkable to previous generations, that I could only wish that mine had not been guilty of it," he said.

• • •

about the potential risks that such massive environmental releases might pose to public health and the earth's ecology.

Because they are alive, genetically engineered products are inherently more unpredictable than chemical products. Genetically engineered products can reproduce, mutate, and migrate. Once released, it would be virtually impossible to recall them to the laboratory.

Environmental scientists have compared the release of genetically engineered organisms to the introduction of exotic plants and animals to North American habitats. While most of these organisms have adapted to our ecosystems without causing undue dislocation, several, including the gypsy moth, Dutch elm disease, the kudzu vine, and chestnut blight, have wreaked environmental havoc.

Carp and salmon are currently being engineered to grow twice as large as they do in nature. But after release into the wild, will they also consume twice as much food? Will they drive other animal or plant species to extinction?

In addition, the U.S. military is involved in dozens of projects involving genetically engineered organisms. More than fifty corporate and university labs are currently involved in genetics research for the Department of Defense. Could this technology spur a deadly biological arms race among nations? What if deadly new organisms escape from a laboratory?

It would seem logical to suppose that genetic engineering would increase biodiversity by creating new forms of life. On the contrary, it is likely that the technology will have the opposite effect. Once scientists develop what is considered to be the "perfect" salmon or the "perfect" chicken, these will be the ones patented and reproduced in large numbers; all other "less desirable" species would fall by the wayside, decrease in number, and even become extinct. "Perfect" animals and plants might even be cloned —reproduced as exact genetic copies—even further reducing the pool of available genes on the planet.

LAWS ARE NEEDED

In the United States, there are no congressionally mandated laws or regulations to address the release of genetically engineered organisms into the environment. Instead, considerable confusion has been generated as several federal agencies, including the Environmental Protection Agency, the Department of Agriculture, the Department of Defense, and the National Institutes of Health, have attempted to graft existing laws and regulations onto this unique new technology.

Current laws and regulations pertaining to chemicals and toxic substances, however, cannot possibly protect the environment from new, live, genetically altered organisms. As a result of this confusion, there has been virtually nothing to stop any scientist or corporation from releasing experimental, genetically engineered life forms into the environment—except for an occasional lawsuit by an environmental or watchdog organization.

It is unlikely that we will ever be able to ensure the safety of genetically altered organisms because we have no way of predicting or judging risk. It is precisely for this reason that insurance companies have refused to insure the field tests of biotech companies. Insurance companies know that the cost of recompensing for widespread environmental loss, such as that caused by gypsy moths or chestnut blight, would bankrupt them. If insurance companies are unwilling to take the risk, then why should we?

AWASH IN MILK

While genetically engineered products and processes are likely to benefit a priviledged few, they are also likely to have a negative effect on many others. Nowhere is the economic battle over biotechnology more intensely felt than in agriculture where the first major genetically engineered product is being readied for commercial application. The product is called bovine growth hormone or BGH (also known as bovine somatotropin—BST). BGH is a genetically engineered version of a bovine hormone produced naturally by cows. When injected into an animal, BGH increases milk production by 10 to 20 percent or more. The hormone is present in the milk.

Four chemical and pharmaceutical companies—Monsanto, Eli Lilly, Upjohn, and American Cyanamid have invested nearly a billion dollars in research and development of BGH and project a worldwide market of a billion dollars or more per year.

Most of the country's leading farm organizations, including the National Family Farm Coalition and the National Farmers Union oppose BGH fearing that it will result in a glut of milk on the market and depress prices and force them out of business. They have good reason to be concerned. One study prepared by researchers at Cornell University for Monsanto predicted that within three years of the introduction of BGH, more than 30 percent of all American dairy farmers might be forced out of business by milk surpluses and falling prices. This kind of dramatic downturn could prove devastating to the rural economies in dairy states throughout the Northeast and Midwest. A University of Wisconsin study predicted a 100 million dollar loss per year within five years of the introduction of BGH.

Animal protection and environmental organizations including The Humane Society of the U.S., the American Society for the Prevention of Cruelty to Animals (ASPCA), and the National Wildlife Federation also oppose the introduction of BGH, citing studies that show an increase in animal health problems due to massive doses of hormone. Some studies have shown an increased incidence of mastitis, infertility, and lactation burnout from the hormone injections.

Consumer organizations, including the Consumers Union of the U.S., oppose BGH, arguing that increased health risks to the animals may necessitate increased use of antibiotics, which, in turn, would enter the milk supply and could affect human health. The Consumers Union has also raised other potential human health questions and has recommended long-range studies before clearing milk containing BGH for commercial use.

Finally, public opinion surveys show overwhelming opposition to the use of BGH to produce milk and dairy products. Many consumers are not willing to risk their families' health or have the government use additional tax dollars to buy up the anticipated overproduction in milk that will result from the use of BGH.

The BGH controversy is a classic illustration of the difference in thinking that separates conventional ideas of progress and the new Green concept of progress. The chemical and pharmaceutical companies naturally define progress as increased output and market performance. The new Green constituencies, on the other hand, are beginning to define progress in a more sophisticated and integrated fashion. To be progressive, a new technology or product must promote the well-being of the larger community—consumers, workers, and animals—not just the commercial interest of the companies—and steward the resources and protect the rights of future generations. By this standard of progress, BGH would seem to have no redeeming social value.

Rep. Peter Smith (R-VT) introduced a bill in Congress "to prohibit the sale, for a three-year period, of milk produced by cows injected with the bovine growth hormone."

In addition, the key milk-producing states of Wisconsin and Minnesota passed legislation imposing a one-year moratorium on the commercial sale of BGH milk and dairy products even if the

SEEDS OF DESTRUCTION

Genetic engineers claim that biotechnology will benefit the environment through the introduction of safer, nonchemical pest controls that will reduce the need for toxic pesticides and herbicides. But interestingly, just the opposite is occurring. In order to sell more of their products, several major chemical conglomerates have recently acquired most of the world's leading seed companies and are now genetically engineering crops to be resistant to the companies' own herbicides. The development of such plants will permit the spraying of poisonous herbicides on farm fields in amounts large enough to kill weeds—but without killing the conglomerates' patented plants.

Through this ingenious scheme, a handful of chemical companies have created a potentially enormous market. They will be able to sell both the herbicide-resistant plant seeds and the herbicide to farmers—but at the expense of a poisoned earth.

The advent of biotechnology has brought still another problem —the "raiding" of third world genetic resources in the South by the transnational corporations of the North. Such companies obtain the traditional native plants of developing countries, "improve" them through genetic engineering, patent them, and then sell them back to the third world.

This process delivers a double whammy to the poor because their now "inferior" agricultural products can no longer compete with the new genetically "improved" ones of the developed world. In just a short period of time, for example, it is expected that vanilla genetically engineered to grow in the laboratory will put entire regions of poor vanilla-bean farmers out of business.

The economic impact of biotechnology on impoverished countries will likely worsen in coming years as more and more of the genetic resources of the planet come under the control of a small number of multinational corporations. At the current rate of corporate acquisition, it has been predicted that by the year 2000, the global seed market will likely be controlled by just twelve giant multinationals, primarily chemical and petrochemical conglomerates.

product is cleared for commercial use by the U.S. Food and Drug Administration before the moratorium is over. The European Community (EC) has imposed a similar ban for its member nations.

PICKING THE PERFECT GENES

Genetic engineering has opened a virtual Pandora's box of social and ethical questions that society will have to contend with in the coming decades. Diagnostic testing, genetic screening, and increasing use of DNA-based identification systems are resulting in violations of privacy and cases of discrimination against individuals and groups.

While few people would regard the development of genetic tests that can help prevent, predict, or identify serious illness as a bad thing, such sophisticated tests have also brought a host of problems to society at large. Already, people who have been diagnosed as having genetic predispositions to certain diseases have had trouble getting health or life insurance, or a job.

The Human Genome Project, a three-billion-dollar, fifteen-year project recently approved by Congress, will attempt to identify every human gene, thus providing a biochemical blueprint of the human species. When the map is complete, science will have advanced humankind's ability to classify individuals and ethnic and racial groups by their genetic printouts. The social implications are enormous and far reaching.

Employers are already looking to the day when they will be able to screen prospective employees in order to match their genetic predispositions and traits with the appropriate job. Workers whose genetic predispositions make them vulnerable to cancer, hypertension, depression, and other health problems may well find themselves targets of discrimination in hiring practices and evaluation for promotions.

DNA "fingerprinting," by which individuals can be identified through their unique genetic profile, is already being used by police departments around the country. The states of Arizona, Wash-

"Let's concentrate on technology for a couple thousand years, and then we can develop a value system.

© REX F. MAY.

ington, and Virginia already require certain criminals to be identified by means of their DNA. Maryland recently passed a law that
allows DNA analysis to be used as evidence in the courtroom.
Often, identification can be made through bodily material as small
as a strand of hair or an eyelash. Unlike a fingerprint, however,
DNA reveals a lot more about a person than just his or her identity
—it reveals a person's entire genetic makeup.

To ensure that the new genetic-screening technology is not
misused and abused, **Rep. John Conyers (D-MI)** has introduced
the Human Genome Privacy Act, which would "safeguard individual privacy of genetic information from the misuse of records
maintained by [federal] agencies or their contractors or grantees for
the purpose of research, diagnosis, treatment, or identification of
genetic disorders, and to provide to individuals access to records
concerning their genome which are maintained by agencies for any
purpose."

If such legislation is not passed soon, many of us may become
victims of genetic discrimination.

GENETIC ENGINEERING: THE GREEN VOTE

☑ Impose a moratorium on the granting of patents on genetically engineered animals so that the myriad ethical, social, environmental, economic, and legal dilemmas posed by the new technology can be publicly deliberated.

☑ Impose a moratorium on the release of genetically engineered organisms into the environment.

☑ Exempt farmers from having to pay royalties each time the offspring of a patented farm animal is sold by a farmer—in order to diminish the incentive for engineering and patenting animals.

☑ Prohibit the sale of milk and dairy products from cows injected with genetically engineered bovine growth hormone.

☑ Protect the privacy of every citizen by ensuring that genetic information is not used as a tool for discrimination by government agencies and their contractors.

SAVING ENDANGERED SPECIES AND PRESERVING BIODIVERSITY

Humankind has so far identified and classified about 1.4 million species of plants and animals that live on the earth. But scientists think that there are actually between 5 and 80 million species. We don't even know the amount of diversity on the planet to the nearest order of magnitude; yet scientists now estimate that every hour, one animal or plant species disappears forever into the eternal void of extinction.

While extinctions have occurred as part of the natural evolutionary process over the millennia, the National Science Board predicts that the rate of extinctions over the next few decades will rise to at least 1,000 times its former rate—an event unprecedented in 65 million years. Scientists predict that one quarter to one half of all species on earth will become extinct within the next thirty years.

Recently, the Scientific Advisory Board of the Environmental Protection Agency ranked "species extinction and overall loss of biological diversity" as one of our greatest environmental problems; and *Time* magazine referred to the current staggering loss of biological diversity as "the death of birth."

Since we derive all of our food, and much of our medicine, clothing, and shelter from the biological richness all around us, the viability of Homo sapiens, too, is threatened by the irretrievable loss of species, ecosystems, gene pools, and ecological processes.

Plants, for example, currently supply nearly one quarter of the world's pharmaceuticals. Yet extinctions of newly discovered, or as yet unknown, plant species are occurring before we can determine their medicinal qualities.

Worldwide, a potentially catastrophic reduction in the gene pool of edible plants and animals has occurred in just a few decades and is rapidly worsening. This has been brought on by a combination of economic factors, new agricultural practices, and loss of habitat. In the United States, for example, 90 percent of all chicken eggs now sold are laid by one breed of chicken; two varieties of peas account for 96 percent of the annual pea harvest. In Japan, two thirds of the local rice varieties have been lost in this century. India had 30,000 varieties of rice fifty years ago, but today depends upon just 10 strains. A new disease that afflicts just one major crop species upon which many depend for food could easily result in widespread famine.

In addition, animals and plants are becoming extinct before we can find out what critical role they may have played in maintaining the delicate balance of ecosystems upon which all life depends. How many species can an ecological system lose before it no longer operates as a system? Biologists Anne and Paul Ehrlich answer that with another question: How many rivets could one unscrew from an airplane before the craft no longer held together and plummeted, in pieces, to earth? No one knows.

And what of the psychic value to humans of the vast richness of life on earth? The plants and animals that surround us certainly have aesthetic value; they make the world more beautiful. More importantly, however, they provide us with a sense of familiarity, a sense of place and day-to-day continuity that is vital in maintaining our sense of security in the world.

But certainly they have more than utilitarian value. Many of us would assert that simply by virtue of their existence the plants and animals with which we share the earth have an inherent worth, apart from any usefulness they may have to humankind, and thus have a right to continued existence. This is surely a fundamental tenet of the Green political vision, and perhaps the ultimate reason for conserving biodiversity.

Saving endangered species has become a politically charged issue in the halls of Congress, where several legislators have attempted to garner support on Capitol Hill for some of the world's most loved and most endangered animals. Bills to save the great whales, the African elephant, Australian kangaroos, the northern spotted owl, and wolves, among others, have been introduced with varying degrees of success.

The Trouble with Whales

Humankind may soon find itself deprived of the joy of sharing the world with some of the most intelligent animals on earth, the great whales. Whales and their smaller cetacean cousins, the dolphins, possess a full consciousness and intelligence, in many ways different from ours, but no less complex. In these mysterious animals perhaps lies humankind's best chance of ever communicating across species lines. Yet the great "mind in the waters," as anthropologist Joan McIntyre so aptly titled her 1974 classic book on cetaceans, continues to be besieged.

Whales and dolphins are strangled by the debris and sickened by the toxins that we dump into the oceans. They are caught and drowned in vast fishing nets; they are being crowded out of the seas by humankind's relentless exploration of the oceans for oil and minerals, by increased shipping, by oil spills, by overfishing, and by underwater weapons tests.

The most immediate threat to these great air-breathing mammals, however, is probably hunting. Although all of the great whale species teeter on the brink of extinction, whales are still hunted and killed for their meat.

In 1982, the International Whaling Commission (IWC), an international regulatory body formed by treaty and composed of representatives from some forty-one countries, declared a world-wide moratorium on the commercial killing of whales to take effect in 1986 and to last indefinitely. Since the ban, however, more than 14,000 whales have been killed by several defiant nations which have at one time or another included Brazil, Denmark, Iceland, the Soviet Union, Chile, China, Japan, Peru, Portugal, South Korea, North Korea, Norway, Spain, and Taiwan.

Currently, only Japan continues to kill whales; Norway and

Iceland only recently—and reluctantly—stopped their whaling operations. Japan hunts under the guise of what the Japanese claim is "scientific research." However, the guise is a very transparent one since most of the meat from the "studied" whales ends up on the menus of Japanese restaurants.

Continued hunting of these magnificent animals could not be occurring at a worse time. A devastating decade-long survey of the world's whale populations off the coast of Antarctica by the IWC's highly regarded scientific committee found only 453 blue whales (the largest animal ever to have lived on earth) when they had expected to find at least ten times as many. The survey turned up only 4,047 humpback whales, when at least 10,000 were anticipated.

Although the IWC has strongly condemned the continued killing, it has no enforcement powers. Enforcement is left to the nations of the world which can, at their disgression, impose various economic sanctions upon non-cooperating countries. U.S. law provides for strong sanctions to be imposed against nations that violate international treaties to protect endangered species, other wildlife, and fishing rights. However, because the imposition of sanctions is discretionary rather than mandatory, the Bush and Reagan administrations have been reluctant to impose sanctions, particularly against U.S. allies; and they have steadfastly refused to impose severe enough economic penalties against Japan, which is by far the worst offender.

SAVE THE WHALES

"Personally, Mr. President, I would like to see not a moratorium, or even an extention of a moratorium on the commercial killing of whales. I would like to see a ban, an end, period; no more killing of the world's whales."

—Sen. Joseph Lieberman (D-CT)

Several members of Congress have repeatedly submitted legislation over the years that would help protect whales. In recent years, **Rep. Gus Yatron (D-PA), Sen. Claiborne Pell (D-RI), Sen. Daniel Patrick Moynihan (D-NY), Sen. John Kerry (D-MA),** and **Rep. Robert Roe (D-NJ)** have been at the forefront.

Sen. Pell and Rep. Yatron introduced companion resolutions calling for "a U.S. policy of promoting the continuation, for a minimum of an additional 10 years, of the International Whaling Commission's moratorium on the commercial killing of whales" and to express the sense of the Congress that whales, dolphins, and porpoises should be protected. The resolution passed both the House and Senate.

Sen. Kerry and Rep. Yatron introduced companion resolutions "calling for a United States policy of strengthening and maintaining indefinitely" the IWC moratorium, which passed both the House and Senate in the 101st Congress. Rep. Roe also submitted a resolution calling on all nations to comply with the moratorium.

Rep. Yatron submitted yet another resolution, passed by the House, that called for "U.S. sanctions against nations which conduct unjustified lethal whale research."

LAWS WITH TEETH

Sen. Daniel Patrick Moynihan (D-NY), Rep. Wayne Owens (D-UT) and **Rep. Don Young (R-AK)** have proposed rewrites of U.S. law that would enable the President to more easily impose economic sanctions on countries that violate domestic and international fisheries and wildlife laws. Such sanctions would not only be useful in protecting whales, but all endangered species.

Rep. Young's bill is the simplest. It would grant the President greater discretion in imposing economic sanctions against offending countries. Currently, the President can choose to embargo fish products from offending nations under what is known as the Pelly Amendment to the Fishermen's Protective Act; he can choose to revoke any permits that an offending nation may have for fishing in U.S. waters; or he can choose to do nothing. Rep. Young's bill would expand the reach of the Pelly Amendment by simply allowing the President to embargo *any* product of an offending nation—not just fish products.

Sen. Moynihan's bill would make actions that undermine international agreements to protect endangered and threatened species unfair trade practices under the U.S. Trade Act of 1974. This would enable the United States to selectively retaliate against all kinds of imports from offending countries.

"If countries such as Japan and Hong Kong fail to comply with laws protecting endangered species such as the whale, the caiman, or the African elephant, retaliatory action, for example, could fall on sophisticated electronics or automotive producers' imports from these nations," Sen. Moynihan told his colleagues.

Sen. Moynihan's bill would also grant private parties the right to petition the U.S. Trade Representative for relief against the failure of foreign governments to comply with international agreements.

Rep. Owens' bill is the strongest. It would mandate what are currently discretionary sanctions by requiring the Secretary of the Treasury to immediately impose an embargo of 20 percent of the monetary value of the fish or wildlife imports from an offending country. This amount would automatically double each year of noncompliance until the embargo is complete, or the nation has stopped offending. The secretary would also have the option of embargoing other products of equal value.

Rep. Owens' bill is appealing because enforcement of international law would not depend upon the discretion of an uncooperative President.

"In a world filled with the tusks, whalebone, horns, skin, and teeth of endangered animals, the irony of the Pelly Amendment is that it is extraordinarily toothless," Rep. Owens told his colleagues in the House. "Nations which violate international conservation agreements, including the resolutions of the International Whaling Commission, must know that the United States has a bite to back up its annoying bark. We all want to protect endangered species, but we must have better tools for the job. This bill provides those tools, giving teeth to what we had only given lip service before."

Last Chance for Elephants

"Mr. Speaker, 28 years ago I went to Africa for the first time to meet the leaders of several African nations. Seeing the herds of elephants and giraffes firsthand will live on in my memory as one of the most beautiful moments I have ever experienced.

"Last week, I opened up an issue of *National Geographic* to an article describing the activities of poachers in Africa who, right now, are gunning down 200 to 300 elephants per day with submachine guns, and removing their tusks with chain saws. I felt sick to my stomach."

—The late Rep. Silvio Conte (R-MA)

While the endangered blue whale is the largest animal ever to have lived, the African elephant is the largest land animal now living. But by the turn of the century, we may refer to both animals in the past tense. For as we rush toward the year 2000, both animals almost certainly appear to be headed toward extinction.

Current estimates of the African elephant population now hover at less than 400,000 animals, down from 1.3 million in 1980; recently the population has been decreasing by about 10 percent a year. Ironically, the African elephant is one of the world's most beloved animals, yet it is the world's love for jewelry and statues carved from the animals' ivory tusks that has brought this most majestic creature to its knees. The fact is, that while the African elephant survived the last Ice Age, it may not survive the affluent shopper.

Although human population growth in Africa has reduced elephant habitat and contributed to the demise of this species and many others, the primary cause for the animals' disappearance has been the world's seemingly insatiable demand for ivory.

The temptation for impoverished people to kill elephants has been great since until quite recently exorbitant ivory prices ensured that a poacher would earn more in one day than most African workers earn in a year. This kind of competition for survival, pitting humans against the animal kingdom, is common in poor nations and has led many environmentalists to the realization that self-reliant, sustainable development must take root in these countries before they can hope to preserve their diverse biological heritage. Fortunately, an increasing number of U.S. legislators have come to the same realization.*

SAVE THE ELEPHANTS

Significant steps have been taken in the past two years to try and save the elephant. A worldwide ban on trade in ivory was declared in the fall of 1989 at the seventh Conference of the Parties of the Convention on International Trade in Endangered Species of Wild Fauna and Flora (CITES), a treaty to which 102 nations are signatories. Since the African elephant was given most-protected status by the CITES nations, ivory prices have plummeted, making it no longer worthwhile to poach elephants at this time.

Bowing to public pressure, President Bush agreed to ban ivory imports into the United States in the summer of 1989. His Administration, however, has been slow to the point of negligence in placing the African elephant on the endangered species list. While environmental and animal protection groups petitioned the government in early 1989 to list the African elephant as endangered under the Endangered Species Act, the Department of the Interior had still not confered most-protected status as late as the summer of 1991. Instead, the agency published a proposal to list as endangered only elephants from certain African countries and not from others. Such a "split listing," however, would only encourage poaching and trophy hunting by reviving the ivory trade.

---

* For more on what legislators are doing to promote self-reliant, sustainable development in the third world, see "Sustainable International Development," pp. 107–27.

Scenes from the year 2000:
The last elephant hides in the
last rain forest.

REPRINTED BY PERMISSION: TRIBUNE MEDIA SERVICES.

FRIENDS OF ELEPHANTS

Several legislators have been influential in trying to save the African elephant. In the spring of 1989, **Rep. Frank Horton (R-NY)** sponsored a resolution urging the Secretary of the Interior "to take expedited action to list the African elephant as endangered under the Endangered Species Act." In another resolution, **Rep. Anthony Beilenson (D-CA)** called on the Bush administration to take measures to curtail the ivory trade and assist African countries in protecting their elephant populations. At the same time, the late **Rep. Silvio Conte (R-MA)** submitted a bill to place "an immediate ban" on the importation of ivory and other elephant products by classifying the animal as endangered under the Endangered Species Act.

The Elephant Protection Act, introduced by **Rep. Brian Donnelly (D-MA),** would have revoked the most-favored-nation status of any country that continued to traffic in ivory or ivory products. It would also have denied tax credit on income derived from the sale of ivory and ivory products and would have imposed criminal penalties on individuals who continued ivory trafficking.

Rep. John Kasich (R-OH) submitted a bill early in the 101st Congress that would have banned the importation of all ivory products into the United States and would have revoked most-favored-nation treatment of products from countries that do not have or enforce protections for indigenous populations of elephants. The bill also urged the President to work to obtain similar ivory product bans in other trading nations.

Rep. Jack Fields (R-TX) sponsored a bill that would have prohibited the importation of fish and wildlife from the People's Republic of China because China had objected to, and had refused to cooperate with, the listing of the African elephant as a most-protected species under CITES.

THE MASSACRE DOWN UNDER

The Australian government frequently employs the image of the kangaroo, joey in pocket, hopping happily through advertisements promoting Australian tourism. Such ads, however, belie the terrible truth that some 4 million kangaroos are killed every year in indiscriminate government-sanctioned hunts. The killing comprises the largest deliberate slaughter of wild animals in the world, and one of the most inhumane.

The animals are hated by ranchers and farmers, who claim that kangaroos compete for forage with cattle and other livestock, and damage crops. The Australian government has given the go-ahead to the wholesale massacre of these animals. Wildlife biologists believe that the killings could lead to the extinction of several species of kangaroos if they coincide with one of the country's frequent droughts.

Because the animals are so hated, kangaroo hunts have been

reported to be unusually brutal. Kangaroos are often hunted at night by truckloads of hunters who mow down large groups with automatic weapons. Photographs and film footage also reveal that kangaroos are sometimes purposefully run down by cars, skinned alive, or beaten to death.

Although the Australian government claims the animals are killed because they are pests, the skin and meat of these animals supplies a huge industry that makes pet food, golf bags, handbags, and athletic shoes.

Kangaroos were declared threatened under the U.S. Endangered Species Act in 1974 after many kangaroo species were driven to near extinction by habitat loss caused by livestock grazing, as well as sport and bounty hunting. A ban was imposed on the importation of kangaroo parts and products into the United States until such time as the Australian government certified that the killing of kangaroos would not prove detrimental to the species.

In 1981, following years of pressure by the Australian government, the U.S. ban on the importation of kangaroo parts and products was lifted, although the animals remain classified as threatened on the endangered species list. The United States is now the number one consumer of finished kangaroo products (primarily running shoes and other athletic footwear), and the third largest consumer of raw kangaroo products.

In 1989, several animal protection and environmental organizations filed a petition to reimpose the ban with the U.S. Fish and Wildlife Service (FWS), which enforces the Endangered Species Act. In 1990, the FWS shocked the environmental community by proposing not only to continue the trade in kangaroo parts, but to remove kangaroos from the endangered species list!

Rep. Robert Mrazek (D-NY) has introduced the Kangaroo Protection Act, which would prohibit the importation of kangaroo parts and products to the United States. Specifically, the bill "provides that any administrative exception made under the Endangered Species Act of 1973 permitting the importation of kangaroos, their parts, and products, shall not apply to kangaroos removed from the wild." The bill won 104 cosponsors in the 101st Congress and is still attracting cosponsors in the current session of Congress.

POLITICALLY ENDANGERED

The Endangered Species Act is highly vulnerable to political interventionism. Nowhere has this been more apparent than in the contentious four-year-long debate that continues to rage within Congress and between Congress, the Bush administration, and environmentalists over the fate of the northern spotted owl, the old-growth forests, and the timber workers of the Northwest.

The northern spotted owl is on the brink of extinction because most of its habitat, the old-growth forests of the Northwest, has been destroyed by logging. Nearly all the remaining acres of old growth are on publicly owned lands managed by the U.S. Forest Service and the Bureau of Land Management (BLM). Industry, however, wants to continue cutting down what little is left of the publicly owned old-growth forests and claims that thousands of timber workers will lose their jobs if the forests are closed to logging.

The Endangered Species Act requires that animals and plants on the verge of extinction be protected from further destruction. But under heavy pressure from the Bush administration to accommodate the timber industry, the Forest Service and the U.S. Fish and Wildlife Service (FWS) have repeatedly failed to carry out their mandate under the law.

In 1989, environmental groups, presenting evidence of the spotted owl's decline, petitioned the courts to have the owl protected. The FWS initially refused to list the owl as threatened or endangered, but, following a court order, listed it as a threatened species in June 1990. FWS violated the Endangered Species Act again by failing to designate critical habitat, the minimum habitat required to maintain the viability of the spotted owl, as required.

In May 1991, U.S. District Court Judge William L. Dwyer ordered most timber sales in the national forests of the Northwest suspended until federal agencies produced an effective protection plan for the owl. In his ruling, the judge noted that when the Forest Service finally began to develop such a plan earlier in 1990, the Secretaries of Agriculture and the Interior had quietly stopped the effort.

"More is involved here than a simple failure by an agency to comply with its governing statute," Dwyer's ruling stated. "The most recent violation of [the law] exemplifies a deliberate and systematic refusal by the Forest Service and the [Fish and Wildlife Service] to comply with the laws protecting wildlife. This is not the doing of the scientists, foresters, rangers and others at the working levels of these agencies. It reflects decisions made by higher authorities in the executive branch of government."

Dwyer also noted that the timber industry is in decline, not because of the spotted owl, but because of several independent economic factors that have conspired over time. "Job losses in the wood products industry will continue regardless of whether the northern spotted owl is protected," he said.

SAVED FROM THE "GOD COMMITTEE" — ALMOST

For the most part, the 101st Congress shied away from a decisive resolution of the debate. Most congressmen from the Northwest, however, were more concerned about the timber industry than preserving the spotted owl or the old-growth forests. Sen. Bob Packwood (R-OR), for example, submitted an amendment to the 1991 Interior appropriations bill that would have derailed normal decision making on the spotted owl by channeling its fate to the Endangered Species Committee. Also known as the "God Committee," this Cabinet-level panel has legal authority to overrule the Endangered Species Act in cases involving severe economic hardship. Packwood felt that the committee would be more inclined to rule in favor of industry than the environment. Fortunately, the Senate voted down the Packwood amendment 62–32.

In mid-1991, the FWS finally determined that 11.6 million acres of Northwestern forest comprise the critical habitat that must be preserved to ensure the owl's survival. A few months later, however, FWS revised its recommendation and reduced the size of the critical habitat to 8.2 million acres by cutting out all private lands and some state lands.

In August of 1991, a bipartisan group of Northwestern legislators in the 102nd Congress, introduced a comprehensive bill that they hoped would appease all warring factions. The bill was denigrated on all sides, however. Industry, labor, and environmentalists could not agree. By September 1991, as many as fourteen bills to address the conflict had been introduced into Congress. Only two of these, which would create a preserve for the tiny bit of old-growth forest remaining, introduced by **Rep. Jim Jontz (D-IN)** and **Sen. Brock Adams (D-WA)**, were truly Green.*

In September 1991, Interior Secretary Manuel Lujan decided to convene the God Committee to resolve the owl vs. timber issue; the committee's decision was expected in February 1992.

THE OWL, SYMBOL OF BIODIVERSITY

The debate over the northern spotted owl has, by now, become symbolic of the critical need to save the few remaining old-growth forests and the tremendous biological diversity they support. The spotted owl is an "indicator species" and as such provides a measure of the health of the forests.

Old-growth forests differ dramatically from the sterile, monocultured, same-age tree plantations that timber companies cultivate on the vast tracts of private and federal lands that once teemed with diverse life. The old forests are rich and voluptous, full of ancient standing trees, fallen trees, snags, and massive decaying vegetation that provide shelter and food to life forms that can live nowhere else.

Not long ago, these ancient forests covered the western parts of Washington, Oregon, and northern California from the coastal mountains to the sea. Now less than 10 percent of the ancient forest remains.

---

* For more on what Rep. Jontz is doing to save the old-growth forests, see "Protecting Forests and Wetlands", pp. 189–94. Also see Rep. Bryant's bill to preserve biodiversity in forests, in this chapter, pp. 263–66.

RETURN OF A NATIVE?

More than seventy years ago, Congress passed legislation to exterminate wolves from the land. Among the last were the wolves of Yellowstone Park, who were killed off by government hunters in 1926. By the time the Endangered Species Act was passed in 1966, wolves were virtually extinct in the lower forty-eight states, and they were listed as a protected species under the act.

Now Congress and the nation seem to be coming full circle on the issue of the wolf, the once universally hated predator. Reflecting the environmental concerns of the times, the House voted in June 1991 to direct the U.S. Fish and Wildlife Service (FWS) to reintroduce gray wolves to their natural and rightful place in the ecological system of Yellowstone Park. If the Senate agrees, the howl of the wolf may be heard in the park as early as 1994.

Despite the storm of controversy that has been stirred up by plans to reintroduce the gray wolf, these animals have been returning slowly to Montana and Idaho from Canada of their own accord. There are fears, however, that naturally returning wolves, and any who may be purposefully introduced, will be killed by ranchers.

FWS studies show that domestic livestock is rarely killed by wolves. At least one organization, Defenders of Wildlife, has set up a program to reimburse ranchers the full value of any livestock preyed upon by wolves. However, none of this has served to quell the ranchers' opposition to wolf reintroduction.

Just as the eradication of the wolf was a political act, the wolf's return is more a matter of politics than protecting endangered wildlife. The Endangered Species Act requires the FWS to restore endangered species. The National Park Service, too, is required to restore and maintain all species of plants and animals indigenous to its parks. Yet, although a plan for reintroducing the gray wolf to Yellowstone was drawn up several years ago, the FWS and Park Service have not implemented it because of political pressure applied by the livestock industry and some Western members of

"What really galls me is that he's on the endangered species list and we're not."
© *1990* BY S. GROSS. PUBLISHED IN AUDUBON.

Congress. The scenario is a virtual rerun of the northern spotted owl controversy.

Rep. Wayne Owens (D-UT) is one member of Congress who has championed the restoration of wolves for several years. In 1987, during the 100th Congress, Rep. Owens introduced a bill directing the National Park Service to restore gray wolves to Yellowstone within three years. In the 101st Congress, Owens introduced another bill, which directed the Secretary of the Interior to comply with the National Environmental Policy Act by submitting an environmental impact statement on the proposed reintroduction of wolves to Yellowstone. Ninety-three cosponsors signed on to Rep. Owens' latest bill.

Despite the large number of wolf supporters in Congress, legislators from Western states, including Sen. Steven Symms (R-ID) and Rep. Ron Marlenee (R-MT), who is a rancher himself, had succeeded in blocking any movement on the issue until recently.

Sen. Max Baucus (D-MT) also opposes the reintroduction of wolves, but favors natural wolf recovery.

Whether the FWS complies with the law and restores this endangered species may soon be decided by the Senate.

Slow Down, Save Lives

In another effort to protect endangered species and all wildlife, **Rep. Charles Bennett (D-FL)** has introduced legislation that would increase the maximum fine that may be imposed for violating posted speed limits in the National Forest System, the National Parks System, and the National Wildlife Refuge System.

The Humane Society of the U.S. has estimated that, every day, 1 million animals, both wild and domestic, are hit and killed by motor vehicles. The terrible toll can be witnessed alongside the nation's roads, particularly during birthing season or at times when food is scarce. The percentage of endangered and threatened species affected is not known.

Rep. Bennett's bill would raise the fine for speeding in protected areas to a maximum of $1,000.

Preserving the Gene Pool

While Congress has, in the past, moved to protect specific species of animals, it has been slow to recognize the importance of maintaining overall biological diversity. However, a handful of legislators have begun to turn their attention to this pressing issue.

Rep. James H. Scheuer (D-NY), Sen. Daniel Patrick Moynihan (D-NY), and **Rep. Gerry E. Studds (D-MA)** have introduced comprehensive legislation to make the preservation of biological diversity a national goal. Unlike the Endangered Species Act, all three of these bills seek to preserve species and ecosystems long before they become endangered.

"At best, the Endangered Species Act serves as a 'biological Superfund'—providing emergency room care only after the catastrophe has occurred," Scheuer told his colleagues in Congress. "The time has come for a statute aimed at preventing the loss of biological diversity through science, planning, and coordination."

Indeed, as of June 1991, the U.S. Endangered Species Act protected only 597 plants and animals in the United States and another 521 species in other countries, while an additional 3,700 species thought to be threatened or endangered still awaited government processing. Of these, 550 required emergency listing. At the rate of 60 species a year—the average number processed annually by the U.S. Fish and Wildlife Service—it would take nine years just to process the emergency backlog.

The nearly identical legislation of Rep. Scheuer and Sen. Moynihan, titled the National Biological Diversity Conservation and Environmental Research Act, "establishes a national policy for the conservation of biological diversity, creates a national Center for Biological Diversity and Conservation Research, ensures that biological diversity be considered [by federal agencies] in environmental impact statements, and creates an interagency working group on biological diversity to plan and implement a federal strategy for the conservation of biological diversity."

The bills would encourage research to catalog the nation's largely unknown inventory of biological wealth through the new center (to be established at the Smithsonian Institution), and would require "identification of those biotic communities, species, and populations that appear to be in decline" as well as ameliorative action to preserve them. Furthermore, the Environmental Protection Agency administrator would be required to reject any federal proposals that would "result in a significant reduction in biological diversity." Federal agencies would be required to report their progress in preserving diversity annually to the President, the White House Council on Environmental Quality, and Congress.

A National Scientific Advisory Committee on Biological Diversity would be responsible for implementing the national strategy. The Agency for International Development would be required to hire experts in the conservation of biological diversity and sustainable development to expand biodiversity conservation in its foreign aid programs.

Rep. Studds' bill, the National Biological Diversity Conservation Act, is similar. It would establish "the Interagency Working Committee of Biological Diversity to prepare a coordinated federal strategy for the conservation of biological diversity, and establish a national Center for Biological Diversity and Conservation Research."

The bill also "requires the Secretary of the Interior to protect lands for purposes of maintaining viable populations of plants, animals, and self-sustaining natural communities."

SAVING THE SEED

Congress has also begun to turn its attention to other programs to preserve genetic biodiversity, including efforts to buttress the National Germplasm Storage System.

The U.S. Department of Agriculture runs the National Plant Germplasm System in which seed samples from plant species from around the world are held at regional repositories and are backed up by duplicate samples at the National Seed Storage Laboratory (NSSL) in Fort Collins, Colorado. The director of the national system, which was set up seventeen years ago, has reported that 25 to 35 percent of the system's seed samples are in danger and that it will take at least twelve years to replenish just the emergency cases.

A 1990 study by the National Academy of Sciences, however, found an even worse situation—that almost 50 percent of the laboratory's seeds are not being properly cared for. The International Board for Plant Genetic Resources recently found that the majority of the world's stored germplasm—including the collection at the NSSL—is not securely stored and that much of it has been irretrievably lost.

The fundamental problem with the NSSL is that it sees its mission primarily as a resource for agribusiness and research—not as the safekeeper for posterity of much of the world's genetic inheritance. One result of this failure of mission is that the NSSL's collection is composed almost exclusively of currently commercially valuable strains of agricultural plants such as wheat, potatoes, corn, rice, and cotton. Heirloom plants that the world's food

EXTINCTIONS IN AGRICULTURE:
A DISASTER WAITING TO HAPPEN

Many varieties of food plants and breeds of domesticated animals have quietly vanished from America's farms in recent decades. For example:

- More than 6,000 known varieties of apples (86 percent of those ever recorded) have become extinct since 1900.
- 2,300 pear varieties have disappeared since 1900.
- Nearly 98 percent of the forty-six asparagus varieties available in 1903 are extinct.
- Nearly 95 percent of the 578 varieties of garden beans available in 1903 are extinct.
- 94 percent of the 288 varieties of beets available in 1903 are extinct.
- 90 percent of all chicken eggs sold are laid by one breed, the white Leghorn.
- 70 percent of the nation's dairy herd is Holstein.
- Two varieties of peas account for 96 percent of the yearly pickings.
- Three varieties of oranges provide 90 percent of Florida's annual harvest.
- Four varieties of potatoes make up nearly three quarters of the yearly crop; and one variety represents the bulk.
- 80 of the 175 varieties of livestock in North America are threatened—including Guernsey cows and other animals that were common when many of us were children.

> —Martin Teitel, *The Rain Forest in Your Kitchen: The Hidden Connection Between the Extinction Crisis and the Supermarket Shelf;* and, Cary Fowler and Pat Mooney, *Shattering: Food, Politics, and the Loss of Genetic Diversity*

supply may need in the future, such as nuts, fruits, vegetables, and herbs, receive little attention. No effort is made to preserve and protect native (North and Meso-American) plant germplasm, such as wild rices, jojoba, and Indian corn.

Rep. George Brown (D-CA) introduced into the 1990 Omnibus Farm Bill language that would establish a National Genetics Resources Program. The program, which became law with the passage of the Food and Agriculture Act, provides for the "collection, preservation, and dissemination of genetic material of importance to American food and agricultural production." The program which is to be administered by the Secretary of Agriculture, is to include genetic material from microbes, plants, insects and other animals, and will make such material available upon request "without charge and without regard to the country from which such a request originates."

The intention behind the new genetic resources program is laudable and will fill a serious vacuum. However, the law does not specifically limit the uses to which such genetic material can be put by those who request it. Materials requested from the program could thus be used for the genetic engineering of new forms of life —or even new weapons—that prove to be detrimental, and could even result in the further reduction of the gene pool.*

SAVE THE TREES, SAVE THE FOREST

Rep. John Bryant (D-TX) takes yet another tack in the attempt to preserve biodiversity with his proposed legislation, the Forest Biodiversity and Clear-cutting Prohibition Act. The bill would prohibit the forestry practice of clear-cutting on all federally controlled lands and require all government agencies that regulate federal lands to maintain the native biodiversity of those lands.

Clear-cutting, or even-age logging, is the most ecologically devastating method of harvesting timber ever devised. Widely practiced on public and privately owned lands, it involves the complete stripping of all trees—commercially valuable and un-

---

* For more on genetic engineering, see "A Genetically Engineered Nature," pp. 226–42.

THINK GLOBALLY, ACT LOCALLY
BIODIVERSITY IN A BACKYARD

Fort Collins, Colorado, is the first city in the country to be certified as an urban wildlife sanctuary. In the summer of 1987, the
city council adopted a resolution that designated the city an
urban wildlife sanctuary under the auspices of the National Institute for Urban Wildlife in Columbia, Maryland. Since then, an
abundance of wildlife has been attracted by the city's extraordinary efforts to reclaim and preserve biodiversity within its borders.

City Hall has a separate division of natural resources, staffed
by full-time wildlife biologists, whose sole job is to identify urban wildlife and ensure that it's protected. Fort Collins is believed to be the only city in the country to have wildlife biologists on the city payroll.

One of the city's awarding-winning projects has been the
creation of a 10-acre nature preserve in the heart of downtown. In
addition to restoring wetlands on the site, volunteers working
with the city are completely restoring two acres of riparian wood-
land, including the reintroduction of original grasses and wild-
flowers that were native to the area before the city was built.

A city program to identify and certify homeowners' backyards as wildlife habitats involves hundreds of citizen participants. In order to be certified, homeowners must make improvements to their yards to attract wildlife, such as letting nature
reclaim their lawns—which involved a modification of existing
weed control ordinances.

The city's master plan analyses the overall habitat system
needed to support ecological communities and outlines the
means of achieving this goal, including the acquisition of properties and balancing the needs of nature against proposed development and public works.

> "Clearcutting is the practice of completely destroying a forest,
> stripping it of every standing tree and reducing it to a muddy field
> in an effort to take from it every commercially valuable stick of
> timber.
>
> "This practice results in fields and mountainsides stripped bare
> of everything but tree stumps. It is a sight that is shocking to see,
> and anyone who sees it knows instinctively that it cannot be a
> prudent method of managing the national forests that belong to the
> American people.
>
> "Clearcutting ignores the need for natural species diversity as a
> requirement for a healthy forest and environment. Clearcutting to-
> tally eliminates species diversity of plants and animals."
>
> —*Rep. John Bryant (D-Texas)*

• • •

wanted trees alike—from a forest. Valuable trees are transported to
lumber mills, while the remaining vegetation is bulldozed and
burned. When cleared, the site is replanted with only one species
of tree, a commercially valuable one. Devoid of the counterbalances
of nature, such monocultures are highly vulnerable to natural diseases and insects.

It takes little imagination to understand how clear-cutting
completely destroys ecological systems and biological diversity,
and how devastating is the loss. Many Americans became convinced of the profound value of North American forests during the
highly publicized discovery two years ago that the Pacific yew, a
"worthless" tree that was regularly bulldozed and burned during
clear-cutting operations, contains taxol, a potentially lifesaving
drug for cancer patients.

Clear-cutting is the same devastating process that is responsible for the destruction of rain forests around the world—a loss that
the world decries. During the past three decades, however, millions of acres of federally owned land in the United States have also
been lost to this destructive form of forestry "management," or,
more accurately, mismanagement.

"It will continue to be impossible to lecture other regions of
the world about natural resource protection, about the dangers of

stripping the forests bare, as long as we continue to pursue waste-ful management practices ourselves," Bryant told his colleagues after a recent trip to the Amazon rain forests in Brazil.

Bryant's bill, which he developed with the aid and support of the Audubon Society, Wilderness Society, and Friends of the Earth, would affect hundreds of thousands of acres of lands regu-lated by the Forest Service, the Bureau of Land Management, the Bureau of Indian Affairs, the Fish and Wildlife Service, and various divisions of the Department of Defense, among others.*

Curtains of Death

Like the forests, the oceans too are home and habitat to countless numbers of animal and plant species—most of which we have not even discovered. The oceans and seas are so large, so deep, and contain so much life that it is almost impossible to imagine that there could ever come a time when there wouldn't be enough fish to fish for, or that simple fishing nets could decimate populations of sea mammals, seabirds, and other marine creatures.

But a relatively new fishing technology employing vast nets called driftnets has, in a few short years, nearly depleted the oceans of certain types of fish; and caused the near-extinction of at least one species. Driftnets, known to environmentalists as "curtains of death," have virtually strip-mined the seas, ensnaring and killing every form of animal life too large to pass through its fine mesh. What clear-cutting is to the forest, driftnetting is to the sea.

Driftnets are lightweight monofiliment nylon nets that can be 30 to 40 miles long and 30 to 50 feet deep. Deployed from flotillas of fishing boats, the nets sweep up any and all marine life from the water's surface to 30 to 50 feet below. Thousands of miles of net can be set daily.

Japan has the largest driftnet fleet in the world, with about 450 vessels in the North Pacific. Taiwan and South Korea are the next largest with about 150 vessels each. At one point, these ves-

---

* For more on what legislators are doing to protect forests, see "Protecting Forests and Wetlands," pp. 189–94.

sels were setting some 30,000 miles of netting nightly in certain portions of the North Pacific.

Driftnets are so efficient, they indiscriminately kill millions of nontarget animals. The unwanted carcasses are simply tossed back into the ocean when the nets are reeled in.

Countless numbers of unintended victims—whales, dolphins, porpoises, seals, sea lions, and other marine mammals as well as sea turtles are caught in these nets and, because they are air-breathers, they drown. Millions of seabirds, attracted to the commotion of life caught up in the nets, also become ensnared and drown. Untold numbers of nontarget fish are killed and wasted.

A report submitted to the United Nations in mid 1991 by an international conference of scientists stated that, in 1990 alone, the Japanese driftnet fishery killed more than 41 million marine animals in the North Pacific while catching 106 million squid. The unwanted catch included 700,000 sharks, more than 39 million other fish, 270,000 seabirds, 26,000 marine mammals, and 406 sea turtles.

All the great whales and all species of sea turtles are endangered or threatened. More than one species of dolphin has been seriously affected.

"Ghost nets," pieces of netting that are lost at sea, continue to kill indefinitely until they sink with the weight of decomposing bodies.

BAN THE DRIFTNETS

For several years, official U.S. policy has been to oppose the use of driftnets. Congress adopted the Driftnet Impact Monitoring, Assessment, and Control Act in 1987, and the 101st Congress expanded its mandate by banning the use of large-scale driftnets (those more than 1.5 miles long) in U.S. waters by both domestic and foreign fleets. The law also bans large-scale driftnet use by U.S. fishermen anywhere in the world. Other legislation passed by the 101st Congress prohibits the importation into the United States of any fish caught in driftnets, beginning in the summer of 1992.

Many nations have long recognized the destructive effects of these nets and have banned their use in coastal waters, but driftnetting is still a major problem on the high seas. The 102nd Congress took early action on the matter and passed several resolutions favoring a worldwide ban on the use of large-scale driftnets.

In 1989, the United Nations adopted a resolution calling for a moratorium on the use of driftnets in the South Pacific by the summer of 1991, and a worldwide ban on driftnetting in international waters by July 1992. Also in 1989, Australia, New Zealand, Fiji, and twelve other South Pacific nations signed a declaration calling for an international ban on driftnetting on the high seas.

In 1991, the Bush administration took a strong stance in opposing the use of driftnets and threatened to impose trade sanctions against Taiwan and South Korea if they do not stop using them by the July 1992 U.N. moratorium deadline. At this writing, no similar threat had been made against Japan, however.

Several members of Congress have been active on the driftnet issue for several years. **Sen. Frank Murkowski (R-AK)** and **Rep. Jolene Unsoeld (D-WA)** each sponsored bills in the 101st Congress to "require that the Secretary of State seek to secure an international agreement to ban the use of driftnet fishing on the high seas."

Sen. Daniel Inouye (D-HI) and **Rep. Eni Faleomavaega (D-DL-American Samoa)** sponsored concurrent resolutions in support of regional efforts to end driftnet fishing in the South Pacific, where overfishing with driftnets resulted in the near-extinction of one species of fish, an albacore tuna. The resolution, which passed in the House during the 101st Congress, also demanded an immediate end to Japanese and Taiwanese driftnet fishing in the South Pacific and urged the Secretary of State to work toward an international convention banning the use of driftnets. **Rep. Robert Lagomarsino (R-CA)** introduced a bill similar to the resolution.

Also in the 101st Congress, **Rep. Peter DeFazio (D-OR)** submitted a bill "to prohibit the importation into the United States of fish or marine animal products of Japan, Taiwan, or the Republic of Korea until those countries cease the practice of driftnet fishing."

In the 102nd Congress, Rep. Unsoeld submitted two resolutions pertaining to driftnets. One expressed the sense of Congress that the President should direct the Secretary of the Treasury to prohibit the importation of fishery products from countries that fail to enter into and implement driftnet monitoring and enforcement agreements. Rep. Unsoeld's other resolution, passed by the House and Senate, states that the President and the Secretaries of State and Commerce should work toward the implementation of the international moratorium or a permanent ban on driftnetting worldwide.

Identical resolutions by **Rep. Gerry Studds (D-MA)** and **Sen. John Kerry (D-MA)** to express the sense of the House and Senate that the "Secretary of State should encourage the European Commission to vote to ban all large-scale driftnet fishing by all European Community fishing fleets," were also passed into law during the 102nd Congress.

A tough bill by **Sen. Bob Packwood (R-OR),** to provide economic sanctions against nations that continue to use driftnets after the U.N. moratorium deadline, was passed by the Senate during the 102nd Congress. Rep. Studds also submitted a bill directing the President to enforce sanctions against all nations that fail to comply with the U.N. moratorium on driftnetting.

ENDANGERED SPECIES AND BIODIVERSITY: THE GREEN VOTE

☑ Work to extend indefinitely the International Whaling Commission's moratorium on the killing of whales.

☑ Immediately list the African elephant as an endangered species in *all* African countries under the U.S. Endangered Species Act and work to ensure that the worldwide ban on the ivory trade stays in place.

☑ Ban the importation into the United States of kangaroo parts and products.

☑ Adopt legislation that would *require* the imposition of strong economic sanctions against countries that break international endangered species, wildlife conservation, and fisheries agreements. Expand the list of products that can be embargoed to include *all* products of an offending country, not just fisheries products.

☑ Immediately implement a plan of action to save the threatened northern spotted owl by designating critical habitat as required by the U.S. Endangered Species Act.

☑ Immediately implement plans to restore the wolf to its native habitat as required by the U.S. Endangered Species Act, and provide protections against vigilante killings of such wolves.

☑ Raise the maximum fine for violating posted speed limits in the National Forests, National Parks, and National Wildlife Refuges.

☑ Establish and implement a national plan for the conservation of biological diversity.

☑ Prohibit the practice of clear-cutting forests; require all government agencies that regulate federal lands to maintain the native biodiversity of those lands.

☑ Impose strong economic sanctions against any nation that continues to employ large-scale driftnets after July 1992 when a worldwide moratorium on the use of driftnets, proposed by the United Nations, takes effect.

THE GREEN PLATFORM FOR 1992

GLOBAL WARMING: THE GREENHOUSE EFFECT

The Green Vote:

☑ Reduce CO_2 emissions by at least 20 percent by the year 2000 through energy conservation programs and a switch to renewable sources of energy.

☑ Require the Secretary of Agriculture to accelerate the government's tree-planting program in the United States. Instruct the Secretary of State to promote tropical forestry conservation programs in developing nations.

☑ Appoint an ambassador to represent the United States in negotiations on global warming.

☑ Establish federal standards governing energy conservation in all federal buildings and facilities and all new homes and offices.

☑ Encourage the transfer of energy efficient and renewable energy technologies to developing nations.

☑ Impose a carbon tax on producers and importers of primary fossil fuels to encourage conservation and a shift to renewable sources of energy.

☑ Extend unemployment benefits, financial assistance, and train-

271

ing for workers displaced as a consequence of implementing global warming legislation, the Clean Air Act, and other environmental laws.

RESTORING THE OZONE LAYER

The Green Vote:

☑ Phase out all chlorofluorocarbons, halons, methyl chloroforms, tetrachloride, hydrochlorofluorocarbons, and other ozone-depleting chemicals by 1997.

☑ Impose an excise tax on the manufacturers of ozone-depleting chemicals to encourage producers to shift to alternatives.

☑ Establish a fund to assist developing nations in their efforts to switch from ozone-depleting chemicals to safe substitutes.

☑ Label all products that contain CFCs or that have used CFCs in the production process to encourage Green consumers to seek alternatives in their purchases.

ENERGY

The Green Vote:

☑ Require all federal agencies to retrofit their facilities and provide cash bonuses to agency personnel who implement innovative new energy conservation programs.

☑ Promulgate uniform energy efficiency standards for all federally assisted housing. Require the establishment of an energy rating system for all homes so that buyers can make informed choices.

☑ Expand the government's research, development, and commercialization program on alternative energy technologies, including solar, wind, hydrogen, geothermal, and biofuels.

☑ Amend the Export-Import Bank Act and the Small Business Act to include loans to small businesses for the promotion of renewable energy technology for export. Direct the Secretary of the Treasury, the International Monetary Fund, and the Inter-American Development Bank to provide financing for renewable energy development.

TRANSPORTING AMERICA

The Green Vote:

☑ Raise the average automobile fuel efficiency standards to 34 miles per gallon by 1996 and 40 miles per gallon by the year 2000.

☑ Impose a gas-guzzler tax on automobile manufacturers, with revenues passed on as rebates for purchasers of fuel efficient cars.

☑ Amend the Internal Revenue Service code to exclude from an individual's gross income employer subsidies for carpooling and mass transit.

☑ Establish a government research and development program for electric and solar vehicles.

☑ Increase the excise tax on gasoline with part of the revenue going to the Mass Transit Account in the Highway Trust Fund; the additional funds to be used to assist mass transit in localities around the country.

☑ Require the Federal Railway Administration to establish a National High-Speed Rail Transportation Policy to promote the commercialization of high-speed rail systems in the United States.

☑ Earmark at least 3 percent of the funds apportioned to federal aid to highway systems for bicycle lanes and pedestrian walkways.

TURNING ARMS INTO A GREEN DIVIDEND

The Green Vote:

☑ Impose sanctions against any company violating the Missile Technology Control Regime Pact. Any company found guilty of selling equipment or technology that could contribute to the acquisition of nuclear-capable missiles would be denied U.S. export licenses and U.S. government contracts. Violators would also be prohibited from importing their products into the United States.

☑ Impose economic sanctions against any foreign person or government that knowingly attempts to acquire or use chemical and biological weapons.

☑ Impose criminal penalties on anyone who knowingly develops, produces, stockpiles, acquires, or possesses biological agents, toxins, or delivery systems designed for use as a weapon.

☑ Outlaw the use of outer space for military purposes.

☑ Terminate the Strategic Defense Initiative Program within the Department of Defense.

☑ Require the President to provide a war impact statement before seeking a declaration of war from Congress. The statement should include an assessment of the expected number of U.S. and foreign casualties, an estimate of the cost and duration of the war, and a plan for how the funds to wage the war will be raised.

☑ Reduce U.S. military assistance and arms sales to developing nations and work toward a worldwide reduction in military spending of 50 percent by the year 2000.

☑ Allow those conscientiously opposed to war to place that portion of their taxable income that would go to the military into a Peace Tax Fund. The tax monies collected by the fund would be used to help finance peace and disarmament activities and improvements in international health, education, welfare, and environmental protection programs.

☑ Require all defense contracting firms to establish a conversion planning committee as a prerequisite for eligibility for military contracts.

☑ Earmark federal government funds to assist communities affected by a reduction or elimination of military production contracts. Provide financial assistance to help convert existing defense-contracting companies to non-military production.

☑ Provide up to two years of adjustment benefits, including benefits for education and retraining for all workers displaced by the scaling down or elimination of defense contracts.

SUSTAINABLE INTERNATIONAL DEVELOPMENT

The Green Vote:

☑ Increase emergency food assistance and long-term development assistance, to sub-Saharan Africa.

☑ Ensure that U.S. assistance to Africa, the Caribbean, Latin America, and other regions of the world, promotes development that is equitable, participatory, self-reliant, and environmentally sustainable. Ensure that local populations that are supposed to benefit from development aid be consulted and involved in designing and implementing aid programs.

☑ Expand the U.S. Agency for International Development's micro-enterprise lending program; and increase the number of micro-enterprise loans to women and the poorest of the poor.

☑ Direct U.S. foreign development aid to work toward the elimination of the worst aspects of poverty by the year 2000, and set specific goals by which the success of such aid can be measured.

☑ Implement the plan of action adopted by the 1990 Summit for Children to meet specific goals to help the world's poor and disadvantaged children by the year 2000.

☑ Increase the percentage of women receiving U.S. development aid in proportion to their traditional participation in targeted activities, or to their proportion of the population. Increase the numbers, and level of responsibility, of women aid providers within the U.S. Agency for International Development and the Peace Corps.

☑ Ensure that U.S. foreign policy and development assistance promotes and defends the rights of indigenous and tribal peoples throughout the world. Require the U.S. Agency for International Development to employ a cultural survival officer at each of its missions in countries in which indigenous peoples are politically underrepresented or would benefit from measures to preserve areas of environmental significance.

☑ Require U.S. foreign development assistance to encourage increased use of modes of transportation that are affordable, meet basic human needs, and protect the global environment.

A BIOSPHERE FOREIGN POLICY

The Green Vote:

☑ Encourage and allow developing nations with external debt to reduce or eliminate their debt by taking actions to preserve and maintain their tropical rain forests and other environmentally significant areas. Promote only those U.S. initiatives that do not force developing nations to adopt economic policies and programs that will have a negative effect on the environment and the poor.

☑ Require U.S. representatives of multilateral development banks to insist that environmental impact statements accompany all development proposals, promote only environmentally sustainable development projects, and veto any projects that do not have an accompanying environmental impact statement or that are not environmentally sustainable. Require U.S. multilateral bank representatives to work closely with U.S. and indigenous environmental protection organizations.

☑ Impose a duty—an environmental protection tax—on manufactured goods exported to the United States from countries that do not impose and enforce pollution controls on their industries. Require that the funds collected be funneled into programs to help such nations adopt pollution controls.

☑ Require all federal agencies to consider the effects of their proposed actions in the United States and overseas on the *global* environment—not just the environment of the United States.

OPENING THE GLOBAL COMMONS

The Green Vote:

☑ Impose heavy fines and up to one year of imprisonment, or both, for negligent violations of the Ocean Dumping Act.

☑ Increase liability limits for oil spills, making owners and operators of oil tankers liable for the cost of containment and cleanup, property loss or damage, damage to the environment, loss of earnings, loss of tax revenue to local and state governments, and the increased cost of public services during the cleanup activities.

☑ Support a $1 billion oil spill liability trust fund to cover any additional costs of cleanup and compensation beyond the liability limits imposed on the owner/operator of responsible vessels.

☑ Require double-hull construction on all oil tankers and barges operating in U.S. waters or subject to U.S. jurisdiction, by the year 2000.

☑ Require the President to intervene and coordinate containment and cleanup efforts for oil spills that pose a substantial threat to public health or the environment.

☑ Preserve the continent of Antarctica as a global commons. Prohibit all commercial mining and oil exploration.

☑ Establish regulations to control tourism and minimize waste disposal on the Antarctic continent.

Toward an Ecological Agriculture

The Green Vote:

☑ Promote incentives to farmers to plant legumes as part of an integrated crop rotation system. Legumes offer an alternative means of adding nitrogen to the soil, reducing or eliminating the need to use petrochemical fertilizers. Allow farmers to count legumes as part of their program crop acreage when determining federal payments.

☑ Establish a Farmer's Conservation Service within the USDA to assist farmers in implementing a low-input sustainable agricultural production system. Provide scientific and technical expertise to farmers making the transition from chemical to organic farming practices.

☑ Make the conversion to and maintenance of low-input agricultural production eligible for operating loans.

☑ Establish a federal matching grant program to assist state efforts at promoting low-input sustainable agriculture programs.

☑ Establish a national training program in sustainable agriculture. Require at least 20 percent of all federal extension service staff to participate in the training.

☑ Establish uniform national standards governing the labeling of organically produced food to allow consumers to make informed choices in their purchases and to encourage farmers to begin producing organically grown crops.

☑ Prohibit the export and sale abroad of any pesticide banned from use in the United States.

☑ Prohibit the importation of food into the United States if banned chemical pesticides were used during its production.

☑ Assist other countries in making the transition away from chemical pesticides to nontoxic sustainable pest management practices.

☑ Adopt laws to ensure that veal calves and all other farm animals are provided with an environment that satisfies their basic physical and psychological needs.

STEWARDING PUBLIC LANDS

The Green Vote:

☑ Designate the coastal plain of the Alaska National Wildlife Refuge as wilderness thus rendering it off limits to oil and gas development.

☑ Join with Canada to create an international Arctic refuge composed of the Alaska National Wildlife Refuge and contiguous protected Canadian lands.

☑ Stop inappropriate and harmful uses of wildlife refuges, including hunting and trapping, commercial and industrial uses, and invasive recreational uses. Turn the refuges back into the inviolate sanctuaries for wildlife they were intended to be.

☑ Raise the fees for grazing on public rangelands as a first step in reducing the number of cattle and other livestock grazing on and destroying public lands.

☑ Stop the wholesale slaughter of predators and "nuisance" animals on public lands, and promote the participation of the public in decisions affecting wildlife.

☑ Make the killing or harassing of wild horses and burros a felony offense and promote biodiversity on public lands.

☑ Repeal or reform the General Mining Law of 1872 to eliminate the practice of patenting, require miners to pay royalties, empower regulatory agencies to deny mining claims and to control environmental impacts, require bonding and reclamation of mines, and promote the participation of the public in land-use decisions.

☑ Create the American Heritage Trust to provide a self-perpetuating trust fund for land acquisition and historic preservation at the national, state, and local levels, and to ensure that all monies available for such purposes are spent.

PROTECTING FORESTS AND WETLANDS

The Green Vote:

☑ Prohibit commercial logging in the old-growth forests of the Pacific Northwest.

☑ Establish a national policy of no net loss of forests.

☑ Require all tropical wood products to be labeled indicating their country of origin and the wood used to produce them so that consumers can make informed choices in their purchases.

☑ Promote urban forestry programs and provide technical and financial assistance to states and localities to plant trees in and around urban areas.

☑ Establish a no net loss of wetlands policy.

CHAMPIONING THE RIGHTS OF ANIMALS

The Green Vote:

☑ Amend the Animal Welfare Act to grant any person or organization standing to sue the U.S. Department of Agriculture on behalf of any animal to compel enforcement of the act.

☑ Amend the Animal Welfare Act in order to include mice, rats, and birds under its protections.

☑ Ban toxicity tests on animals.

☑ Reduce the numbers of animals used in experiments by eliminating the duplication of animal experiments.

☑ Require federally funded school lunch programs to provide vegetarian meals to all students and teachers who conscientiously abstain from eating meat.

☑ Outlaw the steel-jaw leghold trap.

☑ Ban the importation of wild-caught birds for the pet trade.

☑ Ban the practice of setting fishing nets on dolphins to catch tuna; require observers aboard all tuna-fishing vessels to ensure compliance; and promote the development of fishing technologies that do not involve the harassment or killing of dolphins and other marine mammals.

☑ Amend the Marine Mammal Protection Act to allow states to ban the taking of marine mammals from state waters for public display.

☑ Require the sterilization of all dogs and cats who pass through the nation's pound and shelter system.

☑ Ban decompression and other inhumane methods of animal euthanasia.

☑ Promote the idea that animals have inherent rights.

A GENETICALLY ENGINEERED NATURE

The Green Vote:

☑ Impose a moratorium on the granting of patents on genetically engineered animals so that the myriad ethical, social, environmental, economic, and legal dilemmas posed by the new technology can be publicly deliberated.

☑ Impose a moratorium on the release of genetically engineered organisms into the environment.

☑ Exempt farmers from having to pay royalties each time the offspring of a patented farm animal is sold by a farmer—in order to diminish the incentive for engineering and patenting animals.

☑ Prohibit the sale of milk and dairy products from cows injected with genetically engineered bovine growth hormone.

☑ Protect the privacy of every citizen by ensuring that genetic information is not used as a tool for discrimination by government agencies and their contractors.

SAVING ENDANGERED SPECIES AND PRESERVING BIODIVERSITY

The Green Vote:

☑ Work to extend indefinitely the International Whaling Commission's moratorium on the killing of whales.

☑ Immediately list the African elephant as an endangered species in *all* African countries under the U.S. Endangered Species Act and work to ensure that the worldwide ban on the ivory trade stays in place.

☑ Ban the importation into the United States of kangaroo parts and products.

☑ Adopt legislation that would *require* the imposition of strong economic sanctions against countries that break international endangered species, wildlife conservation, and fisheries agreements. Expand the list of products that can be embargoed to include *all* products of an offending country, not just fisheries products.

☑ Immediately implement a plan of action to save the threatened northern spotted owl by designating critical habitat as required by the U.S. Endangered Species Act.

☑ Immediately implement plans to restore the wolf to its native habitat as required by the U.S. Endangered Species Act, and provide protections against vigilante killings of such wolves.

☑ Raise the maximum fine for violating posted speed limits in the National Forests, National Parks, and National Wildlife Refuges.

☑ Establish and implement a national plan for the conservation of biological diversity.

☑ Prohibit the practice of clear-cutting forests; require all government agencies that regulate federal lands to maintain the native biodiversity of those lands.

☑ Impose strong economic sanctions against any nation that continues to employ large-scale driftnets after July 1992 when a worldwide moratorium on the use of driftnets, proposed by the United Nations, takes effect.

SECTION III

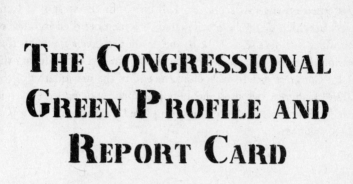

THE CONGRESSIONAL GREEN PROFILE AND REPORT CARD

The Green report card that follows is the most comprehensive ranking of members of Congress on Green-oriented issues ever compiled. We scanned more than 2,000 bills introduced in the 101st Congress (1989–1990) and first quarter of the 102nd Congress (January through June 1991) and selected 264 Green-oriented bills on which to score the 535 members of Congress. Since most of these bills never reached a floor vote, we awarded points for sponsorship and cosponsorship. A bill's primary sponsor received 6 points. Cosponsors of a bill each received 3 points. If the bill came to a vote, each member received 3 points if he or she voted for the pro-Green legislation. Sponsors of resolutions received 2 points and cosponsors of resolutions received 1 point.

Members of Congress were judged on the basis of their performance in both the 101st Congress and the first quarter of the 102nd Congress. All the members of the House and Senate were ranked from first to last based on their raw point scores and then assigned grades along a classical bell curve. The grades are A, B, C, D, F. If a congressperson's score placed him or her in the top 10 percent of the House or Senate, he or she received an A. Everyone whose score placed in the next 20 percent of the chamber received a B. Everyone whose score placed in the next 40 percent of the chamber received a C. If a congressperson's score placed in the next 20 percent, he or she received a D. Those members whose score placed in the bottom 10 percent, received an F. A total of 379 representatives and 93 senators fully participated in both the 101st Congress and the first quarter of the 102nd Congress.

If a member of Congress served only one term, his or her grade was based on the raw score and bell curve for the session of Congress in which he or she participated. If a member died in office or left office during a session, he or she did not receive a grade for that session. In a few cases in which legislators entered office during the 101st Congress or left just before the end of the first quarter of the 102nd Congress, we used our best judgment and graded them on the combined bell curve if they completed a significant portion of both sessions.

THE GREEN PROFILE

The Green profile that emerges is striking. Green elected officials are overwhelmingly Democrats and represent states and districts in the East and along the West Coast of the United States. Of the thirty-nine members of the House who received A's on the Green report card all but two are Democrats. On the other hand, of the thirty-seven House members who received F's, thirty-two are Republicans. The same holds true for the Senate. Of the ten senators who received an A, all are Democrats. But of the nine senators receiving an F, eight are Republicans.

The geographic differences are every bit as dramatic as the party differences. In the House, of the thirty-nine representatives receiving A's, seventeen are from the East and thirteen are from the Pacific Coast. However, only one is from the West, three are from the South, and five are from the Midwest. Of the thirty-seven representatives receiving F's, however, only four are from the East and three are from the Pacific Coast, while eight are from the West, fifteen are from the South, and seven are from the Midwest.

In the Senate, five of the ten senators receiving A's are from the East, two are from the Pacific Coast, two are from the West, only one is from the South, and none are from the Midwest. However, of the nine senators who received F's on the Green report card, only one is from the East, none are from the Pacific Coast, four are from the West, three are from the South, and one is from the Midwest.

Rhode Island has the Greenest delegation in Congress, with

the highest average score on Green legislation. The other nine Greenest state delegations in descending order of rank are from Massachusetts, New York, Connecticut, Hawaii, California, New Jersey, Vermont, Oregon, and Washington. With the exception of Hawaii, all of the states with the Greenest congressional delegations are in the East or along the Pacific Coast.

The least Green state delegation is from Wyoming, followed by those from Mississippi, Kentucky, Louisiana, Alabama, Iowa, Arkansas, Idaho, Virginia, and Montana.

Even more interesting is the gender and race breakdown. Women and African-Americans make up a much higher percentage of Green leaders than do white males. Of the eleven highest ranking members of the House, three are women and five are African-Americans. (These figures include one African-American woman.) There are no women or African-Americans among the thirty-seven members of the House who received an F; all are white males.

While only 6.6 percent of the House of Representatives are women, they make up more than 25 percent of the Green leadership in the House. More surprisingly, while African-Americans make up only 5.3 percent of the House of Representatives, they comprise 45 percent of the top Green politicians in the House. This is likely to come as a surprise to many political analysts who have long accepted the conventional wisdom that Green issues are of less concern to African-Americans and poor Americans than to white, middle-class, and upper-middle-class voters.

Other surprises emerged from the Green report card. Although many political observers continue to entertain the misconception that Green politicians are simply ultraliberal politicians dressed up in a new guise, the Green report card suggests that Green politics is emerging as a new, distinct, and independent force. Of the top eleven Green members of the House, only four appear on the Americans for Democratic Action (ADA) list of liberal legislators with a 100 percent liberal voting record. Of the thirty-nine members of the House who received an A on the Green report card, only eleven received a 100 percent ranking on the ADA report card. Interestingly, eighteen House members who received a perfect score on the ADA scorecard do not appear on the Green "A

List." On the Senate side, only one of the top ten Green politicians has a 100 percent ADA voting record. While many of the nation's best-known liberal politicians score above average on the Green scale, their voting records fall well short of the Green leadership. For example, Sen. Edward Kennedy (D-MA), who enjoys a 100 percent ADA voting record and is ranked among the top liberal legislators in the Senate, only received a B on the Green report card. Sen. Frank Lautenberg (D-NJ), another one of the top four liberal legislators on the ADA list, also received a B on the Green scale.

On the House side, Rep. Henry Waxman (D-CA), who has a 100 percent ADA voting record, only received a B on the Green report card. Rep. Patricia Schroeder (D-CO), who also has a 100 percent ADA voting record, also received a B on the Green scale. Rep. Thomas Downey (D-NY), another congressperson with a perfect score on the ADA scale, barely received a low B on the Green scale.

Perhaps the biggest surprise of all is the close affinity between Green politicians and organized labor. Although Green issues and labor concerns have often been viewed as incompatible, the Green profile shows that the top eleven Green politicians in the House all enjoy a lifetime AFL-CIO voting record of 88 percent or better. A similar pattern emerges in the Senate. Of the top ten Green senators, four are ranked 90 percent or higher on the AFL-CIO scale; and another five scored 80 percent or better.

The two highest ranking Green members of the House of Representatives are Barbara Boxer (D-CA) and Ted Weiss (D-NY). The two highest ranking Green members of the Senate are Albert Gore (D-TN) and John Kerry (D-MA).

The point spread on the Green scale is particularly noticeable in both the House and the Senate. It shows a small but committed group of Green legislators scoring well above their colleagues and a large contingent of representatives and senators who are ideologically opposed to bills that reflect the new Green orientation. Clearly the Congress of the United States is deeply split, with the new Green-oriented legislators pushing a visionary new agenda for the country while the conventional politicians of both parties continue to represent the old way of thinking.

It is clear from an analysis of the Green scores and rankings in Congress that the fledgling Green contingent is fighting an uphill battle against an entrenched leadership in both chambers. For the most part, those who hold positions of power in Congress are antiGreen. Of those holding key party positions, not one received an A on the Green report card. For example, House Majority Leader Richard Gephardt (D-MO) ranked in the lower middle of the House of Representatives, receiving a low C. The House Minority Leader Robert Michel (R-IL) ranked at the bottom of the chamber with a zero Green score and a grade of F. The House Minority Whip, Newt Gingrich (R-GA), did somewhat better, with a grade of low C.

On the Senate side, the Majority Leader, George Mitchell (D-ME), received a C with a raw score of only 36. By contrast, Sen Albert Gore (D-TN), the most Green member of the Senate, had a raw score of 115 or 3 times the point score of Sen. Mitchell. Assistant Majority Leader Wendell Ford (D-KY) ranked even lower than Mitchell, barely receiving a grade of C. The Senate Minority Leader Robert Dole (R-KS) received a low D, while the Senate Republican Whip, Alan Simpson (R-WY), received an F.

A similar pattern shows up in the chairmanship of powerful congressional committees. Of ten key House committees that oversee the issue areas covered in the Green report card, only one chairperson, **Rep. George Brown (D-CA),** chairman of the Committee on Science, Space, and Technology, received an A on the Green report card. In the Senate, only two of seven committee chairpersons received an A—**Patrick Leahy (D-VT),** chairman of the Commitee on Agriculture, Nutrition, and Forestry, and **Claiborne Pell (D-RI),** chairman of the committee on Foreign Relations.

The Green contingent in Congress is a potentially powerful new political force. Whether it will be able to overcome both an entrenched political establishment and special interest groups to pass Green-oriented legislation will depend, in the final analysis, on the American electorate.

The 102-issue positions contained in the "Green Platform for 1992" provide a framework by which to judge candidates for office in the upcoming state and national elections. The Green report card provides a measure for judging incumbents on their Green record in Congress.

Voting for Green-oriented candidates in the upcoming elections will help assure the emergence of a strong new Green voice in American electoral politics in the 1990s. We have written this *Voting Green* guide in the hope that the 1990s will become the Green decade.

The Bell Curve Calculations

House of Representatives, Combined 101st + 102nd Congresses

Grade	Rank	Number of Members	Point Span
A	1–39	39	236–141
B	40–118	79	138–80
C	119–271	153	79–19
D	272–346	75	18–6
F	347–383	37	5–0

Senate, Combined 101st + 102nd Congresses

Grade	Rank	Number of Members	Point Span
A	1–10	10	115–68
B	11–28	18	64–39
C	29–65	37	37–13
D	66–84	19	10–4
F	85–93	9	3–0

Note: The individual bell curves for the 101st Congress and the individual bell curves for 102nd Congress are not depicted.

U.S. House of Representatives

DISTRICT / REPRESENTATIVES	ATMOSPHERIC PROTECTION	ENERGY AND TRANSPORTATION	DEFENSE	INTERNATIONAL DEVELOPMENT AND FOREIGN POLICY #	AGRICULTURE	PUBLIC LANDS, FORESTS AND WETLANDS	ANIMAL RIGHTS π	ENDANGERED SPECIES AND BIODIVERSITY	RAW SCORE	GRADE
ALABAMA										
1. H.L. "Sonny" Callahan-R	0	0	0	0	0	0	1	0	1	F
2. William L. Dickinson-R	3	0	0	0	0	0	0	0	3	F
3. Glen Browder-D	3	0	0	0	0	3	0	4	10	D
4. Tom Bevill-D	3	3	0	0	0	6	7	3	22	C
5. Ronnie G. Flippo-D ★	0	0	1	0	0	3	1	0	5	D
6. Bud Cramer-D ✪	0	3	0	3	0	0	0	0	6	C
7. Ben Erdreich-D	3	0	3	6	0	9	1	0	22	C
8. Claude Harris-D	3	0	3	6	0	15	1	0	28	C
ALASKA										
At Large—Don Young-R	0	0	0	6	0	0	3	17	26	C
ARIZONA										
1. John J. Rhodes III-R	3	3	0	9	0	0	0	1	16	D
2. Morris K. Udall-D	9	6	12	12	0	18	3	11	71	C
3. Bob Stump-R	0	0	0	0	0	0	0	1	1	F
4. Jon Kyl-R	0	6	0	0	0	0	0	0	6	D
5. Jim Kolbe-R	6	3	0	6	0	0	0	0	15	D

ARKANSAS										
1. Bill Alexander-D	0	3	0	0	0	12	3	1	19	C
2. Tommy F. Robinson-R ★	0	6	0	3	0	6	3	3	21	C
2. Ray Thornton-D ✪	0	0	0	0	0	0	0	0	0	F
3. John P. Hammerschmidt-R	0	0	0	0	0	0	0	1	2	F
4. Beryl F. Anthony, Jr-D	3	0	0	0	3	6	1	1	14	D
CALIFORNIA										
1. Douglas H. Bosco-D ★	12	0	10	18	3	9	20	22	94	A
1. Frank Riggs-R ✪	0	3	0	3	0	0	3	10	19	C
2. Wally Herger-R	3	0	0	0	0	0	0	4	7	D
3. Robert T. Matsui-D	9	21	16	19	0	18	17	16	116	B
4. Vic Fazio-D	6	21	21	24	6	3	13	23	117	B
5. Nancy Pelosi-D	12	15	37	37	12	36	22	37	208	A
6. Barbara Boxer-D	12	27	46	36	9	27	44	35	236	A
7. George Miller-D	12	12	4	19	12	15	19	24	117	B
8. Ronald V. Dellums-D	12	24	25	33	6	33	41	38	212	A
9. Fortney "Pete" Stark-D	33	12	31	16	9	27	34	19	181	A

KEY TO CONGRESSIONAL REPORT CARD

Scores and grades are for performance in the 101st and 102nd Congresses combined unless otherwise noted, as below:

★ = Served in the 101st Congress.

✪ = Served in the 102nd Congress.

✓ = Term incomplete as a result of death, resignation, appointment, or midterm election.

NG= Incomplete terms were not graded.

▲ = For reasons of protocol, the Speaker of the House does not introduce or cosponsor legislation. As a result, Thomas Foley (D-WA) cannot be scored.

π = For purposes of simplification, Genetic Engineering has been combined with Animal Rights in the report card. With the exception of one bill, all genetic engineering bills pertain to the potential abuse of animals with this new technology.

= Global Commons, which includes legislation concerning the oceans and Antarctica, has been combined with International Development and Foreign Policy in the report card.

DISTRICT	REPRESENTATIVES	ATMOSPHERIC PROTECTION	ENERGY AND TRANSPORTATION	DEFENSE	INTERNATIONAL DEVELOPMENT AND FOREIGN POLICY #	AGRICULTURE	PUBLIC LANDS, FORESTS AND WETLANDS	ANIMAL RIGHTS π	ENDANGERED SPECIES AND BIODIVERSITY	RAW SCORE	GRADE
10.	Don Edwards-D	12	15	19	22	12	18	27	19	144	A
11.	Tom Lantos-D	12	12	7	24	12	24	32	14	137	B
12.	Tom Campbell-R	3	9	9	9	0	18	9	4	61	C
13.	Norman Y. Mineta-D	9	15	19	16	0	30	23	30	142	A
14.	Norman D. Shumway-R ★	0	3	0	3	0	0	0	1	7	D
14.	John Doolittle-R ✪	0	0	0	0	0	0	0	0	0	F
15.	Tony Coelho-D ★ ✓	0	0	0	3	0	0	3	0	9	NG
15.	Gary Condit-D ✪	0	0	0	0	0	0	1	3	7	C
16.	Leon Panetta-D	9	3	3	18	6	18	10	24	113	B
17.	Charles J. Pashayan-R ★	3	0	25	0	0	0	1	0	4	D
17.	Calvin Dooley-D ✪	0	0	0	0	0	0	0	0	0	F
18.	Richard H. Lehman-D	9	6	6	0	9	6	6	9	51	C
19.	Robert J. Lagomarsino-R	0	12	3	18	3	3	14	26	79	C
20.	William M. Thomas-R	0	0	3	3	0	0	0	0	3	F
21.	Elton Gallegly-R	0	6	3	3	0	0	11	2	25	C
22.	Carlos J. Moorhead-R	0	9	6	6	0	0	6	3	24	C
23.	Anthony C. Beilenson-D	12	18	16	19	9	36	15	28	153	A
24.	Henry A. Waxman-D	9	9	25	9	0	21	15	20	108	B
25.	Edward R. Roybal-D	12	9	19	21	3	18	18	14	114	B
26.	Howard L. Berman-D	12	6	34	27	3	27	6	17	132	B
27.	Mel Levine-D	9	12	19	28	9	21	30	26	154	A

28. Julian C. Dixon-D	6	6	10	30	6	18	15	22	113	B
29. Augustus F. Hawkins-D ★	12	3	6	15	3	12	22	10	83	B
29. Maxine Waters-D ✪	0	0	3	0	6	3	0	0	6	C
30. Matthew G. Martinez-D	12	6	10	19	6	12	34	23	122	B
31. Mervyn M. Dymally-D	12	12	34	24	0	21	21	20	144	A
32. Glenn M. Anderson-D	6	3	3	9	3	6	13	10	53	C
33. David Dreier-R	0	0	3	3	0	3	0	0	9	D
34. Esteban E. Torres-D	12	9	15	21	9	21	19	23	129	B
35. Jerry Lewis-R	0	3	0	6	0	0	11	5	25	C
36. George E. Brown, Jr.-D	12	24	37	28	6	24	22	26	179	A
37. Alfred A. McCandless-R	0	0	0	0	0	0	0	0	0	F
38. Robert K. Dornan-R	0	0	3	0	6	0	39	9	57	C
39. William E. Dannemeyer-R	0	3	0	0	3	0	8	4	18	D
40. C. Christopher Cox-R	0	3	0	3	0	6	4	2	15	D
41. Bill Lowery-R	0	3	0	3	0	0	4	1	7	D
42. Dana Rohrabacher-R	0	0	0	0	0	6	0	1	7	D
43. Ron Packard-R	0	3	3	3	0	0	0	3	12	D
44. Jim Bates-D ★	15	9	25	15	6	24	3	21	118	A

KEY TO CONGRESSIONAL REPORT CARD

Scores and grades are for performance in the 101st and 102nd Congresses combined unless otherwise noted, as below:

★ = Served in the 101st Congress.

✪ = Served in the 102nd Congress.

✔ = Term incomplete as a result of death, resignation, appointment, or midterm election.

NG= Incomplete terms were not graded.

▲ = For reasons of protocol, the Speaker of the House does not introduce or cosponsor legislation. As a result, Thomas Foley (D-WA) cannot be scored.

π = For purposes of simplification, Genetic Engineering has been combined with Animal Rights in the report card. With the exception of one bill, all genetic engineering bills pertain to the potential abuse of animals with this new technology.

= Global Commons, which includes legislation concerning the oceans and Antarctica, has been combined with International Development and Foreign Policy in the report card.

DISTRICT REPRESENTATIVES	ATMOSPHERIC PROTECTION	ENERGY AND TRANSPORTATION	DEFENSE	INTERNATIONAL DEVELOPMENT AND FOREIGN POLICY #	AGRICULTURE	PUBLIC LANDS, FORESTS AND WETLANDS	ANIMAL RIGHTS π	ENDANGERED SPECIES AND BIODIVERSITY	RAW SCORE	GRADE
44. Randy Cunningham-R ✪	0	0	0	0	0	0	0	0	0	F
45. Duncan Hunter-R	3	0	0	0	0	0	0	1	4	F
COLORADO										
1. Patricia Schroeder-D	6	6	21	21	9	21	12	7	103	B
2. David E. Skaggs-D	9	18	10	19	0	21	7	12	96	B
3. Ben Nighthorse Campbell-D	3	9	18	3	0	3	0	4	40	C
4. Hank Brown-R ★ ✪	0	3	0	0	0	0	0	0	3	F
4. Wayne Allard-R ✪	0	0	0	0	0	0	0	0	0	F
5. Joel Hefley-R	0	6	0	0	0	0	3	3	12	D
6. Dan Schaefer-R	3	0	0	15	0	0	0	4	22	C
CONNECTICUT										
1. Barbara B. Kennelly-D	3	6	6	15	3	21	15	12	81	B
2. Sam Gejdenson-D	12	12	34	34	6	12	25	36	171	A
3. Bruce A. Morrison-D ★	12	9	6	14	30	15	9	14	109	A
3. Rosa DeLauro-D ✪	0	0	0	0	3	3	3	6	15	C
4. Christopher Shays-R	9	15	12	10	9	36	31	31	153	A
5. John G. Rowland-R ★	3	0	0	0	0	6	6	4	19	C
5. Gary Franks-R ✪	0	0	0	0	0	0	0	3	3	D
6. Nancy L. Johnson-R	3	3	3	6	0	9	6	9	39	C

	9	3	7	9	0	21	21	21	91	B
DELAWARE										
At Large—Thomas R. Carper-D	0	0	0	9	0	3	7	1	20	B
FLORIDA										
1. Earl Hutto-D	0	0	0	9	0	3	7	1	20	C
2. Bill Grant-R ★	0	0	1	3	0	0	6	4	14	C
2. Pete Peterson-D ✪	0	0	3	9	0	0	3	3	18	C
3. Charles E. Bennett-D	9	3	7	12	12	36	25	53	157	A
4. Craig T. James-R	0	3	0	3	0	9	6	2	23	C
5. Bill McCollum-R	0	0	0	0	0	3	4	3	10	D
6. Clifford B. Stearns-R	0	0	0	0	0	3	0	0	3	F
7. Sam Gibbons-D	3	0	0	6	6	15	21	9	60	C
8. C. W. (Bill) Young-R	0	0	0	0	6	3	6	0	15	D
9. Michael Bilirakis-R	0	3	0	0	0	3	4	3	13	D
10. Andy Ireland-R	0	0	0	0	0	6	16	7	29	C
11. Bill Nelson-D ★	6	3	3	0	0	15	4	7	38	C
12. Jim Bacchus-D ✪	0	3	3	0	0	12	6	4	22	C
12. Tom Lewis-R	0	6	3	3	0	0	19	8	39	C

KEY TO CONGRESSIONAL REPORT CARD

Scores and grades are for performance in the 101st and 102nd Congresses combined unless otherwise noted, as below:

★ = Served in the 101st Congress.
✪ = Served in the 102nd Congress.
✓ = Term incomplete as a result of death, resignation, appointment, or midterm election.
NG= Incomplete terms were not graded.
▲ = For reasons of protocol, the Speaker of the House does not introduce or cosponsor legislation. As a result, Thomas Foley (D-WA) cannot be scored.
π = For purposes of simplification, Genetic Engineering has been combined with Animal Rights in the report card. With the exception of one bill, all genetic engineering bills pertain to the potential abuse of animals with this new technology.
= Global Commons, which includes legislation concerning the oceans and Antarctica, has been combined with International Development and Foreign Policy in the report card.

DISTRICT / REPRESENTATIVES	ATMOSPHERIC PROTECTION	ENERGY AND TRANSPORTATION	DEFENSE	INTERNATIONAL DEVELOPMENT AND FOREIGN POLICY #	AGRICULTURE	PUBLIC LANDS, FORESTS AND WETLANDS	ANIMAL RIGHTS π	ENDANGERED SPECIES AND BIODIVERSITY	RAW SCORE	GRADE
13. Porter Goss-R	3	6	3	6	0	9	27	18	72	C
14. Harry A. Johnston-D	9	0	7	18	6	21	6	10	77	C
15. E. Clay Shaw, Jr.-R	0	0	0	7	6	0	25	7	45	C
16. Lawrence J. Smith-D	9	3	19	15	6	24	38	21	135	B
17. William Lehman-D	9	3	16	15	6	15	22	10	96	B
18. Claude Pepper-D ★ ✓	6	0	3	6	3	6	6	3	33	NG
18. Ileana Ros-Lehtinen-R ★	0	0	0	0	0	0	9	1	10	NG
18. Ileana Ros-Lehtinen-R ✪	0	0	0	0	0	3	0	3	6	C
19. Dante B. Fascell-D	3	12	6	18	6	12	10	16	83	B
GEORGIA										
1. Robert Lindsay Thomas-D	3	0	0	6	0	0	10	0	19	C
2. Charles Hatcher-D	3	3	0	3	0	3	0	0	12	D
3. Richard Ray-D	0	3	0	0	0	0	1	1	5	F
4. Ben Jones-D	3	3	0	12	0	21	1	9	49	C
5. John Lewis-D	12	18	31	32	6	33	25	29	186	A
6. Newt Gingrich-R	6	0	0	3	0	6	1	9	25	C
7. George "Buddy" Darden-D	3	3	0	6	0	36	10	6	64	C
8. J. Roy Rowland-D	6	3	0	3	0	9	1	0	22	C
9. Ed Jenkins-D	0	3	0	0	0	15	1	4	23	C
10. Doug Barnard, Jr.-D	3	6	3	1	0	21	11	4	49	C

HAWAII										
1. Patricia Saiki-R ★	6	3	0	12	4	6	12	26	69	B
1. Neil Abercrombie-D ✪	0	6	6	9	3	6	6	2	38	B
2. Daniel K. Akaka-D ★ ✓	9	9	9	12	3	6	18	18	84	NG
2. Patsy Mink-D ✪	0	3	0	9	0	3	4	1	20	C
IDAHO										
1. Larry E. Craig-R ★	0	3	0	0	0	0	1	1	5	D
1. Larry LaRocco-D ✪	0	0	3	0	0	0	3	0	6	C
2. Richard H. Stallings-D	3	6	3	6	0	0	13	7	38	C
ILLINOIS										
1. Charles A. Hayes-D	12	0	31	21	6	18	25	13	126	B
2. Gus Savage-D	12	0	13	15	6	6	11	7	70	C
3. Marty Russo-D	3	6	4	15	12	12	16	1	69	C
4. George E. Sangmeister-D	9	0	10	3	0	15	0	2	39	C
5. William O. Lipinski-D	9	6	6	13	6	30	12	37	119	B
6. Henry J. Hyde-R	0	0	7	6	0	0	25	3	41	C

KEY TO CONGRESSIONAL REPORT CARD

Scores and grades are for performance in the 101st and 102nd Congresses combined unless otherwise noted, as below:

★ = Served in the 101st Congress.

✪ = Served in the 102nd Congress.

✓ = Term incomplete as a result of death, resignation, appointment, or midterm election.

NG= Incomplete terms were not graded.

▲ = For reasons of protocol, the Speaker of the House does not introduce or cosponsor legislation. As a result, Thomas Foley (D-WA) cannot be scored.

π = For purposes of simplification, Genetic Engineering has been combined with Animal Rights in the report card. With the exception of one bill, all genetic engineering bills pertain to the potential abuse of animals with this new technology.

= Global Commons, which includes legislation concerning the oceans and Antarctica, has been combined with International Development and Foreign Policy in the report card.

DISTRICT	REPRESENTATIVES	ATMOSPHERIC PROTECTION	ENERGY AND TRANSPORTATION	DEFENSE	INTERNATIONAL DEVELOPMENT AND FOREIGN POLICY #	AGRICULTURE	PUBLIC LANDS, FORESTS AND WETLANDS	ANIMAL RIGHTS π	ENDANGERED SPECIES AND BIODIVERSITY	RAW SCORE	GRADE
7.	Cardiss Collins-D	12	27	31	35	6	36	19	24	190	A
8.	Dan Rostenkowski-D	3	0	0	0	0	6	0	0	9	D
9.	Sidney R. Yates-D	9	15	4	10	9	24	24	26	121	B
10.	John E. Porter-R	3	3	12	12	6	12	16	24	88	B
11.	Frank Annunzio-D	3	0	6	0	3	18	10	4	44	C
12.	Philip M. Crane-R	0	0	3	6	0	0	0	1	10	D
13.	Harris W. Fawell-R	6	3	9	12	0	12	11	16	69	C
14.	J. Dennis Hastert-R	0	0	0	0	0	0	10	4	14	D
15.	Edward Madigan-R	0	0	0	3	1	0	10	1	18	D
16.	Lynn Martin-R ★	3	0	0	3	3	0	1	7	17	C
16.	John Cox, Jr.-D ☻	0	0	0	3	0	9	0	0	12	C
17.	Lane Evans-D	12	15	16	19	9	24	19	10	124	B
18.	Robert H. Michel-R	0	0	0	0	0	0	0	0	0	F
19.	Terry L. Bruce-D	3	12	16	9	0	6	6	12	64	C
20.	Richard J. Durbin-D	9	3	13	13	3	24	6	10	81	B
21.	Jerry F. Costello-D	3	9	4	3	0	12	18	23	72	C
22.	Glenn Poshard-D	3	6	13	6	0	15	0	10	53	C
INDIANA											
1.	Peter J. Visclosky-D	3	0	6	0	0	9	0	1	19	C
2.	Philip R. Sharp-D	3	27	3	4	0	12	12	0	61	C

										Grade
3. John Hiler-R ★	0	0	0	6	0	0	0	3	9	D
3. Tim Roemer-D ✪	0	0	0	0	0	3	0	3	6	C
4. Jill Long-D	3	3	4	6	0	0	10	7	33	C
5. Jim Jontz-D	6	6	25	23	15	42	16	24	157	A
6. Dan Burton-R	0	0	3	6	0	0	16	1	26	C
7. John T. Myers-R	0	3	3	0	0	0	0	7	13	D
8. Frank McCloskey-D	6	0	4	12	3	12	11	6	54	C
9. Lee H. Hamilton-D	3	9	10	3	3	12	1	9	50	C
10. Andrew Jacobs, Jr.-D	3	3	13	21	6	27	55	14	142	A

IOWA

										Grade
1. Jim Leach-R	0	0	13	9	0	3	4	7	36	C
2. Thomas J. Tauke-R ★	0	0	0	0	3	3	1	0	7	D
2. Jim Nussle-R ✪	0	0	0	0	0	0	0	0	0	F
3. David R. Nagle-D	6	0	4	1	6	9	1	9	36	C
4. Neal Smith-D	3	0	0	0	0	3	0	0	6	D
5. Jim Lightfoot-R	0	0	0	0	0	0	0	1	1	F
6. Fred Grandy-R	0	0	0	3	0	0	0	0	3	F

KEY TO CONGRESSIONAL REPORT CARD

Scores and grades are for performance in the 101st and 102nd Congresses combined unless otherwise noted, as below:

★ = Served in the 101st Congress.

✪ = Served in the 102nd Congress.

✓ = Term incomplete as a result of death, resignation, appointment, or midterm election.

NG= Incomplete terms were not graded.

▲ = For reasons of protocol, the Speaker of the House does not introduce or cosponsor legislation. As a result, Thomas Foley (D-WA) cannot be scored.

π = For purposes of simplification, Genetic Engineering has been combined with Animal Rights in the report card. With the exception of one bill, all genetic engineering bills pertain to the potential abuse of animals with this new technology.

= Global Commons, which includes legislation concerning the oceans and Antarctica, has been combined with International Development and Foreign Policy in the report card.

DISTRICT / REPRESENTATIVES	ATMOSPHERIC PROTECTION	ENERGY AND TRANSPORTATION	DEFENSE	INTERNATIONAL DEVELOPMENT AND FOREIGN POLICY #	AGRICULTURE	PUBLIC LANDS, FORESTS AND WETLANDS	ANIMAL RIGHTS π	ENDANGERED SPECIES AND BIODIVERSITY	RAW SCORE	GRADE
KANSAS										
1. Pat Roberts-R	0	0	0	0	0	3	0	0	3	F
2. Jim Slattery-D	9	18	4	7	6	9	7	4	64	C
3. Jan Meyers-R	3	9	0	18	0	12	25	17	84	B
4. Dan Glickman-D	9	3	13	7	6	9	0	4	51	C
5. Robert Whitaker-R ★	0	0	0	0	0	0	1	0	1	F
5. Dick Nichols-R ✪	0	0	0	0	0	0	0	0	0	F
KENTUCKY										
1. Carroll Hubbard, Jr.-D	3	0	0	3	0	3	7	1	17	D
2. William H. Natcher-D	3	0	1	0	0	0	0	0	4	F
3. Romano L. Mazzoli-D	3	0	4	9	3	18	4	1	42	C
4. Jim Bunning-R	3	0	0	0	0	0	1	4	8	D
5. Harold Rogers-R	3	0	0	0	0	0	0	0	3	F
6. Larry J. Hopkins-R	3	0	0	0	0	0	0	9	12	D
7. Carl C. Perkins-D	3	0	9	0	3	0	6	7	28	C
LOUISIANA										
1. Bob Livingston-R	0	0	0	0	0	0	1	0	1	F
2. Corrine "Lindy" Boggs-D ★	3	0	0	12	0	6	0	1	22	C
2. William Jefferson-D ✪	0	3	3	12	3	6	6	11	44	A

Name									Grade
3. W. J. "Billy" Tauzin-D	0	0	3	0	6	1	1	11	D
4. Jim McCrery-R	0	0	0	0	6	1	1	8	D
5. Jerry Huckaby-D	0	3	3	3	12	0	10	31	C
6. Richard H. Baker-R	0	0	3	0	0	0	1	1	F
7. James A. Hayes-D	3	0	3	3	6	10	7	29	C
8. Clyde C. Holloway-R	0	0	0	0	0	0	0	0	F
MAINE									
1. Joseph E. Brennan-D ★	6	3	3	3	3	1	0	22	C
1. Thomas Andrews-D ✪	0	3	6	6	6	4	3	25	B
2. Olympia J. Snowe-R	3	0	3	15	9	4	2	36	C
MARYLAND									
1. Roy Dyson-D ★	6	0	0	7	0	9	2	24	C
1. Wayne Gilchrest-R ✪	0	3	0	9	3	0	0	15	C
2. Helen Delich Bentley-R	3	0	3	6	3	16	7	38	C
3. Benjamin L. Cardin-D	9	6	7	9	15	16	5	73	C
4. C. Thomas McMillen-D	6	9	3	6	9	19	11	63	C
5. Steny H. Hoyer-D	3	0	3	6	3	7	4	26	C

KEY TO CONGRESSIONAL REPORT CARD

Scores and grades are for performance in the 101st and 102nd Congresses combined unless otherwise noted, as below:

★ = Served in the 101st Congress.

✪ = Served in the 102nd Congress.

✓ = Term incomplete as a result of death, resignation, appointment, or midterm election.

NG= Incomplete terms were not graded.

▲ = For reasons of protocol, the Speaker of the House does not introduce or cosponsor legislation. As a result, Thomas Foley (D-WA) cannot be scored.

π = For purposes of simplification, Genetic Engineering has been combined with Animal Rights in the report card. With the exception of one bill, all genetic engineering bills pertain to the potential abuse of animals with this new technology.

= Global Commons, which includes legislation concerning the oceans and Antarctica, has been combined with International Development and Foreign Policy in the report card.

DISTRICT / REPRESENTATIVES	ATMOSPHERIC PROTECTION	ENERGY AND TRANSPORTATION	DEFENSE	INTERNATIONAL DEVELOPMENT AND FOREIGN POLICY #	AGRICULTURE	PUBLIC LANDS, FORESTS AND WETLANDS	ANIMAL RIGHTS π	ENDANGERED SPECIES AND BIODIVERSITY	RAW SCORE	GRADE
6. Beverly B. Byron-D	3	6	0	6	0	9	3	1	28	C
7. Kweisi Mfume-D	6	6	22	24	3	27	22	14	124	B
8. Constance A. Morella-R	6	9	13	29	6	27	16	14	120	B
MASSACHUSETTS										
1. Silvio O. Conte -R ★	6	3	0	16	16	3	3	1	48	C
1. Silvio O. Conte-R ⊗ ✓	0	0	0	0	0	0	0	0	0	NG
1. John Olver-D ⊗ ✓	0	3	0	0	0	3	0	0	6	NG
2. Richard E. Neal-D	6	6	10	0	3	21	17	8	71	C
3. Joseph D. Early-D	6	0	3	0	0	6	0	0	9	D
4. Barney Frank-D	12	9	28	24	9	27	19	23	151	A
5. Chester G. Atkins-D	15	21	28	32	9	33	19	26	183	A
6. Nicholas Mavroules-D	9	6	27	13	6	24	23	11	119	B
7. Edward J. Markey-D	9	24	34	13	3	24	28	18	153	A
8. Joseph P. Kennedy II-D	9	21	18	18	3	12	9	14	104	B
9. Joe Moakley-D	6	3	0	0	0	0	0	0	9	D
10. Gerry E. Studds-D	12	9	31	37	12	21	12	21	155	A
11. Brian J. Donnelly-D	12	3	1	6	3	21	18	16	80	B
MICHIGAN										
1. John Conyers, Jr.-D	9	3	22	18	6	18	23	12	111	B
2. Carl D. Pursell-R	3	0	1	6	0	0	3	9	22	C

3. Howard Wolpe-D	12	12	25	36	3	30	22	35	175	A
4. Frederick S. Upton-R	3	0	1	3	3	9	16	7	42	C
5. Paul B. Henry-R	6	6	7	9	0	12	6	16	62	C
6. Bob Carr-D	3	0	7	9	0	6	0	1	26	C
7. Dale E. Kildee-D	9	0	19	12	0	21	9	10	80	B
8. Bob Traxler-D	3	3	4	18	0	3	13	3	47	C
9. Guy Vander Jagt-R	0	0	0	3	0	0	0	0	3	F
10. Bill Schuette-R ★	3	0	0	0	0	0	7	13	23	C
10. Dave Camp-R ✪	0	0	0	0	0	0	0	0	0	F
11. Robert W. Davis-R	3	0	16	9	0	0	1	0	13	D
12. David E. Bonior-D	9	6	16	13	0	36	15	25	120	B
13. George W. Crockett-D ★	12	3	0	18	16	9	6	14	78	B
13. Barbara-Rose Collins-D ✪	0	0	3	3	0	0	0	2	8	C
14. Dennis M. Hertel-D	6	0	13	18	0	12	6	11	66	C
15. William D. Ford-D	6	3	7	12	0	18	6	17	69	C
16. John D. Dingell-D	3	3	3	3	0	6	0	3	21	C
17. Sander M. Levin-D	6	3	10	13	3	12	13	23	83	B
18. William S. Broomfield-R	3	0	3	0	6	3	9	5	29	C

KEY TO CONGRESSIONAL REPORT CARD

Scores and grades are for performance in the 101st and 102nd Congresses combined unless otherwise noted, as below:

★ = Served in the 101st Congress.

✪ = Served in the 102nd Congress.

✓ = Term incomplete as a result of death, resignation, appointment, or midterm election.

NG= Incomplete terms were not graded.

▲ = For reasons of protocol, the Speaker of the House does not introduce or cosponsor legislation. As a result, Thomas Foley (D-WA) cannot be scored.

π = For purposes of simplification, Genetic Engineering has been combined with Animal Rights in the report card. With the exception of one bill, all genetic engineering bills pertain to the potential abuse of animals with this new technology.

= Global Commons, which includes legislation concerning the oceans and Antarctica, has been combined with International Development and Foreign Policy in the report card.

DISTRICT / REPRESENTATIVES	ATMOSPHERIC PROTECTION	ENERGY AND TRANSPORTATION	DEFENSE	INTERNATIONAL DEVELOPMENT AND FOREIGN POLICY #	AGRICULTURE	PUBLIC LANDS, FORESTS AND WETLANDS	ANIMAL RIGHTS π	ENDANGERED SPECIES AND BIODIVERSITY	RAW SCORE	GRADE
MINNESOTA										
1. Timothy J. Penny-D	3	3	16	27	6	15	0	10	80	B
2. Vin Weber-R	0	0	3	0	0	3	1	0	7	D
3. Bill Frenzel-R ★	0	0	0	6	0	0	1	1	8	D
4. Jim Ramstad-D ✪	0	0	0	9	0	6	0	0	15	C
5. Bruce F. Vento-D	9	3	19	34	0	24	18	21	128	B
5. Martin Olav Sabo-D	6	6	10	13	6	15	0	7	63	C
6. Gerry Sikorski-D	12	18	16	25	0	24	15	36	146	A
7. Arlan Stangeland-R ★	3	0	0	0	0	0	0	0	3	F
7. Collin Peterson-D ✪	0	3	0	3	0	6	0	0	12	C
8. James L. Oberstar-D	9	6	22	28	6	9	7	14	101	B
MISSISSIPPI										
1. Jamie L. Whitten-D	3	0	0	0	0	0	0	0	3	F
2. Mike Espy-D	3	3	12	27	0	3	0	1	49	C
3. "Sonny" Montgomery-D	0	0	0	0	0	0	1	1	2	F
4. Mike Parker-D	0	0	0	1	0	0	6	1	8	D
5. Larkin I. Smith-R ★ ✓	0	0	0	0	0	0	0	0	0	NG
5. Gene Taylor-D ★ ✓	0	0	0	0	0	0	0	0	0	NG
5. Gene Taylor-D ★ ✪	0	0	0	0	3	0	0	0	3	D

MISSOURI										
1. William "Bill" Clay-D	12	3	12	9	0	21	18	16	91	B
2. Jack Buechner-R ★	3	0	0	3	3	6	7	18	37	C
2. Joan Kelly Horn-D ⊙	0	0	0	0	3	0	3	3	9	C
3. Richard A. Gephardt-D	6	0	3	6	0	6	0	1	22	C
4. Ike Skelton-D	3	3	3	0	0	3	1	4	17	D
5. Alan Wheat-D	6	3	19	16	0	15	7	4	70	C
6. E. Thomas Coleman-R	0	0	0	3	0	0	1	0	4	F
7. Melton D. "Mel" Hancock-R	0	3	0	0	0	0	3	0	3	F
8. Bill Emerson-R	3	3	0	9	0	0	1	0	16	D
9. Harold L. Volkmer-D	3	3	3	0	0	3	0	3	15	D
MONTANA										
1. Pat Williams-D	6	6	4	12	0	3	12	1	44	C
2. Ron Marlenee-R	0	0	0	0	0	0	0	0	0	F
NEBRASKA										
1. Doug Bereuter-R	0	0	13	22	0	12	7	11	65	C
2. Peter Hoagland-D	3	3	1	3	0	15	0	1	26	C

KEY TO CONGRESSIONAL REPORT CARD

Scores and grades are for performance in the 101st and 102nd Congresses combined unless otherwise noted, as below:

★ = Served in the 101st Congress.

⊙ = Served in the 102nd Congress.

✓ = Term incomplete as a result of death, resignation, appointment, or midterm election.

NG= Incomplete terms were not graded.

▲ = For reasons of protocol, the Speaker of the House does not introduce or cosponsor legislation. As a result, Thomas Foley (D-WA) cannot be scored.

π = For purposes of simplification, Genetic Engineering has been combined with Animal Rights in the report card. With the exception of one bill, all genetic engineering bills pertain to the potential abuse of animals with this new technology.

= Global Commons, which includes legislation concerning the oceans and Antarctica, has been combined with International Development and Foreign Policy in the report card.

District / Representatives	Atmospheric Protection	Energy and Transportation	Defense	International Development and Foreign Policy #	Agriculture	Public Lands, Forests and Wetlands	Animal Rights π	Endangered Species and Biodiversity	Raw Score	Grade
3. Virginia Smith-R ★	0	0	0	0	0	0	0	0	0	F
3. William Barrett-R ✪	0	0	0	0	0	0	0	0	0	F
NEVADA										
1. James H. Bilbray-D	12	6	0	16	9	6	35	14	98	B
2. Barbara F. Vucanovich-R	0	0	0	3	0	0	3	1	7	D
NEW HAMPSHIRE										
1. Robert C. Smith-R ★	0	0	3	0	3	15	22	3	46	C
1. Bill Zeliff-R ✪	0	0	0	0	0	3	0	0	3	D
2. Chuck Douglas-R ★	3	0	0	0	3	6	0	0	12	D
2. Dick Swett-D ✪	0	6	3	3	0	6	7	3	28	B
NEW JERSEY										
1. James J. Florio-D ★✔✪	0	3	0	6	0	6	13	6	34	NG
1. Robert Andrews-D ✪	0	3	0	0	0	0	0	0	3	D
2. William J. Hughes-D	6	15	18	28	3	18	20	20	128	B
3. Frank Pallone, Jr.-D	9	15	10	13	6	27	28	38	146	A
4. Christopher H. Smith-R	6	0	3	9	0	9	20	2	49	C
5. Marge Roukema-R	3	0	4	9	0	9	3	0	28	C
6. Bernard J. Dwyer-D	12	18	24	16	6	24	34	25	159	A

7. Matthew J. Rinaldo-R	3	3	0	13	6	33	39	33	130	B
8. Robert A. Roe-D	9	9	13	15	0	18	27	35	126	B
9. Robert G. Torricelli-D	6	3	3	9	6	18	39	13	97	B
10. Donald M. Payne-D	9	0	19	18	3	12	21	13	95	B
11. Dean A. Gallo-R	0	6	0	3	0	6	26	1	42	C
12. James Courter-R ★	0	3	0	0	3	6	5	3	20	C
12. Richard Zimmer-R ✪	0	9	0	0	0	12	4	4	29	B
13. Jim Saxton-R	0	3	0	16	3	15	28	18	83	B
14. Frank J. Guarini-D	3	6	0	3	6	18	32	14	82	B
NEW MEXICO										
1. Steven Schiff-R	3	0	0	9	0	0	3	0	15	D
2. Joe Skeen-R	0	3	3	3	0	0	1	0	10	D
3. Bill Richardson-D	9	6	7	33	0	3	13	7	78	C
NEW YORK										
1. George J. Hochbrueckner-D	12	15	16	28	9	27	20	27	154	A
2. Thomas J. Downey-D	12	3	19	3	3	9	19	13	81	B
3. Robert J. Mrazek-D	12	0	22	16	9	27	29	36	151	A

KEY TO CONGRESSIONAL REPORT CARD

Scores and grades are for performance in the 101st and 102nd Congresses combined unless otherwise noted, as below:

★ = Served in the 101st Congress.

✪ = Served in the 102nd Congress.

✓ = Term incomplete as a result of death, resignation, appointment, or midterm election.

NG = Incomplete terms were not graded.

▲ = For reasons of protocol, the Speaker of the House does not introduce or cosponsor legislation. As a result, Thomas Foley (D-WA) cannot be scored.

π = For purposes of simplification, Genetic Engineering has been combined with Animal Rights in the report card. With the exception of one bill, all genetic engineering bills pertain to the potential abuse of animals with this new technology.

= Global Commons, which includes legislation concerning the oceans and Antarctica, has been combined with International Development and Foreign Policy in the report card.

DISTRICT	REPRESENTATIVES	ATMOSPHERIC PROTECTION	ENERGY AND TRANSPORTATION	DEFENSE	INTERNATIONAL DEVELOPMENT AND FOREIGN POLICY #	AGRICULTURE	PUBLIC LANDS, FORESTS AND WETLANDS	ANIMAL RIGHTS π	ENDANGERED SPECIES AND BIODIVERSITY	RAW SCORE	GRADE
4.	Norman F. Lent-R	0	3	0	3	0	3	1	0	10	D
5.	Raymond J. McGrath-R	3	0	3	0	6	15	31	3	61	C
6.	Floyd H. Flake-D	6	9	7	18	3	18	16	5	82	B
7.	Gary L. Ackerman-D	9	12	43	25	9	21	40	25	184	A
8.	James H. Scheuer-D	12	18	25	29	9	45	25	47	210	A
9.	Thomas J. Manton-D	3	0	0	18	6	12	24	29	92	B
10.	Charles E. Schumer-D	12	9	12	3	6	18	28	14	102	B
11.	Edolphus Towns-D	9	6	28	29	6	27	50	42	197	A
12.	Major R. Owens-D	12	9	37	28	6	30	39	33	194	A
13.	Stephen J. Solarz-D	9	3	12	19	3	21	26	20	113	B
14.	Guy V. Molinari-R ★ ✓	0	0	0	0	0	3	0	0	3	NG
14.	Susan Molinari-R ✪	0	0	0	3	3	6	5	0	17	C
15.	Bill Green-R	0	12	9	12	0	33	7	7	80	B
16.	Charles B. Rangel-D	6	18	19	21	9	21	21	18	133	B
17.	Ted Weiss-D	12	21	46	38	3	27	30	42	219	A
18.	Robert Garcia-D ★ ✓	6	3	0	9	15	9	3	9	54	NG
18.	Jose Serrano-D ✪	0	6	0	9	3	6	0	3	27	B
19.	Eliot L. Engel-D	9	18	18	25	6	12	17	21	126	B
20.	Nita M. Lowey-D	9	15	10	27	12	18	21	11	123	B
21.	Hamilton Fish, Jr.-R	9	15	6	19	3	24	26	36	138	B
22.	Benjamin A. Gilman-R	9	0	16	42	6	9	19	18	119	B

23.	Michael McNulty-D	6	4	15	3	6	5	10	55	C
24.	Gerald B. H. Solomon-R	0	3	0	0	6	9	8	29	C
25.	Sherwood L. Boehlert-R	9	1	16	0	12	6	12	62	C
26.	David O'B. Martin-R	3	3	3	0	3	0	3	15	D
27.	James T. Walsh-R	9	4	16	0	9	16	15	78	C
28.	Matthew F. McHugh-D	3	14	24	0	6	4	6	63	C
29.	Frank Horton-R	15	7	21	3	12	26	13	103	B
30.	Louise Slaughter-D	6	13	16	3	30	6	17	97	B
31.	Bill Paxon-R	0	0	0	0	0	0	0	0	F
32.	John J. LaFalce-D	6	7	15	0	15	0	0	49	C
33.	Henry J. Nowak-D	6	10	3	0	9	12	13	59	C
34.	Amory Houghton-R	3	3	12	0	6	3	6	39	C

NORTH CAROLINA

1.	Walter B. Jones-D	3	3	21	0	3	0	9	39	C
2.	Tim Valentine-D	6	9	10	8	6	33	22	23	117	B
3.	H. Martin Lancaster-D	9	0	6	19	3	15	4	9	65	C
4.	David E. Price-D	9	3	3	10	0	21	11	13	70	C

KEY TO CONGRESSIONAL REPORT CARD

Scores and grades are for performance in the 101st and 102nd Congresses combined unless otherwise noted, as below:

★ = Served in the 101st Congress.

✪ = Served in the 102nd Congress.

✓ = Term incomplete as a result of death, resignation, appointment, or midterm election.

NG= Incomplete terms were not graded.

▲ = For reasons of protocol, the Speaker of the House does not introduce or cosponsor legislation. As a result, Thomas Foley (D-WA) cannot be scored.

π = For purposes of simplification, Genetic Engineering has been combined with Animal Rights in the report card. With the exception of one bill, all genetic engineering bills pertain to the potential abuse of animals with this new technology.

= Global Commons, which includes legislation concerning the oceans and Antarctica, has been combined with International Development and Foreign Policy in the report card.

DISTRICT	REPRESENTATIVES	ATMOSPHERIC PROTECTION	ENERGY AND TRANSPORTATION	DEFENSE	INTERNATIONAL DEVELOPMENT AND FOREIGN POLICY #	AGRICULTURE	PUBLIC LANDS, FORESTS AND WETLANDS	ANIMAL RIGHTS π	ENDANGERED SPECIES AND BIODIVERSITY	RAW SCORE	GRADE
5.	Stephen L. Neal-D	9	15	12	13	6	27	16	27	125	B
6.	Howard Coble-R	0	0	0	3	0	3	7	1	14	D
7.	Charles Rose-D	6	3	1	22	0	18	34	7	91	B
8.	W. G. "Bill" Hefner-D	9	0	0	0	0	9	1	7	26	C
9.	J. Alex McMillan-R	0	0	0	0	0	3	3	3	9	D
10.	Cass Ballenger-R	0	0	0	0	4	0	4	1	5	F
11.	James McClure Clarke-D ★	0	0	0	3	0	9	7	5	28	C
11.	Charles Taylor-R ✪	0	0	0	3	0	9	0	1	4	C
NORTH DAKOTA											
At Large—	Byron L. Dorgan-D	6	6	16	21	6	0	0	4	59	C
OHIO											
1.	Thomas A. Luken-D ★	3	3	0	3	3	9	13	8	42	C
1.	Charles Luken-D ✪	0	0	0	3	0	3	3	0	9	C
2.	Willis D. Gradison, Jr.-R	0	0	0	0	0	6	0	0	6	D
3.	Tony P. Hall-D	3	9	4	21	0	9	9	3	58	C
4.	Michael G. Oxley-R	3	0	0	0	0	0	3	4	10	D
5.	Paul E. Gillmor-R	3	0	0	0	0	0	3	3	6	D
6.	Bob McEwen-R	3	3	3	6	0	0	3	4	26	C
7.	Michael DeWine-R ★	3	0	0	3	0	6	7	4	16	C
7.	David Hobson-R ✪	0	0	0	0	0	0	0	0	0	NG

									Total	Grade
8. Donald "Buz" Lukens-R ★✓	0	0	0	0	7	0	0	9	22	NG
8. John Boehner-R ✪	0	0	0	0	0	0	0	0	0	F
9. Marcy Kaptur-D	9	9	10	9	0	15	20	30	102	B
10. Clarence E. Miller-R	3	0	0	6	0	9	7	0	25	C
11. Dennis E. Eckart-D	6	18	16	12	0	21	18	37	128	B
12. John R. Kasich-R	3	0	3	3	0	3	4	11	27	C
13. Don J. Pease-D	9	9	13	15	0	15	15	9	85	B
14. Thomas C. Sawyer-D	3	0	10	9	0	12	0	4	38	C
15. Chalmers P. Wylie-R	0	0	0	0	0	3	13	5	21	C
16. Ralph Regula-R	3	0	0	0	0	3	7	3	16	D
17. James A. Traficant, Jr.-D	6	12	7	12	6	24	28	22	117	B
18. Douglas Applegate-D	3	3	4	12	0	9	0	1	32	C
19. Edward F. Feighan-D	6	0	19	21	6	18	18	4	92	B
20. Mary Rose Oakar-D	6	0	13	9	0	9	9	13	59	C
21. Louis Stokes-D	9	6	13	19	12	15	17	7	98	B
OKLAHOMA										
1. James M. Inhofe-R	0	0	0	3	0	3	1	0	7	D
2. Mike Synar-D	3	6	10	15	15	33	4	4	90	B

KEY TO CONGRESSIONAL REPORT CARD

Scores and grades are for performance in the 101st and 102nd Congresses combined unless otherwise noted, as below:

★ = Served in the 101st Congress.

✪ = Served in the 102nd Congress.

✓ = Term incomplete as a result of death, resignation, appointment, or midterm election.

NG= Incomplete terms were not graded.

▲ = For reasons of protocol, the Speaker of the House does not introduce or cosponsor legislation. As a result, Thomas Foley (D-WA) cannot be scored.

π = For purposes of simplification, Genetic Engineering has been combined with Animal Rights in the report card. With the exception of one bill, all genetic engineering bills pertain to the potential abuse of animals with this new technology.

= Global Commons, which includes legislation concerning the oceans and Antarctica, has been combined with International Development and Foreign Policy in the report card.

DISTRICT / REPRESENTATIVES	ATMOSPHERIC PROTECTION	ENERGY AND TRANSPORTATION	DEFENSE	INTERNATIONAL DEVELOPMENT AND FOREIGN POLICY #	AGRICULTURE	PUBLIC LANDS, FORESTS AND WETLANDS	ANIMAL RIGHTS π	ENDANGERED SPECIES AND BIODIVERSITY	RAW SCORE	GRADE
3. Wes Watkins-D ★	3	3	0	3	0	0	0	0	9	D
3. Bill Brewster-D ✪	0	0	0	0	0	0	0	0	0	F
4. Dave McCurdy-D	0	3	9	3	0	9	0	7	31	C
5. Mickey Edwards-R	0	0	0	0	0	0	6	3	9	D
6. Glenn English-D	3	0	3	0	6	6	0	9	27	C
OREGON										
1. Les AuCoin-D	12	3	37	19	0	3	15	19	108	B
2. Robert F. Smith-R	3	0	0	3	0	0	0	1	7	D
3. Ron Wyden-D	9	9	16	12	0	9	10	12	77	C
4. Peter A. DeFazio-D	12	18	28	25	21	6	36	39	185	A
5. Denny Smith-R ★	0	0	0	0	0	0	0	5	5	D
5. Mike Kopetski-D ✪	0	6	9	9	0	0	0	4	28	B
PENNSYLVANIA										
1. Thomas M. Foglietta-D	9	15	31	31	3	21	22	15	147	A
2. William H. Gray III-D	6	0	4	15	0	6	0	1	32	C
3. Robert A. Borski, Jr.-D	3	3	1	13	3	18	17	7	65	C
4. Joe Kolter-D	6	0	13	3	0	15	13	12	62	C
5. Richard T. Schulze-R	3	0	0	0	0	0	0	3	3	F
6. Gus Yatron-D	3	0	4	1	6	6	11	6	37	C

7. Curt Weldon-R	3	0	0	12	0	9	7	6	37	C
8. Peter H. Kostmayer-D	12	6	25	43	3	36	31	24	180	A
9. Bud Shuster-R	0	0	0	0	0	0	0	1	1	F
10. Joseph M. McDade-R	3	3	0	0	0	6	1	3	16	D
11. Paul E. Kanjorski-D	9	3	12	0	0	9	1	1	35	C
12. John P. Murtha-D	3	3	0	3	0	0	4	1	14	D
13. Lawrence Coughlin-R	3	6	3	0	0	0	3	1	16	D
14. William J. Coyne-D	6	3	9	6	0	18	6	19	67	C
15. Don Ritter-R	3	9	6	0	0	6	1	6	31	C
16. Robert S. Walker-R	0	6	3	0	0	6	0	0	15	D
17. George W. Gekas-R	3	0	0	0	0	0	0	0	3	F
18. Doug Walgren-D ★ ✪	6	9	3	9	4	21	3	9	64	B
18. Rick Santorum-R ✪	0	0	0	0	0	3	0	0	3	D
19. William F. Goodling-R	3	0	1	3	0	0	13	3	23	C
20. Joseph M. Gaydos-D	6	0	0	0	0	6	0	0	12	D
21. Thomas J. Ridge-R	3	0	3	3	0	6	1	6	22	C
22. Austin J. Murphy-D	6	3	6	15	0	12	13	1	56	C
23. William F. Clinger-R	0	3	3	3	0	12	4	2	27	C

KEY TO CONGRESSIONAL REPORT CARD

Scores and grades are for performance in the 101st and 102nd Congresses combined unless otherwise noted, as below:

★ = Served in the 101st Congress.

✪ = Served in the 102nd Congress.

✓ = Term incomplete as a result of death, resignation, appointment, or midterm election.

NG= Incomplete terms were not graded.

▲ = For reasons of protocol, the Speaker of the House does not introduce or cosponsor legislation. As a result, Thomas Foley (D-WA) cannot be scored.

π = For purposes of simplification, Genetic Engineering has been combined with Animal Rights in the report card. With the exception of one bill, all genetic engineering bills pertain to the potential abuse of animals with this new technology.

= Global Commons, which includes legislation concerning the oceans and Antarctica, has been combined with International Development and Foreign Policy in the report card.

DISTRICT / REPRESENTATIVES	ATMOSPHERIC PROTECTION	ENERGY AND TRANSPORTATION	DEFENSE	INTERNATIONAL DEVELOPMENT AND FOREIGN POLICY #	AGRICULTURE	PUBLIC LANDS, FORESTS AND WETLANDS	ANIMAL RIGHTS π	ENDANGERED SPECIES AND BIODIVERSITY	RAW SCORE	GRADE
RHODE ISLAND										
1. Ronald K. Machtley-R	6	6	6	21	6	27	28	24	124	B
2. Claudine Schneider-R ★	12	15	9	34	16	27	18	23	154	A
2. Jack Reed-D ◉	0	3	0	9	0	0	3	6	21	C
SOUTH CAROLINA										
1. Arthur Ravenel, Jr.-R	9	9	3	15	9	39	29	33	146	A
2. Floyd Spence-R	0	0	0	6	0	6	1	0	13	D
3. Butler Derrick-D	3	0	1	6	0	18	1	6	35	C
4. Elizabeth J. Patterson-D	3	3	1	12	3	30	13	8	73	C
5. John M. Spratt, Jr.-D	6	0	4	12	3	12	4	3	44	C
6. Robin Tallon-D	9	0	4	20	0	15	10	17	75	C
SOUTH DAKOTA										
At Large—Tim Johnson-D	9	3	7	16	12	6	7	7	67	C
TENNESSEE										
1. James H. Quillen-R	3	0	0	0	0	0	1	0	4	F
2. John J. Duncan, Jr.-R	3	0	0	0	0	6	0	1	10	D
3. Marilyn Lloyd-D	3	6	0	0	0	9	1	6	25	C
4. Jim Cooper-D	3	3	3	6	3	18	0	6	42	C
5. Bob Clement-D	3	9	3	4	0	12	5	13	49	C

6. Barr Gordon-D	6	18	4	9	3	24	13	10	87	B
7. Don Sundquist-R	0	0	0	0	0	0	1	0	0	F
8. John S. Tanner-D	3	6	0	0	3	6	13	4	14	D
9. Harold E. Ford-D	9	6	7	30	3	24	13	6	98	B
TEXAS										
1. Jim Chapman-D	3	3	6	0	0	0	12	1	25	C
2. Charles Wilson-D	12	3	0	13	6	15	32	30	111	B
3. Steve Bartlett-R ★	0	0	0	0	0	3	4	3	10	D
3. Steve Bartlett-R ✪ ✓	0	0	0	0	0	0	0	0	0	NG
3. Sam Johnson-R ✪ ✓	0	0	0	0	0	0	0	0	0	NG
4. Ralph M. Hall-D	0	3	0	0	0	0	1	3	7	D
5. John Bryant-D	6	3	18	18	6	21	15	28	115	B
6. Joe Barton-R	0	0	0	0	0	0	0	0	0	F
7. Bill Archer-R	0	3	0	6	0	3	0	0	3	F
8. Jack M. Fields, Jr.-R	0	3	0	6	0	0	4	11	24	C
9. Jack Brooks-D	3	0	3	0	0	9	0	1	16	D
10. J. J. Pickle-D	3	0	0	3	3	6	1	1	17	D

KEY TO CONGRESSIONAL REPORT CARD

Scores and grades are for performance in the 101st and 102nd Congresses combined unless otherwise noted, as below:

★ = Served in the 101st Congress.

✪ = Served in the 102nd Congress.

✓ = Term incomplete as a result of death, resignation, appointment, or midterm election.

NG = Incomplete terms were not graded.

▲ = For reasons of protocol, the Speaker of the House does not introduce or cosponsor legislation. As a result, Thomas Foley (D-WA) cannot be scored.

π = For purposes of simplification, Genetic Engineering has been combined with Animal Rights in the report card. With the exception of one bill, all genetic engineering bills pertain to the potential abuse of animals with this new technology.

= Global Commons, which includes legislation concerning the oceans and Antarctica, has been combined with International Development and Foreign Policy in the report card.

DISTRICT / REPRESENTATIVES	ATMOSPHERIC PROTECTION	ENERGY AND TRANSPORTATION	DEFENSE	INTERNATIONAL DEVELOPMENT AND FOREIGN POLICY #	AGRICULTURE	PUBLIC LANDS, FORESTS AND WETLANDS	ANIMAL RIGHTS π	ENDANGERED SPECIES AND BIODIVERSITY	RAW SCORE	GRADE
11. Marvin Leath-D ★	3	0	0	0	0	0	0	1	4	D
11. Chet Edwards-D ✪	0	0	0	0	0	0	0	0	0	F
12. James C. Wright-D ★ ✓	0	0	0	0	0	0	0	0	0	NG
12. Pete Geren-D ★ ✓	0	0	1	3	0	3	0	7	14	NG
12. Pete Geren-D ✪	0	0	0	3	0	3	3	3	12	C
13. Bill Sarpalius-D	3	3	0	0	0	0	1	1	8	D
14. Greg Laughlin-D	0	3	0	3	0	0	0	1	7	D
15. E. "Kika" de la Garza-D	3	0	0	3	0	0	0	1	7	D
16. Ronald D. Coleman-D	3	3	0	3	0	3	3	4	19	C
17. Charles W. Stenholm-D	0	0	0	0	0	0	1	1	2	F
18. Mickey Leland-D ★ ✓	3	3	6	15	0	3	6	9	45	NG
18. Craig Washington-D ★ ✓	0	0	0	0	3	3	0	0	6	NG
18. Craig Washington-D ✪	0	0	3	6	0	9	0	0	18	C
19. Larry Combest-R	0	0	0	0	0	0	0	0	0	F
20. Henry B. Gonzalez-D	6	0	0	3	0	3	1	4	17	D
21. Lamar Smith-R	0	0	0	0	0	3	3	0	6	D
22. Tom DeLay-R	0	0	0	0	0	3	1	0	4	D
23. Albert G. Bustamante-D	6	6	27	21	3	15	16	5	99	B
24. Martin Frost-D	3	9	15	12	6	0	10	7	62	C
25. Michael A. Andrews-D	0	0	3	3	0	12	0	12	30	C

26. Richard K. Armey-R	0	3	0	0	0	0	3	3	9	D
27. Solomon P. Ortiz-D	6	0	0	6	0	6	0	1	19	C
UTAH										
1. James V. Hansen-R	12	0	0	0	0	0	1	1	2	F
2. Wayne Owens-D	0	30	19	37	6	21	13	47	185	A
3. Howard C. Nielson-R ★	3	3	0	6	0	0	0	4	16	C
3. William Orton-D ✪	0	0	0	0	0	0	0	6	6	C
VERMONT										
At Large—Peter Smith-R ★	12	3	0	6	4	9	13	6	53	C
At Large—Bernard Sanders-I ✪	0	6	3	9	3	9	0	3	33	B
VIRGINIA										
1. Herbert H. Bateman-R	0	0	0	6	0	0	1	0	7	D
2. Owen B. Pickett-D	0	6	0	6	0	9	4	4	29	C
3. Thomas J. Bliley, Jr.-R	0	3	0	3	0	0	3	0	9	D
4. Norman Sisisky-D	0	0	0	3	0	6	1	0	10	D
5. Lewis F. Payne, Jr.-D	3	3	0	6	3	9	7	7	38	C

KEY TO CONGRESSIONAL REPORT CARD

Scores and grades are for performance in the 101st and 102nd Congresses combined unless otherwise noted, as below:

★ = Served in the 101st Congress.

✪ = Served in the 102nd Congress.

✓ = Term incomplete as a result of death, resignation, appointment, or midterm election.

NG= Incomplete terms were not graded.

▲ = For reasons of protocol, the Speaker of the House does not introduce or cosponsor legislation. As a result, Thomas Foley (D-WA) cannot be scored.

π = For purposes of simplification, Genetic Engineering has been combined with Animal Rights in the report card. With the exception of one bill, all genetic engineering bills pertain to the potential abuse of animals with this new technology.

= Global Commons, which includes legislation concerning the oceans and Antarctica, has been combined with International Development and Foreign Policy in the report card.

DISTRICT / REPRESENTATIVES	ATMOSPHERIC PROTECTION	ENERGY AND TRANSPORTATION	DEFENSE	INTERNATIONAL DEVELOPMENT AND FOREIGN POLICY #	AGRICULTURE	PUBLIC LANDS, FORESTS AND WETLANDS	ANIMAL RIGHTS π	ENDANGERED SPECIES AND BIODIVERSITY	RAW SCORE	GRADE
6. Jim Olin-D	9	0	3	9	0	9	7	3	40	C
7. D. French Slaughter, Jr.-R	0	3	0	0	0	3	0	0	6	D
8. Stan Parris-R ★	0	3	0	0	3	0	7	0	13	D
8. Jim Moran, Jr.-D ✪	0	6	0	0	0	0	0	0	6	C
9. Rick Boucher-D	6	3	4	12	0	6	7	12	50	C
10. Frank R. Wolf-R	0	6	3	9	0	3	1	4	26	C
WASHINGTON										
1. John Miller-R	3	12	4	16	0	12	17	20	84	B
2. Al Swift-D	3	18	9	12	3	3	9	12	69	C
3. Jolene Unsoeld-D	6	21	22	34	3	9	11	35	141	A
4. Sid Morrison-R	0	3	1	3	3	3	3	0	16	D
5. Thomas S. Foley-D ▲	0	0	0	0	0	0	0	0	0	NG
6. Norman D. Dicks-D	3	3	7	15	0	9	4	9	50	C
7. Jim McDermott-D	12	21	25	22	9	12	18	26	145	A
8. Rod Chandler-R	0	6	4	6	6	6	16	8	52	C
WEST VIRGINIA										
1. Alan B. Mollohan-D	3	0	0	3	6	3	4	3	22	C
2. Harley O. Staggers, Jr.-D	3	3	3	9	3	3	1	0	25	C

3. Robert E. Wise, Jr.-D	6	18	6	9	3	9	9	1	61	C
4. Nick Joe Rahall II-D	3	0	13	12	6	15	16	1	66	C
WISCONSIN										
1. Les Aspin-D	3	0	0	3	0	18	0	1	25	C
2. Robert Kastenmeier-D ★	9	0	6	17	25	18	15	10	100	A
2. Scott Klug-R ☻	0	0	3	0	0	0	3	9	12	C
3. Steve Gunderson-R	9	6	7	15	0	6	4	0	28	C
3. Gerald D. Kleczka-D	9	9	28	7	6	15	23	10	77	C
5. Jim Moody-D	9	9	3	22	0	18	15	13	120	B
6. Thomas E. Petri-R	0	3	3	6	0	9	7	6	34	C
7. David R. Obey-D	3	0	3	3	0	6	0	1	16	D
8. Toby Roth-R	0	0	3	0	0	0	6	2	11	D
9. F. James Sensenbrenner-R	0	0	3	3	0	3	0	0	9	D
WYOMING										
At Large–Richard Cheney-R ✓★	0	0	0	0	0	0	0	0	0	NG
At Large–Craig Thomas-R ★✓	0	0	0	0	0	0	0	1	1	NG
At Large–Craig Thomas-R ☻	0	0	0	0	0	0	0	0	0	F

KEY TO CONGRESSIONAL REPORT CARD

Scores and grades are for performance in the 101st and 102nd Congresses combined unless otherwise noted, as below:

★ = Served in the 101st Congress.

☻ = Served in the 102nd Congress.

✓ = Term incomplete as a result of death, resignation, appointment, or midterm election.

NG= Incomplete terms were not graded.

▲ = For reasons of protocol, the Speaker of the House does not introduce or cosponsor legislation. As a result, Thomas Foley (D-WA) cannot be scored.

π = For purposes of simplification, Genetic Engineering has been combined with Animal Rights in the report card. With the exception of one bill, all genetic engineering bills pertain to the potential abuse of animals with this new technology.

= Global Commons, which includes legislation concerning the oceans and Antarctica, has been combined with International Development and Foreign Policy in the report card.

DELEGATES	ATMOSPHERIC PROTECTION	ENERGY AND TRANSPORTATION	DEFENSE	INTERNATIONAL DEVELOPMENT AND FOREIGN POLICY #	AGRICULTURE	PUBLIC LANDS, FORESTS AND WETLANDS	ANIMAL RIGHTS π	ENDANGERED SPECIES AND BIODIVERSITY	RAW SCORE	GRADE
AMERICAN SAMOA Eni F. H. Faleomavaega-D	3	6	10	10	0	6	2	26	63	C
GUAM Ben Blaz-R	3	0	3	9	0	0	0	11	26	C
PUERTO RICO Jaime B. Fuster-D	6	0	3	30	0	0	7	10	56	C
VIRGIN ISLANDS Ron De Lugo-D	9	6	3	30	0	6	13	25	92	B
DISTRICT OF COLUMBIA Walter E. Fauntroy-D ★	9	9	31	26	3	3	13	19	113	A
Eleanor Holmes Norton-D ✪	0	9	9	12	3	3	0	3	39	B

Note:

Along with 435 elected Representatives, there are four Delegates and one Resident Commissioner in the House of Representatives. They represent American Samoa, Guam, Puerto Rico, the U.S. Virgin Islands, and the District of Columbia. They may propose and cosponsor legislation, and may vote on legislation in committee but not on the House floor.

KEY TO CONGRESSIONAL REPORT CARD

Scores and grades are for performance in the 101st and 102nd Congresses combined unless otherwise noted, as below:

★ = Served in the 101st Congress.

✪ = Served in the 102nd Congress.

✓ = Term incomplete as a result of death, resignation, appointment, or midterm election.

NG= Incomplete terms were not graded.

▲ = For reasons of protocol, the Speaker of the House does not introduce or cosponsor legislation. As a result, Thomas Foley (D-WA) cannot be scored.

π = For purposes of simplification, Genetic Engineering has been combined with Animal Rights in the report card. With the exception of one bill, all genetic engineering bills pertain to the potential abuse of animals with this new technology.

= Global Commons, which includes legislation concerning the oceans and Antarctica, has been combined with International Development and Foreign Policy in the report card.

SENATORS	ATMOSPHERIC PROTECTION	ENERGY AND TRANSPORTATION	DEFENSE	INTERNATIONAL DEVELOPMENT AND FOREIGN POLICY #	AGRICULTURE	PUBLIC LANDS, FORESTS AND WETLANDS	ANIMAL RIGHTS π	ENDANGERED SPECIES AND BIODIVERSITY	RAW SCORE	GRADE
ALABAMA										
Howell T. Heflin-D	3	0	1	0	3	6	1	0	14	C
Richard C. Shelby-D	3	0	0	0	3	3	4	0	13	C
ALASKA										
Frank H. Murkowski-R	0	3	3	9	3	0	1	10	29	C
Ted Stevens-R	3	3	3	0	0	6	0	4	19	C
ARIZONA										
Dennis DeConcini-D	3	15	3	12	0	0	4	0	37	C
John McCain-R	0	3	24	3	0	0	0	3	33	C
ARKANSAS										
Dale Bumpers-D	6	9	1	9	6	9	3	3	46	B
David Pryor-D	1	0	3	0	3	6	1	0	14	C
CALIFORNIA										
Alan Cranston-D	9	15	3	22	15	7	8	10	89	A
Pete Wilson-R ★	0	6	0	0	3	3	1	0	13	C
John F. Seymour-R ✪	0	3	0	0	0	0	0	0	3	D

COLORADO										
William L. Armstrong-R ★	0	6	0	3	0	0	0	0	9	C
Hank Brown ☻	0	3	0	0	0	0	0	0	3	D
Timothy E. Wirth-D	13	27	9	17	3	3	7	3	82	A
CONNECTICUT										
Christopher J. Dodd-D	4	6	9	10	3	6	4	8	50	B
Joseph I. Lieberman-D	16	21	10	14	12	9	3	5	90	A
DELAWARE										
Joseph R. Biden, Jr.-D	3	0	9	5	0	9	7	1	34	C
William V. Roth, Jr.-R	0	0	3	0	0	18	1	1	23	C
FLORIDA										
Bob Graham-D	0	9	1	13	3	3	4	6	39	B
Connie Mack-R	0	0	3	0	0	0	0	0	3	F

KEY TO CONGRESSIONAL REPORT CARD

Scores and grades are for performance in the 101st and 102nd Congresses combined unless otherwise noted, as below:

★ = Served in the 101st Congress.

☻ = Served in the 102nd Congress.

✓ = Term incomplete as a result of death, resignation, appointment, or midterm election.

NG= Incomplete terms were not graded.

▲ = For reasons of protocol, the Speaker of the House does not introduce or cosponsor legislation. As a result, Thomas Foley (D-WA) cannot be scored.

π = For purposes of simplification, Genetic Engineering has been combined with Animal Rights in the report card. With the exception of one bill, all genetic engineering bills pertain to the potential abuse of animals with this new technology.

= Global Commons, which includes legislation concerning the oceans and Antarctica, has been combined with International Development and Foreign Policy in the report card.

SENATORS	ATMOSPHERIC PROTECTION	ENERGY AND TRANSPORTATION	DEFENSE	INTERNATIONAL DEVELOPMENT AND FOREIGN POLICY #	AGRICULTURE	PUBLIC LANDS, FORESTS AND WETLANDS	ANIMAL RIGHTS π	ENDANGERED SPECIES AND BIODIVERSITY	RAW SCORE	GRADE
GEORGIA										
Wyche Fowler, Jr.-D	0	15	0	3	9	9	6	3	45	B
Sam Nunn-D	0	0	3	0	0	4	0	0	7	D
HAWAII										
Spark M. Matsunaga-D ★ ✔	6	6	10	0	0	3	6	0	31	NG
Daniel Akaka-D ★ ✪	0	0	4	0	6	3	6	1	20	NG
Daniel Akaka-D ✪	1	6	0	4	3	9	9	3	35	A
Daniel K. Inouye-D	6	9	1	7	9	3	6	9	50	B
IDAHO										
James A. McClure-R ★	3	0	0	0	0	3	0	1	7	D
Larry Craig-R ✪	0	0	0	3	0	0	0	3	6	C
Steven Symms-R	0	3	0	6	0	6	1	0	16	C
ILLINOIS										
Alan J. Dixon-D	3	0	0	3	0	0	0	0	6	D
Paul Simon-D	7	9	13	13	3	12	7	0	64	B
INDIANA										
Dan Coats-R	3	0	0	0	0	0	0	0	3	F
Richard G. Lugar-R	1	0	7	6	0	0	4	4	22	C

State / Senator										Grade
IOWA										
Charles E. Grassley-R	3	0	0	0	0	0	4	0	7	D
Tom Harkin-D	3	3	19	11	9	9	3	0	57	B
KANSAS										
Robert Dole-R	0	0	6	0	0	1	0	0	7	D
Nancy Landon Kassebaum-R	0	0	3	3	0	0	1	0	7	D
KENTUCKY										
Wendell H. Ford-D	3	6	3	0	0	0	1	3	16	C
Mitch McConnell-R	3	0	0	0	3	3	0	0	6	D
LOUISIANA										
John Breaux-D	0	0	3	3	0	0	1	3	10	D
Bennett Johnston-D	0	0	0	0	0	0	1	0	1	F
MAINE										
William S. Cohen-R	0	6	6	12	3	3	4	3	37	C
George J. Mitchell-D	7	6	3	12	3	0	1	4	36	C

KEY TO CONGRESSIONAL REPORT CARD

Scores and grades are for performance in the 101st and 102nd Congresses combined unless otherwise noted, as below:

★ = Served in the 101st Congress.

✪ = Served in the 102nd Congress.

✓ = Term incomplete as a result of death, resignation, appointment, or midterm election.

NG= Incomplete terms were not graded.

▲ = For reasons of protocol, the Speaker of the House does not introduce or cosponsor legislation. As a result, Thomas Foley (D-WA) cannot be scored.

π = For purposes of simplification, Genetic Engineering has been combined with Animal Rights in the report card. With the exception of one bill, all genetic engineering bills pertain to the potential abuse of animals with this new technology.

= Global Commons, which includes legislation concerning the oceans and Antarctica, has been combined with International Development and Foreign Policy in the report card.

SENATORS	ATMOSPHERIC PROTECTION	ENERGY AND TRANSPORTATION	DEFENSE	INTERNATIONAL DEVELOPMENT AND FOREIGN POLICY #	AGRICULTURE	PUBLIC LANDS, FORESTS AND WETLANDS	ANIMAL RIGHTS π	ENDANGERED SPECIES AND BIODIVERSITY	RAW SCORE	GRADE
MARYLAND										
Barbara A. Mikulski-D	7	9	0	19	9	12	3	3	62	B
Paul S. Sarbanes-D	0	6	0	7	6	9	3	4	35	C
MASSACHUSETTS										
Edward M. Kennedy-D	7	3	6	10	9	12	7	3	57	B
John F. Kerry-D	19	15	16	18	6	9	4	8	95	A
MICHIGAN										
Carl M. Levin-D	1	6	7	7	6	6	3	0	36	C
Donald W. Riegle, Jr.-D	0	0	4	6	0	6	0	3	19	C
MINNESOTA										
Rudy Boschwitz-R ★	6	3	7	9	0	0	1	1	27	B
Paul Wellstone-D ✪	1	3	0	3	3	6	0	3	19	B
David Durenberger-R	3	3	3	13	6	6	1	0	35	C
MISSISSIPPI										
Thad Cochran-R	3	0	0	0	0	3	0	0	6	D
Trent Lott-R	0	0	3	0	0	0	0	3	6	D
MISSOURI										
Christopher Bond-R	3	0	0	0	0	0	1	3	7	D
John C. Danforth-R	3	0	0	0	0	0	0	3	6	D

									Score	Grade
MONTANA										
Conrad Burns-R	0	6	0	0	0	0	1	3	10	D
Max Baucus-D	12	6	0	7	3	3	6	0	37	C
NEBRASKA										
J. James Exon-D	3	0	1	9	0	0	1	0	14	C
J. Robert Kerrey-D	3	3	3	3	3	0	0	0	15	C
NEVADA										
Richard H. Bryan-D	7	18	0	0	9	6	1	3	44	B
Harry Reid-D	9	15	0	10	12	18	15	0	79	A
NEW HAMPSHIRE										
Gordon J. Humphrey-R ★	0	0	3	0	0	3	3	0	9	C
Robert C. Smith-R ✪	0	0	0	0	0	0	0	0	0	F
Warren B. Rudman-R	0	3	0	0	0	0	0	0	3	F

KEY TO CONGRESSIONAL REPORT CARD

Scores and grades are for performance in the 101st and 102nd Congresses combined unless otherwise noted, as below:

★ = Served in the 101st Congress.

✪ = Served in the 102nd Congress.

✓ = Term incomplete as a result of death, resignation, appointment, or midterm election.

NG= Incomplete terms were not graded.

▲ = For reasons of protocol, the Speaker of the House does not introduce or cosponsor legislation. As a result, Thomas Foley (D-WA) cannot be scored.

π = For purposes of simplification, Genetic Engineering has been combined with Animal Rights in the report card. With the exception of one bill, all genetic engineering bills pertain to the potential abuse of animals with this new technology.

= Global Commons, which includes legislation concerning the oceans and Antarctica, has been combined with International Development and Foreign Policy in the report card.

SENATORS	ATMOSPHERIC PROTECTION	ENERGY AND TRANSPORTATION	DEFENSE	INTERNATIONAL DEVELOPMENT AND FOREIGN POLICY #	AGRICULTURE	PUBLIC LANDS, FORESTS AND WETLANDS	ANIMAL RIGHTS π	ENDANGERED SPECIES AND BIODIVERSITY	RAW SCORE	GRADE
NEW JERSEY										
Bill Bradley-D	4	0	3	6	0	9	3	3	28	C
Frank R. Lautenberg-D	6	27	0	9	0	6	4	6	58	B
NEW MEXICO										
Jeff Bingaman-D	3	9	12	3	0	3	0	0	30	C
Pete V. Domenici-R	0	3	0	3	0	0	1	0	7	D
NEW YORK										
Alfonse D'Amato-R	0	12	0	16	0	3	4	6	41	B
Daniel Patrick Moynihan-D	4	12	1	9	6	12	3	21	68	A
NORTH CAROLINA										
Jesse Helms-R	0	0	6	1	0	0	1	2	10	D
Terry Sanford-D	3	12	6	8	3	0	3	1	36	C
NORTH DAKOTA										
Quentin Burdick-D	3	3	7	6	6	3	7	0	35	C
Kent Conrad-D	9	12	12	9	6	0	4	0	52	B
OHIO										
John Glenn-D	3	6	6	0	0	3	3	0	21	C
Howard Metzenbaum-D	9	6	4	7	0	9	1	0	36	C

OKLAHOMA										
David L. Boren-D	0	0	6	6	3	3	1	3	22	C
Don Nickles-R	0	0	0	0	0	0	0	0	0	F
OREGON										
Mark Hatfield-R	3	15	20	6	0	0	12	6	62	B
Bob Packwood-R	0	0	0	3	3	3	3	8	20	C
PENNSYLVANIA										
John Heinz-R ★	3	9	6	6	0	0	1	3	28	B
John Heinz-R ✪ ✓	0	0	0	0	0	0	0	0	0	NG
Harris Wofford-D ✪ ✓	0	0	0	3	0	0	0	0	3	NG
Arlen Specter-R	3	6	0	0	0	3	1	0	13	C
RHODE ISLAND										
John Chafee-R	7	15	0	12	0	15	4	3	56	B
Claiborne Pell-D	13	12	19	11	9	12	7	7	90	A

KEY TO CONGRESSIONAL REPORT CARD

Scores and grades are for performance in the 101st and 102nd Congresses combined unless otherwise noted, as below:

★ = Served in the 101st Congress.

✪ = Served in the 102nd Congress.

✓ = Term incomplete as a result of death, resignation, appointment, or midterm election.

NG= Incomplete terms were not graded.

▲ = For reasons of protocol, the Speaker of the House does not introduce or cosponsor legislation. As a result, Thomas Foley (D-WA) cannot be scored.

π = For purposes of simplification, Genetic Engineering has been combined with Animal Rights in the report card. With the exception of one bill, all genetic engineering bills pertain to the potential abuse of animals with this new technology.

= Global Commons, which includes legislation concerning the oceans and Antarctica, has been combined with International Development and Foreign Policy in the report card.

SENATORS	ATMOSPHERIC PROTECTION	ENERGY AND TRANSPORTATION	DEFENSE	INTERNATIONAL DEVELOPMENT AND FOREIGN POLICY #	AGRICULTURE	PUBLIC LANDS, FORESTS AND WETLANDS	ANIMAL RIGHTS π	ENDANGERED SPECIES AND BIODIVERSITY	RAW SCORE	GRADE
SOUTH CAROLINA										
Ernest Hollings-D	6	6	3	0	0	3	0	5	23	C
Strom Thurmond-R	0	0	0	0	3	0	0	0	3	F
SOUTH DAKOTA										
Thomas Daschle-D	1	9	7	14	6	6	1	0	44	B
Larry Pressler-R	0	0	1	0	0	0	0	3	4	D
TENNESSEE										
Albert Gore, Jr.-D	38	12	12	26	6	12	4	5	115	A
Jim Sasser-D	6	0	0	3	0	6	1	0	16	C
TEXAS										
Lloyd Bentsen-D	3	6	0	0	3	0	1	0	13	C
Phil Gramm-R	0	0	3	0	0	0	0	0	3	F
UTAH										
Jake Garn-R	0	0	3	3	0	0	1	0	7	D
Orrin G. Hatch-R	0	3	0	0	3	0	1	0	7	D
VERMONT										
James Jeffords-R	9	9	4	17	9	3	7	0	58	B
Patrick Leahy-D	9	9	10	4	33	12	3	0	80	A

VIRGINIA										
Charles Robb-D	0	6	3	0	0	0	0	0	9	D
John Warner-R	0	3	0	13	0	0	0	0	16	C
WASHINGTON										
Brock Adams-D	6	18	4	19	6	9	4	5	71	A
Slade Gorton-R	0	15	3	9	0	3	1	4	35	C
WEST VIRGINIA										
Robert Byrd, Jr.-D	6	0	0	0	0	0	1	0	7	D
John D. Rockefeller, IV-D	4	6	0	10	0	3	0	0	23	C
WISCONSIN										
Robert W. Kasten, Jr.-R	0	6	3	0	3	6	6	3	27	C
Herbert H. Kohl-D	3	3	7	12	12	3	3	0	43	B
WYOMING										
Alan Simpson-R	0	0	0	3	0	0	0	0	3	F
Malcolm Wallop-R	0	0	0	0	0	0	0	0	0	F

KEY TO CONGRESSIONAL REPORT CARD

Scores and grades are for performance in the 101st and 102nd Congresses combined unless otherwise noted, as below:

★ = Served in the 101st Congress.

✪ = Served in the 102nd Congress.

✓ = Term incomplete as a result of death, resignation, appointment, or midterm election.

NG= Incomplete terms were not graded.

▲ = For reasons of protocol, the Speaker of the House does not introduce or cosponsor legislation. As a result, Thomas Foley (D-WA) cannot be scored.

π = For purposes of simplification, Genetic Engineering has been combined with Animal Rights in the report card. With the exception of one bill, all genetic engineering bills pertain to the potential abuse of animals with this new technology.

= Global Commons, which includes legislation concerning the oceans and Antarctica, has been combined with International Development and Foreign Policy in the report card.

GREEN LEGISLATION INTRODUCED IN THE HOUSE DURING THE 101ST AND 102ND CONGRESSES

Atmospheric Protection

H.R. 1078	Global Warming Prevention Act of 1989
H.R. 4805	Tax Act on Fuels that Produce Carbon Dioxide
H.R. 1086	Tax Act on Fuels that Produce Carbon Dioxide
H.R. 2699	Stratospheric Ozone Protection Act of 1989
H.R. 3257	Stratospheric Ozone Layer Protection Act
H.R. 1112	Ozone Protection and CFC Reduction Act of 1989
H.R. 503	Labeling of Products with Chlorofluorocarbons Act
H. Amd. 464	Clean Air Employment Transition Assistance Act

Energy and Transportation

H.R. 5521	National Energy Policy Act of 1990
H.R. 2104	Renewable Energy Trade Equity and Promotion Act
H.R. 776	National Energy Efficiency Act of 1991
H.R. 1216	Renewable Energy and Energy Efficiency Technology Competitiveness Act of 1989
H.R. 1196	Comprehensive Energy Conservation Program Act
H.R. 711	State Energy Conservation Programs Improvement Act of 1989
H.R. 117	Public Housing Energy Conservation Act
H.R. 272	Public Housing Energy Conservation Act
H.R. 446	Motor Vehicle Fuel Efficiency Act of 1991
H.R. 1583	Fuel Efficient Vehicle Purchase Incentive Act
H.R. 5560	Motor Vehicle Fuel Efficiency Act of 1990
H.R. 1538	National Electric Vehicle Act of 1991
H.R. 3631	Employee Mass Transit Benefits Act
H.R. 1442	Employee Mass Transit Benefits Act
H.R. 2233	Gasoline Tax for Mass Transit Act
H.R. 861	Gasoline Tax for Mass Transit Act
H.R. 1145	Tax Benefit for Public Transport Act
H.R. 1087	High-Speed Rail Transportation Policy and Development Act
H.R. 193	Tax Benefits for Public Transport Act
H.R. 2265	Tax Benefits for Public Transport Act
H.R. 3396	Tax Benefits for Public Transport Act
H.R. 4043	Tax Benefits for Public Transport Act
H.R. 494	Tax Benefits for Public Transport Act
H.R. 2101	Bicycle and Pedestrian Transportation Improvement Act of 1991
H.R. 4568	Bicycle Transportation Act of 1990

Defense

H.R. 830	Nuclear Non-Proliferation Enforcement Act of 1991
H.R. 5902	Non-Proliferation Act of 1990
H.R. 1635	Limit of Export-Import Bank Financing of Military Materials Act
H.R. 963	Sanctions for Violators of Military Trade Law Act
H.R. 1574	International Security and Satellite Monitoring Act of 1989
H. Amdt. 166	Restriction of SDI Amendment
H.R. 2201	Outer Space Protection Act of 1989
H.R. 3033	Chemical and Biological Warfare Elimination Act
H.R. 2426	Chemical and Biological Weapons Nonproliferation Act
H.R. 696	Chemical and Biological Weapons Control Act of 1989
H.R. 238	Control of Chemical Weapons Resolution
H.R. 237	Biological Weapons Act of 1989
H.R. 475	War Cost Disclosure Act of 1991
H. Con. Res. 259	Harvest of Peace Resolution
H.R. 1870	United States Peace Tax Fund Act
H.R. 1994	United States Peace Tax Fund Act
H.R. 441	Defense Economic Adjustment Act
H.R. 2784	Community Economic Adjustment Funding Act of 1991
H.R. 101	Defense Economic Adjustment Act
H.R. 2852	Economic Diversification and Defense Adjustment Act of 1989
H.R. 699	Economic Conversion Act of 1989
H.R. 3999	Economic Stabilization, Adjustment, and Defense Industry Conversion Act of 1990

International Development, Foreign Policy, and Global Commons

H.R. 594	Global Poverty Reduction Act
H.R. 1510	Africa Famine Recovery and Development Act
H.R. 1454	Horn of Africa Recovery and Food Security Act of 1991
H.R. 4443	Mickey Leland African and Caribbean Development Act of 1990
H.R. 1240	Caribbean Regional Development Act of 1989
H.R. 5934	Micro-enterprise Loans for the Poor Act
H.R. 1608	Micro-enterprise Development Act of 1991
H.R. 951	Women in Development Act of 1989
H.R. 1360	Women in Development Act of 1991
H.R. 879	International Indigenous Peoples Protection Act of 1989
H.R. 1596	International Indigenous Peoples Protection Act of 1989
H.R. 1633	World Summit for Children Implementation Act of 1991
H. Res. 263	Human Needs and Mobility Resolution
H.R. 1704	Tropical Forest Protection Act of 1989
H. Con. Res. 44	Debt for Tropical Forest Exchange Resolution
H.R. 5088	Western Hemisphere Debt for Nature Conversion Act
H.R. 2777	International Banking Environmental Protection Act of 1989

H.R. 3189	National Environmental Policy on International Financing Act of 1989
H.R. 1113	Appropriations Authorization for the Office of Environmental Quality and to Ensure Consideration of the Impact of Major Federal Actions on the Global Environment
H.R. 1271	Appropriations Authorization for the Office of Environmental Quality and to Ensure Consideration of the Impact of Major Federal Actions on the Global Environment
H.R. 4514	Antarctica World Park and Protection Act of 1990
H.J. Res. 415/418	Protection of Antarctica as a Global Ecological Commons Act
H.R. 4210	Antarctica Environmental Protection, Clean-Up, and Liability Act of 1990
H.R. 1920	Antarctic Environmental Protection Act of 1991
H.R. 2826	Antarctica World Park and Protection Act
H. Con. Res. 109	Antarctica Mining Ban Resolution
H.R. 3503	Ocean Dumping Enforcement Improvement Act of 1989
H.R. 1465	Oil Pollution Liability and Compensation Act of 1989
H.R. 1281	Illegal Dumping Prevention Act of 1989
H.R. 1239	Illegal Dumping Prevention Act of 1991
H.R. 2953	Comprehensive Ocean Assessment and Strategy (Coast) Act of 1989

Agriculture

H.R. 3552	Sustainable Agricultural Adjustment Act of 1989
H.R. 4156	Organic Foods Production Act of 1990
H.R. 84	Veal Calf Protection Act
H.R. 252	Protection of Veal Calves Act
H.R. 4219	Pesticide Export Reform Act of 1990
H.R. 2083	Circle of Poison Prevention Act

Public Lands, Forests, and Wetlands

H.R. 39	Alaska Wilderness Act of 1990
H.R. 39	Alaska Wilderness Act of 1991
H.R. 4948	National Wildlife Refuge System Act of 1990
H.R. 2881	National Wildlife Refuge System Act of 1991
H.R. 1693	Refuge Wildlife Protection Act of 1989
H.R. 330	Refuge Wildlife Protection Act of 1991
H.R. 5788	Fair Market Grazing for Public Rangelands Act of 1990
H. Amdt. 863	Federal Grazing Fee Amendment
H.R. 775	Federal Grazing Fee Act
H.R. 944	Fair Market Grazing for Public Rangelands Act of 1991
H.R. 481	Public Rangelands Fee Act of 1991
H.R. 918	Mineral Exploration and Development Act of 1991
H.R. 876	American Heritage Trust Act of 1989
H.R. 3362	Global Forest Emergency Act
H.R. 528	Global Forest Emergency Act
H.R. 5958	Tropical Forest Consumer Information and Protection Act of 1990

H.R. 2854	Tropical Forest Consumer Information and Protection Act of 1991
H.R. 4492	Ancient Forest Protection Act of 1990
H.R. 842	Ancient Forest Protection Act of 1991
H.R. 2144	Urban and Community Forestry Act of 1989
H.R. 1746	Wetlands No Net Loss Act of 1989
H.R. 251	Wetlands No Net Loss Act of 1991

Animal Rights and Genetic Engineering

H.R. 2345	Citizen Suit Provision for Animal Welfare Act
H.R. 2766	Extension of Animal Welfare Act Coverage Act
H.R. 425	Animal Welfare Protection Act of 1989
H.R. 1676	Consumer Products Safe Testing Act
H. Con. Res. 6	Alternative to the Draize Test Resolution
H. Con. Res. 65	Alternative to the Draize Test Resolution
H.R. 560	Information Dissemination and Research Accountability Act
H.R. 1389	Information Dissemination and Research Accountability Act
H.R. 2596	Silver Spring Monkeys Transfer Act
H. Con. Res. 5	School Lunches with Optional Meatless Meals Resolution
H. Con. Res. 64	School Lunch with Optional Meatless Meals Resolution
H.R. 4604	Ban on Steel Jaw Leghold Trap Act
H.R. 1354	Ban on Steel Jaw Leghold Trap Act
H.R. 2540	Wild Bird Protection Act of 1991
H.R. 2926	Dolphin Protection Consumer Information Act of 1989
H.R. 2948	Dolphin Protection Act of 1989
H.R. 261	Dolphin Protection and Fair Fishing Act of 1991
H.R. 3984	Marine Mammal Public Display Reform Act of 1990
H.R. 3132	Marine Mammal Public Display Reform Act of 1991
H.R. 578	Anti–Live Animal Lure Act of 1989
H.R. 318	Anti–Live Animal Lure Act
H.R. 1064	Greyhound Racing and Training Control Act of 1989
H.J. Res. 441	National Prevent-a-Litter Month Resolution
H. Con. Res. 4	Ban on Rapid Decompression as a Method of Euthanasia Resolution
H.J. Res. 254	Animal Rights Awareness Week Resolution
H.R. 3247	Moratorium on Patents for Genetically Altered Animals Act
H.R. 1556	Transgenic Animal Patent Reform Act
H.R. 4004	Bovine Growth Hormone Moratorium Act of 1990
H.R. 5612	Human Genome Privacy Act
H.R. 2045	Human Genome Privacy Act

Biodiversity and Endangered Species

H.R. 1268	National Biological Diversity Conservation and Environmental Research Act
H.R. 585	National Biological Diversity Conservation and Environmental Research Act
H.R. 2082	National Biological Diversity Conservation Act
H.R. 2406	Clear-cutting Restraint Act of 1989

H.R. 1969	Forest Biodiversity and Clear-cutting Prohibition Act of 1991
H. Con. Res. 89	Sanctions Against Nations Violating Driftnet Agreement
H.R. 2958	Marine Resource Protection and Driftnet Use Cessation Act of 1989
H. Con. Res. 113	Moratorium on Use of Large-Scale Driftnets Act
H.R. 3496	Sanctions Against Nations Using Driftnets Act
H.R. 2152	Non-compliance with U.N. Driftnet Moratorium Act
H. Con. Res. 214	Regional Efforts to End Driftnet Fishing in the South Pacific Resolution
H.R. 3373	Establish a Driftnet-Free Zone in the South Pacific Region Act
H. Res. 182	Ban European Community Use of Driftnets Resolution
H. Con. Res. 287	Extension of Whaling Moratorium Resolution
H. Con. Res. 105	Extend Moratorium on Commercial Killing of Whales Resolution
H. Con. Res. 21	Moratorium on the Commercial Killing of Whales Resolution
H. Con. Res. 329	Sanctions Against Lethal Whale Research Resolution
H.R. 4289	Import Sanctions Against Countries Violating International Fish or Wildlife Conservation Agreements Act
H.R. 132	International Fish and Wildlife Protection Act
H. Con. Res. 129	Listing the African Elephant as an Endangered Species Resolution
H. Res. 158	Stop Ivory Trade Resolution
H.R. 2384	Save the Elephant Act of 1989
H.R. 2172	Elephant Protection Act
H.R. 2519	African Elephant Preservation Act of 1989
H.R. 4563	African Elephant Preservation Act of 1990
H.R. 2786	Restoration of Gray Wolves to Yellowstone Park Act
H.R. 1356	Kangaroo Protection Act
H.R. 744	Kangaroo Protection Act
H.R. 2041	Manatee Protection Act of 1991
H.R. 89	Endangered Species Protection Act of 1989
H.R. 61	Endangered Species Protection Act of 1991

GREEN LEGISLATION INTRODUCED IN THE SENATE DURING THE 101ST AND 102ND CONGRESSES

Atmospheric Protection

S. 676	Atmospheric and Environmental Preservation Act
S. 1035	Stratospheric Ozone Layer Protection Act
S. 871	Ozone Layer Conservation Act of 1989
S. 872	Upper-Ozone Chemicals Act of 1989
S. 2666	Ozone Protection Funding Act of 1990
S. 491	Stratospheric Ozone and Climate Protection Act of 1989
S. 201	World Environment Policy Act of 1989
S. 201	World Environment Policy Act of 1991
S. 1052	Motor Vehicle Air Conditioner Ozone Depletion Act
S. Res. 95	Phaseout of Ozone-Destroying Substances Resolution
S. Amdt. 1329	Benefits for Terminated Coal Mine Workers Amendment

Energy and Transportation

S. Amdt. 1107	Housing Affordability Through Energy Efficiency Amendment
S. 488	Renewable Energy and Energy Efficiency Technology Competitiveness Act of 1989
S. 1059	Renewable Energy Trade Equity and Promotion Act of 1989
S. Amdt. 2032	Mortgage Financing Incentives for Energy Efficiency Amendment
S. 326	Comprehensive Energy Conservation Program Act
S. 417	Federal Energy Management Amendments Act of 1991
S. 1040	Government Energy Efficiency Act of 1991
S. 961	Federal Buildings Management Improvement and Recycling Act of 1991
S. 741	National Energy Efficiency and Development Act of 1991
S. 1224	Motor Vehicle Fuel Efficiency Act of 1989
S. 279	Motor Vehicle Fuel Efficiency Act
S. 768	National Electric Vehicle Act of 1991
S. 1522	Tax Benefit for Use of Public Transport Act
S. 26	Tax Benefit for Use of Public Transport Act
S. 129	Tax Benefit for Use of Public Transport Act

Defense

S. 2627	Weapons of Mass Destruction Control Act
S. 3190	War Prevention and Arms Transfer Control Act
S. 1421	Gore-McCain Missile and Proliferation Control Act
S. 1227	Missile Control Act of 1989
S. 195	Chemical and Biological Weapons Control Act of 1989
S. 8	Chemical and Biological Weapons Control Act
S. Amdt. 876	Sanctions Against the Use and Transfer of Chemical and Biological Weapons Amendment
S. 993	Biological Weapons Anti-Terrorism Act of 1989
S. 752	Outer Space Protection Act of 1989
S. Con. Res. 91	Harvest of Peace Resolution
S. 784	United States Peace Tax Fund Act of 1989
S. 689	United States Peace Tax Fund Act of 1991

International Development, Foreign Policy, and Global Commons

S. 369	Global Poverty Reduction Act
S. 985	Horn of Africa Recovery and Food Security Act of 1991
S. 878	World Summit for Children Implementation Act of 1991
S. 971	Micro-enterprise Development Act of 1991
S. 873	Women in Development Act of 1989
S. 1001	Women in Development Act of 1991
S. 748	Pan-American Cultural Survival Act of 1991
S.J. Res. 387	Preserve the Tropical Rain Forests and the Indigenous Tribal Culture of Sarawak Resolution
S. 1622	Environmental Sector Lending Act of 1989
S. 1124	International Economic and Environmental Improvement Act of 1991
S. 1045	National Environmental Policy on U.S. Participation in International Financing Act
S.J. Res. 206	Antarctica as a Global Ecological Commons Resolution
S. 2571	Antarctic Environmental Protection Act of 1990
S. Con. Res. 26	Commercial Mineral Development in Antarctica Prohibition Resolution
S. 686	Oil Pollution Liability and Compensation Act of 1989
S. 1179	Comprehensive Ocean Assessment and Strategy (Coast) Act of 1989
S. 984	International Pollution Deterrence Act of 1991

Agriculture

S. 970	Farm Conservation and Water Protection Act of 1989
S. 1896	Organic Foods Act of 1989
S. 2334	Sustainable Agriculture Research and Education Act of 1990
S. 2108	Organic Foods Production Act of 1990
S. 2346	Veal Calf Protection Act of 1990

S. 2227   Pesticide Export Reform Act of 1990
S. 898   Circle of Poison Prevention Act of 1991

Public Lands, Forests, and Wetlands

S. 39   Arctic Coastal Plain Wilderness Act
S. 344   Northern Yukon-Arctic International Wildlife Refuge Act
S. 370   American Heritage Trust Act of 1989
S. 433   Mining Law Reform Act of 1991
S. 1159   Tropical Forest Consumer Information and Protection Act of
                   1991
S. 1399   Urban and Community Forestry Act of 1989
S.J. Res. 5   Public Lands Policy for Protection of Predators and Scaven-
                   gers Resolution of 1989
S.J. Res. 90   Public Lands Policy to Protect Predators and Scavengers Res-
                   olution of 1991
S. 1508   Protection of Wild Free-Roaming Horses and Burros Act
S.J. Res. 149   National Free-Roaming Wild Horse and Burro Day Resolu-
                   tion

Animal Rights and Genetic Engineering

S. 2044   Dolphin Protection Consumer Information Act of 1990
S. 1259   Steel Jaw Leghold Trap Prohibition Act
S. 1219   A Bill to Enhance the Conservation of Exotic Wild Birds
S. 891   Consumer Products Safe Testing Act
S.J. Res. 229   National Prevent-a-Litter Month Resolution
S.J. Res. 152   Animal Rights Awareness Week Resolution
S. 2169   Moratorium on Patents for Genetically Altered Animals Act
S. 1291   Moratorium on Patents for Genetically Altered Animals Act

Endangered Species and Biodiversity

S. 2368   National Biological Diversity Conservation and Environmen-
                   tal Research Act
S. 58   National Biological Diversity Conservation and Environmen-
                   tal Research Act
S. 261   Sanctions Against Nations that Violate Endangered or
                   Threatened Species Agreements Act
S. 1684   Large-Scale Driftnet Fishing on the High Seas Prohibition
                   Act
S. 884   Driftnet Moratorium Enforcement Act of 1991
S. Res. 144   Ban Driftnets by European Community Resolution
S. Con. Res. 100   End Driftnet Fishing in the South Pacific Resolution
S. Con. Res. 126   Extension of Moratorium on Commercial Killing of Whales
                   Resolution
S. Con. Res. 37   Extension of Moratorium on Commercial Killing of Whales
                   Resolution

GREEN LEADERSHIP FOR THE '90s

SENATE		HOUSE	
Name	*Score*	*Name*	*Score*
Albert Gore (D-TN)	115	Barbara Boxer (D-CA)	236
John Kerry (D-MA)	95	Ted Weiss (D-NY)	219
Joseph Lieberman (D-CT)	90	Ronald Dellums (D-CA)	212
Claiborne Pell (D-RI)	90	James Scheuer (D-NY)	210
Alan Cranston (D-CA)	89	Nancy Pelosi (D-CA)	208
Timothy Wirth (D-CO)	82	Edolphus Towns (D-NY)	197
Patrick Leahy (D-VT)	80	Major Owens (D-NY)	194
Harry Reid (D-NV)	79	Cardiss Collins (D-IL)	190
Brock Adams (D-WA)	71	John Lewis (D-GA)	186
Daniel Moynihan (D-NY)	68	Peter DeFazio (D-OR)	185
		Wayne Owens (D-UT)	185

The "A" List

(Combined 101st and 102nd Congresses)

SENATE		HOUSE	
Name	*Score*	*Name*	*Score*
A. Gore (D-TN)	115	B. Boxer (D-CA)	236
J. Kerry (D-MA)	95	T. Weiss (D-NY)	219
J. Lieberman (D-CT)	90	R. Dellums (D-CA)	212
C. Pell (D-RI)	90	J. Scheuer (D-NY)	210
A. Cranston (D-CA)	89	N. Pelosi (D-CA)	208
T. Wirth (D-CO)	82	E. Towns (D-NY)	197
P. Leahy (D-VT)	80	M. Owens (D-NY)	194
H. Reid (D-NV)	79	C. Collins (D-IL)	190
B. Adams (D-WA)	71	J. Lewis (D-GA)	186
D. Moynihan (D-NY)	68	P. DeFazio (D-OR)	185
		W. Owens (D-UT)	185
		G. Ackerman (D-NY)	184
		C. Atkins (D-MA)	183
		F. Stark (D-CA)	181
		P. Kostmayer (D-PA)	180
		G. Brown (D-CA)	179
		H. Wolpe (D-MI)	175
		S. Gejdenson (D-CT)	171
		B. Dwyer (D-NJ)	159
		C. Bennett (D-FL)	157
		J. Jontz (D-IN)	157
		G. Studds (D-MA)	155
		G. Hochbrueckner (D-NY)	154
		M. Levine (D-CA)	154
		A. Beilenson (D-CA)	153
		E. Markey (D-MA)	153
		C. Shays (R-CT)	153
		B. Frank (D-MA)	151
		R. Mrazek (D-NY)	151
		T. Foglietta (D-PA)	147
		F. Pallone (D-NJ)	146
		A. Ravenel (R-SC)	146
		G. Sikorski (D-MN)	146
		J. McDermott (D-WA)	145

HOUSE

Name	Score
M. Dymally (D-CA)	144
D. Edwards (D-CA)	144
A. Jacobs (D-IN)	142
N. Mineta (D-CA)	142
J. Unsoeld (D-WA)	141

The "F" List

(Combined 101st and 102nd Congresses)

SENATE		HOUSE	
Name	*Score*	*Name*	*Score*
D. Coats (R-IN)	3	C. Ballenger (R-NC)	5
P. Gramm (R-TX)	3	R. Ray (D-GA)	5
C. Mack (R-FL)	3	E. Coleman (R-MO)	4
W. Rudman (R-NH)	3	D. Hunter (R-CA)	4
A. Simpson (R-WY)	3	W. Natcher (D-KY)	4
S. Thurmond (R-SC)	3	J. Quillen (R-TN)	4
B. Johnston (D-LA)	1	T. DeLay (R-TX)	4
D. Nickles (R-OK)	0	B. Archer (R-TX)	3
M. Wallop (R-WY)	0	W. Dickinson (R-AL)	3
		G. Gekas (R-PA)	3
		F. Grandy (R-IA)	3
		M. Hancock (R-MO)	3
		P. Roberts (R-KS)	3
		H. Rogers (R-KY)	3
		R. Schulze (R-PA)	3
		C. Stearns (R-FL)	3
		W. Thomas (R-CA)	3
		G. Vander Jagt (R-MI)	3
		J. Whitten (D-MS)	3
		J. Hammerschmidt (R-AR)	2
		J. Hansen (R-UT)	2
		G. Montgomery (D-MS)	2
		C. Stenholm (D-TX)	2
		R. Baker (R-LA)	1
		H. Callahan (R-AL)	1
		J. Lightfoot (R-IA)	1
		B. Livingston (R-LA)	1
		B. Shuster (R-PA)	1
		B. Stump (R-AZ)	1
		J. Barton (R-TX)	0
		L. Combest (R-TX)	0
		C. Holloway (R-LA)	0
		R. Marlenee (R-MT)	0
		A. McCandless (R-CA)	0
		R. Michel (R-IL)	0
		B. Paxon (R-NY)	0
		D. Sundquist (R-TN)	0

THE TEN HIGHEST RANKING GREEN DELEGATIONS

1. Rhode Island   +58.79
2. Massachusetts   +42.93
3. New York   +42.68
4. Connecticut   +38.79
5. Hawaii   +34.29
6. California   +32.22
7. New Jersey   +31.10
8. Vermont   +22.21
9. Oregon   +17.83
10. Washington   +13.84

THE TEN LOWEST RANKING GREEN DELEGATIONS

1. Wyoming   −51.13
2. Mississippi   −41.89
3. Kentucky   −37.35
4. Louisiana   −36.66
5. Alabama   −34.79
6. Iowa   −33.33
7. Arkansas   −33.13
8. Idaho   −32.96
9. Virginia   −30.88
10. Montana   −29.71

THE STATE CONTINGENT SCORING METHOD

Example: Utah

District + Name	Raw Score
House of Representatives:	
1. James V. Hansen (R)	2
2. Wayne Owens (D)	185
3. Howard C. Nielson (R)	16
3. William Orton (D)	+ 6
Total	209
Senate:	
1. Jake Garn (R)	7
2. Orrin G. Hatch (R)	+ 7
Total	14
Total House & Senate Scores	223
Total House/Senate Districts	5
Average (Total Score/5)	44.60
Deviation (House/Senate Avg. 52.46)	−7.86

The Positions of Power
(SCORE/GRADE)

Speaker of the House▲
Thomas Foley (D-WA)
Not Available

Senate Majority Leader
George Mitchell (D-ME)
36 / C

House Majority Leader
Richard Gephardt (D-MO)
22 / C

Senate Majority Whip
Wendell Ford (D-KY)
16 / C

House Majority Whip
David Bonior (D-MI)
120 / B

Senate Minority Leader
Robert Dole (R-KS)
7 / D

House Minority Leader
Robert Michel (R-IL)
0 / F

Senate Minority Whip
Alan Simpson (R-WY)
3 / F

House Minority Whip
Newt Gingrich (R-GA)
25 / C

▲ For reasons of protocol the Speaker of the House does not introduce or cosponsor legislation. As a result, Thomas Foley cannot be accurately scored.

House of Representatives Committee Leadership Record

COMMITTEE	SCORE/GRADE
1. Committee on Agriculture	
Majority (Chairman): E. de la Garza (D-TX)	7 / D
Ranking Minority: E. Coleman (R-MO)	4 / F
2. Committee on Armed Services	
Majority (Chairman): L. Aspin (D-WI)	25/ C
Ranking Minority: W. Dickinson (R-AL)	3 / F
3. Committee on Energy and Commerce	
Majority (Chairman): J. Dingell (D-MI)	21/ C
Ranking Minority: N. Lent (R-NY)	10/ D
4. Committee on Foreign Affairs	
Majority (Chairman): D. Fascell (D-FL)	83/ B
Ranking Minority: W. Broomfield (R-MI)	29/ C
5. Committee on Interior and Insular Affairs	
Majority (Chairman): G. Miller (D-CA)	117/ B
Ranking Minority: D. Young (R-AK)	26/ C
6. Committee on Merchant Marine and Fisheries	
Majority (Chairman): W. Jones (D-NC)	39/ C
Ranking Minority: R. Davis (R-MI)	13/ D
7. Committee on Public Works and Transportation	
Majority (Chairman): R. Roe (D-NJ)	126/ B
Ranking Minority: J. Hammerschmidt (R-AR)	2 / F
8. Committee on Rules	
Majority (Chairman): J. Moakley (D-MA)	9 / D
Ranking Minority: G. Solomon (R-NY)	29/ C
9. Committee on Science, Space and Technology	
Majority (Chairman): G. Brown (D-CA)	179/ A
Ranking Minority: R. Walker (R-PA)	15/ D
10. Committee on Ways and Means	
Majority (Chairman): D. Rostenkowski (D-IL)	9 / D
Ranking Minority: B. Archer (R-TX)	3 / F

SENATE COMMITTEE LEADERSHIP RECORD

COMMITTEE	SCORE/GRADE
1. Committee on Agriculture, Nutrition, and Forestry	
Majority (Chairman): P. Leahy (D-VT)	80/ A
Ranking Minority: R. Lugar (R-IN)	22/ C
2. Committee on Armed Services	
Majority (Chairman): S. Nunn (D-GA)	7 / D
Ranking Minority: J. Warner (R-VA)	16/ C
3. Committee on Commerce, Science, and Transportation	
Majority (Chairman): E. Hollings (D-SC)	23/ C
Ranking Minority: J. Danforth (R-MO)	6 / D
4. Committee on Energy and Natural Resources	
Majority (Chairman): J. B. Johnston (D-LA)	1 / F
Ranking Minority: M. Wallop (R-WY)	0 / F
5. Committee on Environment and Public Works	
Majority (Chairman): Q. Burdick (D-ND)	35/ C
Ranking Minority: J. Chafee (R-RI)	56/ B
6. Committee on Foreign Relations	
Majority (Chairman): C. Pell (D-RI)	90/ A
Ranking Minority: J. Helms (R-NC)	10/ D
7. Committee on Rules and Administration	
Majority (Chairman): W. Ford (D-KY)	16/ C
Ranking Minority: T. Stevens (R-AK)	19/ C

THE BUSH ADMINISTRATION "GREEN" REPORT CARD

BUSH AND BROKEN PROMISES

In 1989, George Bush brought with him to the White House a long list of campaign promises to protect the environment. In the four years since he took office, however, virtually none of these promises have been fulfilled.

Instead, George Bush, the self-proclaimed "environmental President" has delivered to the nation:

- the most environmentally destructive war in world history
- a shameful distinction as the world's only major power unwilling to take action to slow global warming
- a fossil-fuels-based energy strategy that will worsen already critical pollution problems nationally and globally
- a proposal to drop nearly one third of the nation's ecologically important wetlands from federal protection in order to free them for commercial development
- a scheme to open the irreplaceable Arctic National Wildlife Refuge, North America's only pristine Arctic wilderness, to full-scale oil development
- a series of back-room maneuvers to dismantle the Endangered Species Act, perhaps the most important environmental law in the world

In spite of his many environmental misdeeds, George Bush continually insists that he is an environmentalist. The fact is, George Bush works hard at maintaining his public image. He's a master at turning negative events and decisions around to make himself look good.

The Persian Gulf War is a good example. The "environmental President" was, in large part, responsible for bringing about the most environmentally destructive war the world has ever known. But it was a wise President indeed who banned news coverage of Operation Desert Storm. Bush knew that nightly broadcasts of human, animal, and environmental suffering caused by saturation bombing would provoke vehement opposition to the U.S. war effort. Bush's tactic worked. Almost wholly unaware of the horrors of the war, the nation celebrated its success. And "the environmental President" became a hero.

Bush's handling of the wetlands issue is another artful example of the politics of appearance. Before and after his election, George Bush made repeated promises to do everything in his power to ensure "no net loss of wetlands" throughout the nation. But in the summer of 1991, Bush shocked the environmental community, as well as many long-time Bush supporters, by revising the official definition of "wetlands" so that federal protection for nearly one half of these ecologically sensitive areas would be dropped to open the way for their commercial development. In response to public outrage, Bush later revised his proposal to drop 30 percent, rather than 50 percent, of the nation's wetlands from protection.

In reality, the new wetlands policy is an environmental tragedy; but during the announcement of his proposal, Bush said just the opposite. He said that his new policy marks a "significant step" toward fulfilling his campaign pledge of "no net loss of wetlands." Unfortunately, in the minds of some, the image of the man and the power of his words will likely be remembered after the wetlands are gone.

The fact is, if you read his lips, George Bush sounds like he is the "environmental President." But if you study his program and his agency directives, a far different scenario unfolds.

ENVIRONMENTAL BAIT AND SWITCH

In reviewing President Bush's environmental record, certain other patterns and conclusions emerge:

- A master of "doublespeak," Bush frequently says one thing, does quite another, and then announces to the public that he's done something terrific, or fulfilled a campaign pledge. At other times, he makes strong environmental statements loudly for all to hear, but then retreats, favoring window dressing and symbolic gestures over tough decisions. Some Bush-observers have referred to this dance as the "bait-and-switch approach" to environmental policy.

- President Bush is not a leader; he's a "people pleaser." When it comes to the environment, Bush has a strong tendency to try and placate opposing interests, straddle issues, and buy time. The environment almost always gets bargained or negotiated away.

- President Bush prefers study to action—particularly when strong and courageous leadership is called for. Since taking office, Bush has commissioned studies on all the major issues: global warming, agriculture, mass transportation, competitiveness, science, technology—you name it. He even commissioned a study on his "1000 Points of Light" proposal. Ironically, many of the studies initiated by Bush have yielded recommended courses of action that are at odds with White House politics. These recommendations have been ignored or diluted.

- President Bush has relied on the so-called "terrible troika": former White House Chief of Staff John Sununu, Budget Director Richard Darman, and Vice President Danforth Quayle, when setting environmental policy. The personal biases of these three advisors regularly have determined policy on environmental matters of global importance. While Bush pretends to care for the environment, Sununu and Darman, in particular, have been openly hostile toward even the mention of the word.

- President Bush's administration, like the Reagan administration before it, routinely guts legislation it doesn't like. Contrary to what millions of people think, passing legislation is only the first step in carrying out a law. Legislation passed by Congress and signed by the President must then pass through a veritable maze of administrative processes and procedures and is subject to political manipulation at every stop along the way. A hostile Administration can easily delay for years the writing of regulations, or force federal agencies to write weak regulations and enforcement provisions. In this way the Bush administration has delayed and watered down several vital pieces of legislation carefully designed by Congress to protect human and environmental health.

- President Bush created the Council on Competitiveness, a high-level advisory panel which ostensibly works to improve U.S. industry's competitive edge in the world market, but which actually works almost exclusively to help industry bypass or tamper with laws it doesn't like. The council is the direct successor of the Reagan-era Task Force on Regulatory Relief, which was chaired by then-Vice President George Bush. Now headed by Vice President Quayle, the council has tinkered with, and dramatically altered, scores of regulations unpopular with industry, including regulations written by the Environmental Protection Agency to implement the new Clean Air Act, which Bush signed into law with so much fanfare in 1990. Quayle's council has also had a devastating effect on wetlands policy and has interfered with the regulatory process in such areas as biotechnology, the protection of workers from toxic substances, animal protection, recycling, and automobile efficiency standards, among others. Called a "shadow government" by some, the council allows Bush to appear pro-environment while it guts environmental laws behind-the-scenes.

- President Bush has also used the Office of Management and Budget

(OMB), headed by Richard Darman, to do much of his behind-the-scenes dirty work. OMB routinely demands changes in rules proposed by regulatory agencies, ostensibly to reduce cost or minimize the burden on private industry.

VOTING GREEN

We now present President Bush's environmental report card through November 1991, organized by subject area.

Global Warming

The Rhetoric

"Those who think we are powerless to do anything about the 'greenhouse effect' are forgetting about the 'White House effect.' As President, I intend to do something about it.

"In my first year of office, I will convene a global conference on the environment at the White House. It will include the Soviets, the Chinese, the developing world as well as the developed. All nations will be welcome. . . . The agenda will be clear. We will talk about global warming. . . . And we will act."

—Candidate Bush, Erie Metropark, Michigan,
August 31, 1988

The Reality

George Bush promised to lead the world in taking action to stop global warming, but that turned out to be just a lot of hot air. The Bush administration's position on global warming has been, until quite recently, that the phenomenon does not exist. Campaign promises notwithstanding, Bush's National Energy Strategy clearly shows that the Bush administration has no intention of taking any substantial steps toward slowing or preventing the greenhouse effect. The United States is the world's largest contributor of greenhouse gases. Yet, we now stand alone among nations in denial and defiance of the impending, possibly catastrophic, warming of the earth.

- The first significant action the Bush White House took on global warming was to alter the text of testimony on the dangers of global warming scheduled to be delivered to Congress by Dr. James E. Hansen, director of the National Aeronautics and Space Administration's (NASA) Goddard Institute for Space Studies. Dr. Hansen disavowed the testimony, which he said was changed against his will by the Office of Management and Budget (OMB). Hansen had planned to tell a Senate subcommittee that

enough is known about the dangers of global warming to warrant immediate action to counteract it. The altered text considerably softened the
warning.

Questioned later by reporters about the watered-down testimony,
White House Press Secretary Marlin Fitzwater stated: "The Administration stands behind it." Fitzwater defended the OMB's action and described it as a routine effort to see that prepared testimony conforms to
Administration policy.

- Bush's first year in office ended without his hosting the global environmental conference he had promised during his campaign. Instead, the
  United States sent a delegation to a United Nations–sponsored global
  warming conference in Geneva in May 1989. The Americans were instructed by then-White House Chief of Staff John Sununu—over EPA
  head William Reilly's objections—to support only further study and not
  to endorse a treaty to limit greenhouse gases. A similar scenario unfolded
  at a global warming conference in the Netherlands in November 1989.

- EPA head Reilly, joined by two Cabinet members and the President's
  science advisor, urged Bush to stress the dangers of global warming in a
  February 1990 speech to the U.N.'s Intergovernmental Panel on Climate
  Change. Sununu, however, deleted key points in the speech and empha-
  sized only a need for more research. When questioned by the press later,
  Sununu replied that he was merely stopping a move by "faceless bureaucrats to try to create a policy in this country that cuts off our use of coal,
  oil, and natural gas."

- Less than a week before Earth Day 1990, Bush finally hosted a two-day
  international meeting on global warming in Washington but angered
  environmental ministers and officials from eighteen countries and the European Community when he sidestepped the issue, declining even to utter
  the words "global warming" or "greenhouse effect." While representatives
  of several nations, including those from Germany, the Netherlands, and
  France had come prepared to cut carbon dioxide emissions in their countries by as much as 25 percent in fifteen years, Bush agreed only to more
  research.

  The Administration's strategy of avoidance was based on "Talking
  Points," a document prepared for the U.S. delegation and leaked to the
  press at the conclusion of the conference. Under the heading, "Debates to
  Avoid," the document advised delegates that it is "not beneficial to discuss whether there is or is not warming, or how much or how little
  warming. In the eyes of the public we will lose this debate. A better
  approach is to raise the many uncertainties that need to be better understood on this issue."

  China, a major producer of greenhouse gases, was not invited to Bush's
  conference, despite Bush's campaign promise to include that country.

BY PAUL FELL © 1990, JOURNAL-STAR PRINTING CO..

- At the Economic Summit of Industrialized Nations, in Houston in July 1990, Bush again made it clear that he wants no part of an international timetable to limit CO_2 emissions. Although all of the countries represented at the summit —including Japan and Britain—had by now pledged to stabilize greenhouse gas emissions by the first part of the next century, Bush blocked West German Chancellor Helmut Kohl's proposal to set limits on those emissions. (Bush later referred to Kohl as "a bulldog when it comes to the environment.")

  Dismayed European officials said that the first sign of trouble came when President Bush left EPA administrator William Reilly at home and brought then-White House Chief of Staff John Sununu to the summit meeting instead. Some 150 environmental groups from across the globe gathered in Houston to monitor events and to score the participants' environmental performance. The United States' grade?—F.

> **"They don't want to think about the tough deci-sions they would have to make if they admitted (global warming) is real."**
>
> **—Sen. Albert Gore, Jr. (D-TN)**

- The United States was singled out as "the great polluter" by some eighty environmental ministers at the second World Climate Conference sponsored by the U.N. in Geneva in November 1990. While more than twenty nations, including Germany, Japan, and other industrial countries had by now an-nounced that they could stabilize or cut back on carbon dioxide emissions without harming their economies, the U.S. delegation, under White House orders, continued to dig in its heels.

Unimpressed by a strongly worded consensus document by more than 700 scientists urging all nations to take immediate and significant steps to curb global warming, the U.S. delegation proceeded to dilute the conference declaration. The watered-down statement welcomed the European commitments, but omitted any reference to the responsibilities of other countries.

• The Bush administration finally publicly conceded that global warming is a problem and announced its intention to stabilize greenhouse gases at a February 1991 U.N.-sponsored climate-change conference of 130 nations in Virginia. The meeting was convened to set specific goals and a timetable for reductions in greenhouse gases with the hope of signing of a treaty to that effect by June 1992. The Bush announcement, however, was nothing but a public relations ploy. As everyone at the conference understood, the U.S. pledge could be fulfilled simply by keeping a prior commitment, made in mid 1990, to reduce the production of ozone-destroying chloroflurocarbons (CFCs). (See "Ozone Layer," pp. 360–61.)

> **"The old White House position was, 'This isn't a problem and we're not going to do anything about it. . . .' The new position is, 'Yes, this is a problem, but we're still not going to do anything about it.'"**
> **—Dr. Michael Oppenheimer, Atmospheric Physicist, Environmental Defense Fund**

While most of the industrial countries have strongly favored the adoption of concrete targets and timetables for stabilizing carbon dioxide, the Bush administration has refused to budge—despite a National Academy of Sciences report released in April 1991 that concludes: "The United States could reduce its greenhouse gas emissions by between 10 and 40 percent of the 1990 levels at a very low cost." In fact, under Bush's National Energy Strategy, CO_2 production will significantly increase. (See "Energy," pp. 365–66.)

Grade: F

Ozone Layer

The Rhetoric

"I am an environmentalist, always have been, always will be."
                                        —Candidate Bush, New Jersey rally,
                                        September 2, 1988

The Reality

While President Bush certainly has not led the world in protecting the ozone layer from further deterioration, his Administration has, reluctantly, followed the lead of other countries toward this goal.

- Following Europe's lead, the Bush administration approved a 1990 amendment to the Montreal Protocol of 1987 that calls for a 100 percent phaseout of chlorofluorocarbons (CFCs) and most other ozone-depleting chemicals by 2000. The international treaty had originally committed the United States and other countries to reduce the use and manufacture of CFCs by only 50 percent by 1999.

  In light of new information that ozone depletion is more serious than previously thought, many environmentalists have called for an immediate ban on CFCs. E. I. du Pont de Nemours and Co., the world's largest manufacturer of CFCs, has voluntarily agreed to stop producing these chemicals by 1997.

- Bush instructed U.S. delegates to a U.N.-sponsored international conference on ozone depletion in Geneva, in May 1990, to oppose a globally supported fund to help developing nations reduce their use of CFCs. The fund was proposed to help India and China switch to CFC substitutes and to encourage them to join the Montreal Protocol. The U.S. funding contribution, approved overwhelmingly by the Senate, was only $25 million over a three-year period—a bargain considering that the U.S. Treasury is reaping windfall profit taxes of $5 billion from the CFC industry as it phases down. EPA head Reilly and top State Department officials recommended that the United States support the fund. Sununu and Darman opposed it. Only after intense pressure from European allies, including then-Prime Minister Margaret Thatcher of Britain, did Bush relent and agree to contribute to the fund.

Grade: B

Clean Air

The Rhetoric

"Every American expects and deserves to breathe clean air, and as President, it is my mission to guarantee it—for this generation and generations to come."
> —White House bill overview, East Room of the White House, June 12, 1989

The Reality

In his first year in office, George Bush provided the impetus that pushed Congress to overhaul the outdated and ineffective Clean Air Act of 1970, ending more than a decade of political stalemate. New clean air legislation was signed into law on November 15, 1990 and was the first update of air pollution laws since 1977. Good public relations accompanied the introduction of the legislation and its signing. But, in reality, the Bush administration submitted a disappointing clean air bill to Congress. (As introduced, the Bush bill would have weakened the existing clean air law; and in most respects was weaker than the Reagan administration's clean air proposal.) During the arduous sixteen-month negotiation that followed, the Administration consistently tried to placate industry by opposing and weakening stronger antipollution provisions proposed by members of Congress.

The new clean air law is weak compromise legislation. White House operatives are now in the process of running interference with the regulatory process and gutting this already inadequate law.

- Bush's proposal to fight urban smog was heavily criticized by environmentalists. In the bill he presented to Congress, Bush proposed, among other provisions, that:

    —cities with the worst air pollution be granted another twenty years to meet clean air standards.

    —a new system of averaging auto pollution for various fleets of cars, rather than reducing emissions from individual vehicles, be developed. Under such a system, automakers would be allowed to make some highly polluting car models if emissions from other car models they produce fell below the maximum emission levels allowed by law. Under this scheme "up-to-par" auto makers could sell "pollution rights" to other car manu-

HERBLOCK'S CARTOON APR 16 1989

"WHO'S BEEN REGULATING WHO?"

© 1989 BY HERBLOCK IN THE WASHINGTON POST.

facturers whose cars were not meeting emissions standards. Instead of reducing pollution levels all around, environmentalists have demonstrated that such a system could actually maintain air pollution at current levels or increase it.

—auto emissions be controlled through the use of so-called "clean fuels" such as methanol which is made from coal or natural gas. Although this was one of Bush's more acceptable proposals, he later withdrew his support for it.

- Bush's proposals to combat airborne toxic pollutants—industrial emissions that cause cancer, other illness, and birth defects—were also inadequate. He proposed that:

  —toxic polluters be required to install in their plants "maximum achievable control technology" to curb toxic pollution, but, at the same time, be granted exemptions for claims of financial hardship.

  —emission controls be set on only half of 187 toxic air pollutants that have so far been identified. Bush's proposal did not set a numerical standard by which unhealthful levels of toxic pollutants could be measured, and allowed questions of health to be moderated by cost considerations.

  —clean-up deadlines for toxic pollutants be extended as long as twenty-five years.

- Although far from perfect, Bush's proposals to combat acid rain were the strongest part of his clean air bill. Bush proposed that:

  —sulfur dioxide emissions, the chief cause of acid rain, be reduced by 10 million tons and that a cap be placed on total annual emissions produced after the year 2000.

  —industry be permitted to buy and sell permits to pollute as an incentive to get industry to reduce pollution. Some environmentalists counter, however, that the imposition of mandatory antipollution standards on industry, a timetable for meeting antipollution goals, and penalties for failing to meet air quality standards is the quickest and most efficient way to cleaner air.

- Initially, the Senate passed a fairly strong clean air bill. The Bush administration, however, threatened to influence Republican Senators to filibuster if weakening amendments were not made.

  During Senate and House debates on their respective clean air bills, and later during the conference process, the Administration opposed several strong proposals and amendments. For example, Bush said he would veto any bill that contained an assistance program for workers, especially miners, who would lose their jobs as a result of antipollution controls. (Bush later reversed his position after it became clear that Congress would not adopt clean air legislation without providing for displaced workers.) Bush opposed attempts by Democrats to provide more stringent antismog provisions such as mandatory reductions in the emissions of individual motor vehicles. The Administration supported amendments by Republicans to undercut regulation and to limit citizens' rights to enforce antipollution laws.

- Although the legislation disappointed environmentalists, Congress did pass a stronger antipollution bill than had been proposed by the President, and the President signed it into law.

- The ink was hardly dry, however, before the Bush administration began to dismantle the new law behind the scenes. Over EPA's objections, the White

House inserted a giant loophole into the air pollution permit system, the centerpiece of the antipollution law. The loophole allows industry to increase the amount of pollutants released into the air if state officials fail to veto such an increase within seven days of receipt of notice. Enactment of such a regulation would effectively gut much of the legislation, rendering major portions of the new law virtually unenforceable.

> **"The EPA often produces carefully considered regulatory proposals based on an extensive record and lengthy studies only to see them dismissed out of hand by White House officials eager to protect industry from the cost of regulations."**
> **—Rep. Henry Waxman (D-CA)**

- By mid 1991, Vice President Quayle, as chairman of the President's Council on Competitiveness, had already scrutinized more than 100 key regulations drawn up by the EPA to implement and enforce the new Clean Air Act. At the council's bidding, many of the EPA's regulations were eliminated or dramatically changed to reflect industry concerns. Among them were EPA proposals that would require the recycling of 25 percent of the waste that is usually burned in municipal incinerators and a ban on the burning of toxic lead batteries.

  Rep. Henry Waxman (D-CA), who led the fight for a new clean air bill in the House, uncovered internal memoranda from Quayle's office and the EPA which, Waxman said, is "unmistakable evidence that White House officials, spearheaded by Vice President Dan Quayle . . . are working with industry to undermine implementation of the new clean air law." Waxman said some of the regulatory changes made by Quayle's office violate both the letter and spirit of the clean air law.

  "The ramifications of these rules are devastating," Waxman said in a September 1991 interview with *The New York Times.* "The problem isn't just that they're inconsistent with the law. The whole process is outrageous and flagrantly illegal—to allow polluters, [who] opposed the law, to go through the back door and have the law rewritten to favor their point of view."

  A Quayle aide said that the Vice President had reviewed the EPA proposals with a view toward "making sure that the deregulation gains of the Reagan years are not canceled out by creeping reregulation generated from government bureaucracies." This way of thinking has alarmed environmentalists because the 700-plus-page law is nothing if not a regulatory act.

Grade: D

Energy

The Rhetoric

"I'll put incentives back into the domestic energy industry, for I know from personal experience there is no security for the United States in further dependence on foreign oil."

> —Candidate Bush, accepting the Republican
> presidential nomination in New Orleans,
> August 18, 1988

"Drilling should not take place in those environmentally sensitive areas where the risk of damage is too great."

> —Candidate Bush, San Diego, October 14, 1988

The Reality

Bush's National Energy Strategy (NES), announced on February 20, 1991, shocked not only the Green community but longtime Bush supporters as well. The strategy centers around continued reliance on fossil fuels—an energy package only a former Texas oil man like Bush could love. Sen. Albert Gore (D-TN) has called Bush's energy plan "breathtakingly dumb"; the Sierra Club has called it "an all-out attack on the environment."

An earlier draft energy plan, developed by the Department of Energy (DOE) and pushed by Energy Secretary James Watkins, had originally included several conservation, energy efficiency, and renewable energy options. Two years in the making, the DOE's plan was summarily dismissed by John Sununu, Richard Darman, and Michael Boskin, chairman of the President's Council of Economic Advisors.

Bush's National Energy Strategy includes:

- an emphasis on increased use of fossil fuels and continued dependence on oil, both foreign and domestic.

- the opening of the Arctic National Wildlife Refuge, the only pristine Arctic wilderness left in North America, to full-scale oil and gas drilling. (Bush has said that he will veto any national energy plan that does not include drilling in the refuge.)

- the opening of thousands of miles of the outer continental shelf along the East Coast, the Florida Panhandle, large tracts off Southern California, and vast areas off Alaska, to oil and gas exploration.

- deregulation of the oil and gas industries.

- increased reliance on nuclear power by doubling the number of nuclear reactors to about 150 by 2030, and by extending the life of currently operating plants to sixty years from their current forty—all the while ignoring overwhelming safety, cost, waste, and proliferation problems.

- a speeding up of nuclear-plant licensing by reducing public participation in deciding where nuclear reactors and nuclear waste dumps will be located.

- loopholes that will lower automobile fuel efficiency standards.

- dramatic budget cuts for low-income home energy efficiency programs.

Bush's energy plan does *not* include:

- substantial improvements in all-around energy efficiency.

- major energy conservation programs or incentives.

- significant increases in funding for research and development of alternative renewable energy.

- new tax incentives to reduce fossil fuel use, such as a new gasoline or gas-guzzler tax or a carbon tax.

- new tax credits for renewable energy.

Grade: F

Transportation

The Rhetoric

"I want to be the environmental President."

—Candidate Bush, on the campaign trail, 1988

The Reality

Bush's transportation plan for the nation, the Surface Transportation Assistance Act of 1991, includes:

- an emphasis on increased automobile usage and oil consumption.

- a plan to spend billions on a new federal highway system rather than mass transit.

- a limit on the use of highway funds for mass transit, but unlimited use of transit funds for highways.

- the elimination of operating assistance to 147 mass transit systems in regions with populations of more than one million.

- a plan to discourage the development of new mass transit systems.

Bush's transportation plan does *not* include:

- adequate funding for transportation changes needed by many cities to fulfill Clean Air Act requirements.

- major programs to develop energy-efficient, cost-effective mass transportation or auto use, including renewable-energy-powered transit.

- higher automobile fuel efficiency standards. (The Bush administration joined the auto industry in 1990 to block action by Congress to improve automobile fuel efficiency—a move that would have saved more oil than the United States imports from the Middle East.)

- new tax incentives to reduce dependence on automobiles and oil such as a new gasoline or gas-guzzler tax or a carbon tax.

Grade: F

Defense

The Rhetoric

"We have before us the opportunity to forge for ourselves and for future generations a new world order, a world where the rule of law, not the law of the jungle, governs the conduct of nations."

> —President Bush, in a broadcast from the Oval Office announcing the start of the Persian Gulf War, January 16, 1991

The Reality

George Bush didn't waste any time establishing his "new world order"—the same old way of thinking that has pushed the earth and its inhabitants to the brink of environmental, economic, and social disaster. It wasn't until the disintegration of the Soviet Union and the overthrow of communism in Eastern Europe that Bush agreed to follow the world in a new direction.

New World Order #1

In his first year of office, President Bush ordered the invasion of Panama by 24,000 U.S. troops to capture one man, Panama's President, General Manuel Noriega, on drug charges.

- The invasion, Operation Just Cause, was a gross violation of the U.N. Charter and the U.S. Constitution.

- Twenty-six Americans were killed and more than 300 wounded. Human rights organizations in both countries believe that between 1,000 and 4,000 Panamanian civilians were killed by U.S. forces, in contrast to the official U.S. estimate of 250.

- Noriega was captured, but, by the end of 1991, was still sitting in a U.S. jail planning his legal defense. Meanwhile, the new Panamanian President was sworn in at a U.S. military base and survived a coup attempt only with U.S. assistance.

- The U.S. military still patrols Panama's streets, drug trafficking continues, and the country's economy is in a shambles—with Bush's promise of a billion-dollar aid package still just a promise.

New World Order #2

George Bush said that the Persian Gulf War would not be another Vietnam. But in at least one respect the two wars were similar. Not since U.S. forces sprayed tons of toxic herbicides over Vietnam with disastrous long-term effects on forests, crops, and human and animal health, has war brought such environmental devastation.

In 1990, for the first time in history, major U.S. environmental groups organized to oppose war on the grounds that it could result in catastrophic environmental devastation—not only for the Middle East, but for the world. While Saddam Hussein is to blame for provoking the Persian Gulf War, the "environmental President" bears much of the responsibility for what may be the most environmentally destructive conflict in the history of warfare.

- Bush, eager to go to war, dismissed the advice of several of his advisors, including the Chairman of the Joint Chiefs of Staff, General Colin Powell, to give more time for economic sanctions against Iraq to work.

- Bush clamped down hard on press coverage, and conducted his war in secret. To this day, most Americans are not aware of the full human and environmental devastation caused by the war.

- Months before the war began, the Department of Defense commissioned a secret study on the environmental risks of a war with Iraq. The study reportedly confirmed the dangers of oil well fires and other possibly cataclysmic environmental effects. According to *Scientific American,* the results of the study were suppressed in order to allow Operation Desert Storm to proceed.

- The United States, and all combatants in the Persian Gulf, ignored the U.N. Convention on the Prohibition of Military or Any Other Hostile Use of Environmental Modification Techniques, which was adopted in 1978 and ratified by the United States in 1981.

- The United States ignored a U.N. prohibition against bombing nuclear facilities. While, on November 29, 1990, the U.N. Security Council adopted Resolution 678 which authorized the allies to "use all necessary means" to remove Iraq from Kuwait, the U.N. General Assembly also passed another resolution, on December 4, 1990, which reaffirmed a long-standing ban against military attacks on nuclear facilities. In the 14-to-1 vote to support the resolution, the United States cast the sole dissenting vote; both Israel and Kuwait supported the ban.

  On January 17, 1991, the United States proceeded to bomb Iraqi nuclear facilities, thereby potentially exposing large populations to radio-active materials and poisonous substances.

- The United States and its allies also bombed what are believed to have been storage areas for components of chemical and biological weapons, thus potentially spreading deadly chemicals and disease-causing organisms throughout the region.

- White House reports created the impression that only "smart bombs" were used to make "surgical strikes" on military targets only. On the contrary, most of the weapons used during the war were highly destructive conventional weapons which hit many civilian areas.

  Air Force Chief of Staff General Merrill McPeak has estimated that some 88,550 tons of bombs were dropped on Iraq, or about 59,000 tons per month. (In comparison, 22,000 tons of bombs per month were dropped during the Korean War, and 34,000 tons per month on Vietnam.) Of the 88,500 tons of bombs dropped, only 7.4 percent were "smart" or precision-guided.

- At the war's end, the environment of the Persian Gulf and surrounding region emerged as a principal casualty. Hundreds of oil wells were set afire (70 percent by Iraq, 30 percent by U.S. and allied bombing), spewing tons of toxic black smoke into the atmosphere. The fires were finally extinguished by the end of 1991. Conservative estimates are that the amount of oil burned is as much as twice Kuwait's prewar oil production—some 2.5 to 3 million barrels a day. Atmospheric pollution on such a scale has never occurred before and will undoubtedly have serious health effects on humans, animals, and the entire ecology of the region. Smoke thick with sulfur dioxide and carcinogenic chemicals is causing acid rain and may alter climate patterns and imperil crops in nearby areas of southern Asia.

  Several huge oil spills, including some caused by U.S. forces, have literally choked the Gulf with at least 3.3 million barrels of oil—a spill ten times the size of the 1989 Exxon Valdez spill in Alaska. The oil continues to kill millions of birds and other wildlife as they migrate through the region, destroy marine ecology and the food chain in the Gulf, as well as destroy fisheries and sources of water important for human survival.

BY DANA SUMMERS © 1990, WASHINGTON POST WRITERS GROUP. REPRINTED WITH PERMISSION.

- The human toll of the war has remained largely unpublicized. Of the more than 500,000 U.S. troops involved in Operation Desert Storm, 148 were killed, 35 of these by friendly fire. The true number of Iraqi dead will probably never be known; however, private analysts in the United States estimate that as many as 150,000 Iraqi soldiers were killed during the 43-day war (an average of 3,500 per day). Recent U.S. news reports have revealed that many of them were mercilessly destroyed with air delivery of burning napalm and other fuel-air explosives. *The New York Times* reported that U.S. forces buried alive scores of Iraqi soldiers.

  An unknown number of Iraqi civilians were killed or wounded during the fighting. Moreover, a U.N. report described "near apocalyptic damage" to Iraqi infrastructure that has relegated the country to a "preindustrial age." The U.N. reported that more than 9,000 homes had been destroyed leaving more than 72,000 homeless. Scores of thousands of Iraqi civilians, especially children, are expected to die from unsanitary conditions and lack of adequate food and medical care.

- The estimated financial cost of the war against Iraq ranges from $45 billion to $70 billion. Saddam Hussein remains in power in Iraq.

New World Order #3

The Bush administration is responsible for at least three positive developments in the area of defense—steps that will move the world closer to human and environmental safety. This is the "new world order" that many Americans would like to pursue.

- In late 1990, before Operation Desert Storm, the State Department announced that it was developing regulations to block any U.S. exports that could be used by other nations in clandestine nuclear, missile, or chemical and biological warfare development programs. The change of policy came with the realization that Iraq would use weapons purchased from the United States against U.S. forces. Between 1986 and 1990, the United States sold to Iraq $1.5 billion' worth of technology and products that could be used to develop advanced weapons systems.

- In May of 1991, in the aftermath of the Persian Gulf War, George Bush called for a global ban on chemical weapons by the end of 1992, and pledged to destroy all U.S. chemical weapon stockpiles within ten years of the implementation of a global treaty. Bush also forswore America's right to use chemical weapons even if under chemical attack. Bush had previously stated that the United States would maintain 500 tons of its chemical stocks, about 2 percent of the total.

  At their Washington summit in 1990, Bush and then-Soviet President Mikhail Gorbachev agreed to a draft proposal to reduce chemical weapons inventories. Defense Secretary Richard Cheney subsequently ordered the Army to shut down all chemical weapons production facilities and canceled tests for a new chemical bomb.

- In September 1991, Bush made what may turn out to be the most important decision of his career by ordering a major reduction in U.S. strategic and tactical nuclear arms. Following on the heels of massive change in the Soviet Union and Eastern Europe, President Bush challenged the Soviets to join in what he called a "historic opportunity" to reduce nuclear arsenals and begin to change the Cold War policies that have characterized American-Soviet relations for nearly five decades.

  On September 27, 1991, Bush announced that he had ordered the withdrawal of all ground-based, short-range nuclear weapons worldwide, and the removal of all nuclear-tipped cruise missiles and bombs from U.S. Navy submarines and ships. Bush removed all U.S. strategic bombers from alert status and ordered their bombs to be placed in storage. He lifted from alert status all long-range Minuteman II missiles that had been scheduled for deactivization over a seven-year period under the new Strategic Arms Reduction Treaty, and said he would accelerate their elimination after the treaty was ratified. Bush also voiced a plan to negotiate new agreements with the Soviets to eliminate all missiles carrying multiple warheads.

Bush stressed, however, that his offers would be fulfilled only if the Soviets also agreed to reduce their nuclear arsenal. The President's announcement came at a time when some members of Congress and Western European allies were clamoring for arms reductions in the wake of political changes in the East.

Some observers received Bush's announcement with optimistic caution. Bush's arms reduction offer calls for the withdrawal or destruction of only the least effective, least useful weapons in the U.S. nuclear stockpile, and will not affect development of the Strategic Defense Initiative, the B-2 strategic bomber now in production, and other major weapons systems.

Unfortunately, Bush said that he would not divert military funds to domestic priorities and that there would be "no budget windfall for domestic programs." The badly needed peace dividend—for the environment, social programs, and deficit reduction—is nowhere in sight, at least for now.

Grade: C

Oceans

The Rhetoric

"We need a President who is finally going to clean up that ocean. I am that man."

—Candidate Bush, campaigning in the
Northeast, September 2, 1988

"Our ultimate goal must be the complete restoration of the ecology and the economy of Prince William Sound, including all of its fish, marine mammals, birds, and other wildlife. . . . The excellent safety record that was recorded prior to this incident must be restored and maintained into the future."

—President Bush, April 7, 1989

The Reality

- Delay, neglect, and timidity characterize Bush's response to the tragic *Exxon Valdez* oil spill in Alaska in 1989. Rather than take a leadership role in response to the crisis, Bush waited two weeks after the spill to commit federal resources to the cleanup. The Administration then allowed Exxon to abandon cleanup efforts for the winter in mid September. (Cold weather, however, did not prevent Exxon from continuing to pump and ship Alaskan oil.) The proposed settlement the Administration finally negotiated with Exxon was so weak that a federal judge threw it out.

Doonesbury

G.B. TRUDEAU

- In the wake of the *Exxon Valdez* oil spill disaster, the Bush administration sided with the oil industry on several key points during House consideration of oil spill liability legislation. Bush opposed provisions that would preserve stronger state oil spill laws, require double hulls on oil tankers, and require oil spillers to assume unlimited liability in cases of negligence. Fortunately, all three provisions passed over Bush's objections, although, the third was later reversed on a technicality.

Grade: D

Antarctica

The Rhetoric

"It's unjust to allow the natural splendor bestowed upon us to be compromised."

—Remarks by President Bush at a Ducks Unlimited Symposium, June 8, 1989

The Reality

On October 4, 1991, the United States finally signed an international agreement to ban mineral and oil exploration in Antarctica for the next fifty years. But getting to this point wasn't easy.

In 1990, the President promised Congress that he would push for a long-term worldwide ban on commercial activity in Antarctica, the largest remaining wilderness in the world, and he signed congressional legislation to that effect.

In 1991, after months of painful negotiation, the twenty-six voting-member nations to the 30-year-old Antarctica Treaty, including the United States, agreed to extend protections to the continent another fifty years with the proviso that the protections could be lifted after that time only if all voting members concurred. However, when representatives from the twenty-six nations assembled in Madrid for a signing ceremony on June 23, 1991—the thirtieth anniversary of the Antarctica Treaty—the U.S. delegation shocked everyone by submitting a last-minute counterproposal: at the end of fifty years, any nation that wished to amend the ban could unilaterally withdraw from the agreement if the other nations failed to ratify the amendment within three years.

"[Bush and his administration] are always a last-minute holdout and an obstacle to progress. They grudgingly accept the bare minimum, and always at

the last minute. They haven't provided any genuine leadership for the world community."
—Sen. Albert Gore, Jr. (D-TN)

Apparently, Bush had been persuaded by his advisors that signing the protocol would set a dangerous precedent that could logically be extended to include other ecologically sensitive areas such as the Arctic National Wildlife Refuge which is now threatened by oil development.

Embarrassed by his months of vacillation on the issue, Bush finally agreed to join the treaty if a clause was inserted to the effect that, after fifty years, the treaty can be revised by a two-thirds majority vote.

Grade: B

Public Lands

The Rhetoric

"Nineteen eighty-eight is the year the earth spoke back. Our land, water, and soil support a remarkable range of human activities; but they can only take so much. We must remember to treat them not as a given, but as a gift."
—Candidate Bush, Erie Metropark, Michigan,
August 31, 1988

The Reality

Nowhere does George Bush demonstrate his ideological bent more than in his stance on how our public lands should be managed. Time and time again, Bush has supported programs designed to commercially exploit these lands to the detriment of the environment, wildlife, and the vast majority of Americans who want to preserve and harmlessly enjoy their natural heritage.

- Bush vigorously opposes wilderness designation for the coastal plain of the Arctic National Wildlife Refuge, America's only pristine Arctic wilderness. Indeed, Bush has stated that he will veto any energy bill that does not include oil and gas development there.

- The Bush administration supports what amounts to subsidies for ranchers who use Western public lands for grazing—even in the face of undeniable evidence that subsidization encourages overgrazing which is seriously degrading public lands. The Administration opposes legislation currently before Congress that would increase grazing fees to reflect the market value of the forage. Such an increase would reduce the amount of livestock on public lands and thus improve the condition of the range, as well as return millions of dollars to the Treasury each year.

> ## "We should thank President Bush for saying he is an environmentalist and thank him again when he becomes one."
> —David Brower, President, Earth Island Institute

- The Bush administration opposes the repeal or substantial rewrite of the General Mining Law of 1872, which, after 120 years, still allows the sale of public land for between $2.50 and $5 per acre to private developers. In addition, the law also does not impose any environmental restrictions upon mining operations.

- As an example of the attitude toward public lands that reigns in the Bush administration, the head of the U.S. Bureau of Mines, T. S. Ary, recently called environmentalists "a bunch of nuts" and said that he does not believe in endangered species. "There is this 'Mine-Free by '93 Syndrome,' " Ary told a Denver assembly of miners, loggers, ranchers, farmers, and other advocates of developing public land. "Watch your backside. . . . If they find a way to roll us and repeal that mining law, you people are duck soup," he said.

Grade: F

Wetlands

The Rhetoric

"It is time to stand the history of wetlands destruction on its head."
—Candidate Bush to Ducks Unlimited, 1988

"We have been losing wetlands at a rate of almost a half-million acres per year. . . . Much of the loss comes from inevitable pressure for development, and many of our wetlands are on private property. But we must act to conserve wetlands. Our national goal should be no net loss of wetlands. We can't afford to lose the half of America's wetlands that still remains."
—Candidate Bush, Erie Metropark, Michigan, August 31, 1988

"My position on wetlands is straightforward. All existing wetlands, no matter how small, should be preserved."
—President Bush to *Sports Afield* magazine, 1989

BY JEFF DANZIGER IN THE CHRISTIAN SCIENCE MONITOR © 1990, TCSPS.

The Reality

It seems as though George Bush has made more promises regarding wetlands protection than any other area of environmental concern. A look at the record, however, shows that Bush has also broken more promises concerning wetlands than any other.

- In 1989, Bush signed the North America Wetlands Conservation Act (which authorized $25 million for restoration and acquisition of wetlands) and the Coastal Wetlands Restoration and Protection Act of 1990. But, in February 1990, Bush's White House altered an agreement between the EPA and the Army Corps of Engineers in order to permit exceptions to formerly strict wetlands policies. Since 1977, the Clean Water Act has prohibited the destruction or development of wetlands without obtaining a permit from the Army Corps. The new policy permits exceptions to requirements that protect wetlands from development, or that require the replacement of any wetlands that are destroyed. The new policy also gives the EPA and the Army Corps discretion to waive wetlands protections.
  The changes, which affected 20 percent of the nation's wetlands, were

made at the insistence of then-White House Chief of Staff John Sununu over the objections of EPA head William Reilly, after Alaskan developers, oil companies, and others complained that wetlands policies were too strict.

- As a result of the February decision, the Army Corps of Engineers, in September 1990, decided to remove 60 million acres of cropland from protection as wetlands in response to farmers' complaints that too much of their land, designated as wetlands, was off limits to development. Agricultural wetlands sustain the nation's ducks, other migratory birds and wildlife, provide flood control, filter contaminants out of water, and perform many other vital ecological functions.

- In August 1991, Bush made one of the most environmentally destructive decisions of his career when he proposed a narrowing of the technical definition of "wetlands" so that nearly half of the nation's 100 million acres formerly protected as wetlands could be commercially developed. Incredibly, in his announcement of the proposal, Bush said his new policy marks a "significant step" toward his campaign pledge of "no net loss of wetlands." In truth, he simply defined the wetlands away. Under this proposal, nearly half the nation's wetlands would cease to exist, and twenty-nine states that now have wetlands would no longer have any.

The White House proposal ignited an immediate public uproar. In November 1991, Bush responded by scaling down his proposal so that "only" 30 percent—instead of 50 percent—of the nation's wetlands would be removed from federal protection.

Bush's new wetlands policy constitutes what is probably the most significant weakening of an environmental regulation in U.S. history. Under Bush's proposal, millions of ecologically fragile acres known by scientists to be wetlands, from Alaskan tundra to about half of the Florida Everglades, would be open to development.

> **"The Bush administration is not interested in protecting the environment. The two shouldn't even be in the same sentence."**
> **—Paul Bogart, Greenpeace, Madrid, June 22, 1991**

At the center of the controversy is a field manual used by government agents to identify wetlands. In 1989, the manual was updated and revised by government scientists, but the revision angered development interests who claimed that the definition of "wetlands" in the manual was too broad and covered too much land. In fact, the revised definition did not encompass much more land than in the past.

In response to the developers' complaints, the President's Council on

Competitiveness, headed by Vice President Quayle, quietly set to work to develop its own version of the wetlands field manual. Federal wetlands experts, including government scientists, charged that what was supposed to have been a scientific review of the nation's wetlands turned into a purely political one. Several government scientists resigned from the field-manual project.

In the end, it was White House advisors who made the scientific determinations that now define how wet an area has to be in order to qualify as protected wetlands. At the decisive meeting, the politicos were so ignorant on the subject that they all had to be given a special wetlands glossary.

At a top-level meeting on the subject of wetlands, EPA head William Reilly had argued for strong wetlands protections and quoted Bush's much-repeated promise: "no net loss of wetlands." But Budget Director Richard Darman, in a revealing comment, leaned over the conference table and said, "[Bush] didn't say that. He read what was given to him in a speech."

Grade: F

Forests

The Rhetoric

"The protection of the environment and the conservation and wise management of our natural resources—this whole notion of stewardship—must have a high priority on our national agenda."

—Candidate Bush, speaking at a business
luncheon, Seattle, May 16, 1988

The Reality

The Bush administration, for the most part, has continued the destructive policies of the Reagan administration with regard to the nation's forests. Bush has consistently favored logging at unsustainable levels in the nation's few remaining ancient forests—areas critical to preventing the extinction of the northern spotted owl and other species. The Administration has curbed its timber policies only when forced to by the courts or by highly publicized scientific reports. (See "Endangered Species and Biodiversity," pp. 243–70.)

- Siding with Western senators in October 1990, President Bush threatened to veto legislation if it included a provision to cut millions of dollars from a Forest Service program that builds logging roads in national forests. The federal logging road program is heavily subsidized by the government

($96 million in 1989) and enables logging companies to more easily denude federally owned forests. The Forest Service's network of roads is already *eight times* as long as the interstate highway system and is an environmentalist's nightmare. Nonetheless, in his 1991 budget, Bush proposed spending $181.6 million constructing another 2,300 miles of logging roads. The Forest Service is currently campaigning for another $2 *billion* to build an additional 40,000 miles of new roads through forests in the next decade.

- Before and during the Persian Gulf War, the U.S. Forest Service considered a proposal to lift environmental laws and protections for 191 million acres of Forest Service lands to enable oil companies to boost oil production on those lands. The Forest Service proposal, which came to light in September 1990, stated that because oil supplies were reduced worldwide during the Iraqi invasion of Kuwait, the Forest Service could help make up the difference. The proposal recommended that environmental regulations that would normally govern Forest Service decisions be dropped to enable oil companies to increase domestic supplies of oil. "Drilling should be given the same urgency as [forest] fire," the proposal stated. Apparently, the proposal never got off the ground.

- In 1990, Bush called on the government to join the private sector in planting of billions of trees over the decade. The tree-planting program is one component of what Bush calls his "America the Beautiful" initiative which includes, according to the Administration, government land acquisition and protection of national parks and forests. While laudable, the program was designed to deceive. Many existing programs were simply repackaged as the "America the Beautiful" campaign. Some other new environmental initiatives were created by simply taking funds from other environmental programs.

  Several scientists have characterized the tree-planting program as a public relations ploy designed to get Bush off the hook on his "no action" stance on global warming. One global warming expert called the program a "mere palliative" because no number of trees can compensate for the huge amount of greenhouse gases that will continue to be produced under Bush's National Energy Strategy.

- More than one critic has noted, with some irony, that at the same time Bush was promoting his tree-planting program, he was also promoting the cutting down of vast acres of giant ancient trees in the Pacific Northwest—despite warnings that this would destroy the last ecosystem of its kind in the United States (not to mention its contribution to global warming).

- In what initially appeared to be a positive development, in its budget request for 1990, the Bush administration attempted to phase out logging in a dozen national forests where the government spends more money subsidizing logging than it receives back in timber receipts. However, the Administration withdrew in the face of opposition from conservative Western legislators and did not renew the request in fiscal year 1991. "Below-cost" timber sales take place in two thirds of the national forest system. These sales not only cost taxpayers millions of dollars each year, but they are also highly damaging to the environment since such forests are clear-cut.

- In a positive action, President Bush signed into law a ban on the export of raw logs from most state-owned land in the West, in August 1990. The action represented a reversal for Bush who had previously opposed restrictions on log exports. The law also makes permanent the prohibition on raw-log exports from federal lands in the West. The action was taken in an effort to retain thousands of timber industry jobs. Excessive export of unfinished logs is the primary reason for job loss in the lumber industry and creates pressure for increased logging on federal lands.

Grade: D

Animal Rights

The Rhetoric

"I want a kinder, gentler nation."

—Candidate Bush, televised campaign advertisement, 1988

The Reality

Aside from his affectionate romps with Millie, the White House springer spaniel, George Bush is no friend of animals.

- The Bush administration, following in the deregulatory footsteps of the Reagan administration, has worked behind the scenes to gut the only law that mandates minimum standards of care for millions of animals used in laboratory experiments, as well as those held in zoos, in circuses, and by animal dealers. And they have largely succeeded. Many of the newly released final regulations written to implement and enforce Animal Welfare Act amendments, which Congress mandated in 1985, are weak, virtually unenforceable, and ignore improvements specifically called for by Congress.

  Congress had strengthened the act in response to extensive documentation that appalling, inhumane conditions for animals held in laboratories, zoos, and elsewhere, continued to persist years after the Animal Welfare Act was first adopted in 1966. Congress amended the act to require, among other things, larger cages for animals and exercise for dogs who spend their days locked in cages. Congress also required that primates not be isolated in tiny dark cages, but rather, be provided with an environment that would provide physical and mental stimulation and which would enable them to express a range of natural behaviors.

However, the regulations have in effect transformed these congressional mandates into discretionary options, with compliance in many cases dependent upon the subjective judgment of animal experimenters, zookeepers, and animal dealers—the very entities from which the regulations were supposed to protect animals.

The U.S. Department of Agriculture (USDA) initially had written strong regulations to implement and enforce the amendments. However, over a period of almost seven years, each new revision was rejected by the Office of Management and Budget (OMB), the executive agency that has veto power over proposed rules and regulations. In addition, Vice President Quayle's Council on Competitiveness also became involved and rejected several of the regulations as written by the USDA.

OMB's deliberate stalling tactics, and constant rewrites of steadily weakening regulations, caused immense frustration for members of Congress, the USDA, and animal protection organizations. Although Congress amended the Animal Welfare Act in 1985, final regulations were not issued until the first part of 1991, and not until the Animal Legal Defense Fund had obtained court orders for their release.

The new regulations have greatly pleased the multi-billion-dollar animal research industry. The National Association for Biomedical Research, which was created by the Charles River Company, the largest breeder of laboratory animals in the world, worked closely with the Bush administration to gut this animal-protective legislation. Among the Bush administration players were Science Advisor D. Allan Bromley; James Wyngaarden, former head of the National Institutes of Health and the Office of Science and Technology Policy, and Richard Darman of OMB.

- Bush calls himself the nation's "first hunter," and has engaged in the "sport" of hunting for more than twenty-five years. The President finds nothing wrong with using live animals, especially doves and quail, for target practice.

  "These aren't animals—these are wild quail," said President-elect Bush in 1988 when a reporter asked him how hunting animals jibes with a "kinder, gentler America."

  The following year, a group of antihunting protesters demonstrated at a Texas hunt in which Bush was participating. Referring to the protesters, Bush said to a reporter: "That group that was down there, I cannot identify with that. . . . I do not identify with them at all."

In 1990, Bush told another reporter that: "I'll be a great conservation and environmental President. I plan to fish and hunt as much as I can."

Grade: F

Genetic Engineering

The Rhetoric

"There's something more we owe the generations of the future: stewardship, the safekeeping of America's precious environmental inheritance."

—George Bush, State of the Union Address,
January 30, 1990

The Reality

- Vice President Quayle and his Competitiveness Council, working hand in hand with Budget Director Richard Darman, have been busy for years scuttling EPA and USDA proposals to regulate biotechnology. While Darman has been using his veto power to prevent any biotech rules from being approved, Quayle and his council have proposed that genetically engineered products be considered safe until proven otherwise, and have recommended that no genetically engineered organisms be federally regulated unless there is "substantial evidence that an organism poses significant and unreasonable risk."

  Quayle has recently made the overseeing of biotechnology regulation his pet project. The prospect is frightening indeed! If Quayle and his council are successful in blocking regulation, the door will be opened to massive releases of genetically engineered plants, animals, bacteria, and viruses into the environment—a giant experiment with human and environmental health.

Grade: F

Endangered Species and Biodiversity

The Rhetoric

"A Bush administration will enforce environmental laws aggressively."
—Candidate Bush at a business luncheon,
Seattle, May 16, 1988

The Reality

The Bush administration gets mixed reviews for its performance on preserving biodiversity and endangered species. When it has been easy to do so, the Administration has supported biodiversity. However, when economics enters the picture, industry gets first consideration. The Administration has even attempted to evade and manipulate the Endangered Species Act to comply with industry demands.

- After years of politically motivated delay and subterfuge, in 1990 the U.S. Fish and Wildlife Service (FWS), acting on a court order, finally listed the northern spotted owl as a threatened species under the Endangered Species Act. But presented with evidence that tracts of federally owned ancient forest would have to be closed to the timber industry to prevent the spotted owl from becoming extinct, the Bush administration proposed that the Endangered Species Act be modified "to reflect a better balance" between the interests of endangered species and industry.

  Bush proposed expanding the authority of a little-used Cabinet group, often referred to as the "God Committee" or "God Squad," that is empowered to overrule actions protecting endangered species. The Administration also supported an amendment to the Interior appropriations bill, by Sen. Bob Packwood (R-OR), that would have effectively exempted timber-cutting plans from the provisions of the Endangered Species Act for ten years, ample time for the ancient forests and the spotted owl to disappear forever.

  After receiving the FWS recommendations on the spotted owl, the Bush administration decided to set up its own Inter-Agency Scientific Committee to study the matter. But, upon completion of the study, the Administration rejected the committee's report because it too found that logging would have to be curtailed in order to save the species.

"Bush's efforts at balance, compromise, and consensus-building are killing our world." —Jay Hair, President, National Wildlife Federation

Since then, the Administration has delayed the adoption of a species protection plan for the owl as required by the Endangered Species Act, and has repeatedly attempted to permit heavy logging in critical owl habitat.

Charging the Bush administration with back-room political interventionism and trying to derail the Endangered Species Act, a U.S. District Court judge, in May 1991, ordered most 1991 timber sales in the national forests of the Northwest suspended until federal agencies comply with the law and produce an effective protection plan for the spotted owl.

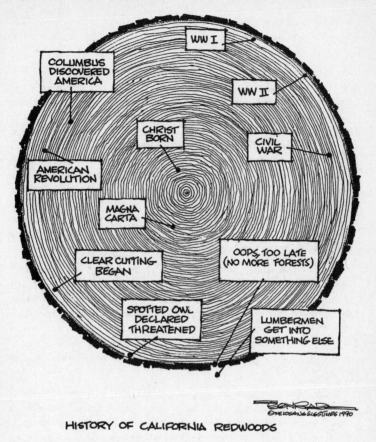

HISTORY OF CALIFORNIA REDWOODS

BY PAUL CONRAD. © 1990, LOS ANGELES TIMES. REPRINTED BY PERMISSION.

The ruling protects 66,000 acres of ancient forest until March 1992 when the Forest Service must present an acceptable spotted owl management plan.

In September 1991, the Bureau of Land Management (BLM) announced that it wants to cut and sell Oregon timber that FWS recommended be preserved to protect the spotted owl. Later in the month, at the request of BLM administrator Cy Jamison, Interior Secretary Manuel Lujan requested the "God Committee" to convene in November. The committee, which is composed of six senior government officials and one Oregon resident appointed by President Bush, is to decide by February 1992 whether or not to grant an exemption to the Endangered Species Act and allow the BLM to proceed with its timber sales—an action that would kill some owls outright and destroy much of the remaining owls' habitat. The momentous decision could have a major effect on the future of the Endangered Species Act which is due for reauthorization in 1992—the presidential election year.

- The Bush administration initially took a surprisingly strong stand on protecting the African elephant. In the summer of 1989, in response to public pressure, Bush agreed to ban ivory imports into the United States. The United States also took a hard line at an international wildlife conservation meeting which resulted in the African elephant being listed as a "most-protected species" internationally. The Administration, however, has been slow to the point of negligence in placing the animal on the U.S. endangered species list. Environmental groups petitioned the government early in 1989 to list the African elephant as endangered, but, as of October 1991, the Interior Department had still not conferred most-protected status on the animal. Instead, the Administration has proposed listing the animal as endangered in some African countries but not others. Such a "split-listing", however, would reopen the world ivory market and encourage poaching and trophy hunting.

- The Bush administration initially opposed protections for sea turtles in the Gulf of Mexico who are endangered primarily as a result of becoming caught in nets used to catch shrimp. However, once a law was passed that requires all shrimp vessels to use turtle-excluder devices (TEDs) which keep turtles out of nets, Secretary of Commerce Robert Mosbacher had the Coast Guard attempt to enforce it. The Administration, however, has so far not used its power to press criminal charges against fishermen who continue to kill endangered sea turtles.

- Bush has been strong on the issue of driftnets and has worked toward an international ban on their use. However, the Administration has steadfastly refused to impose significant economic sanctions against Japan for continually violating the world moratorium on killing whales, other fisheries agreements, and wildlife conservation agreements. Instead, the Administration has used these issues as political and economic bargaining chips with Japan.

Grade: D

Political Appointments

The Rhetoric

"I will put the very best people we can find to work on our environmental agenda."

—Candidate Bush, at a business luncheon,
Seattle, May 16, 1988

The Reality

All the President's men are not environmentalists. Those who are unfortunately do not have much power.

- Environmental Protection Agency Administrator William Reilly, the first career environmentalist to head the EPA, was a fair choice for this position. However, even before accepting his post, Reilly had a reputation as a negotiator with industry who often compromised the environment. Reilly has continued this tradition in office, although it sometimes has been hard to tell whether he has waffled on an issue or whether he was overpowered by the "terrible troika": Sununu, Darman, and Quayle. Reilly's is the strongest proenvironment voice in the executive branch of the government. However, it is precisely for that reason that he is frequently left out of important environmental decisions and international environmental conferences.

- President's Council on Environmental Quality Chairman Michael Deland appears to be a dedicated environmentalist. However, Deland plays a relatively minor advisory role; his voice is regularly reduced to a whisper by the aggressive antienvironmentalists in the Bush administration.

- Secretary of the Interior Manuel Lujan was a bad bet for his post when he was appointed, and he still is. Prior to his appointment, Lujan was a U.S. representative from New Mexico, who, over his twenty-year congressional career, amassed one of the worst environmental voting records ever. According to the League of Conservation Voters, Lujan sided with environmentalists only 23 percent of the time from 1970 to 1988.

  As Interior Secretary, Lujan has promoted oil and gas drilling in environmentally sensitive areas, including the Arctic National Wildlife Refuge and the nation's outer continental shelf. And he once described the nation's public lands as "a place with a lot of grass for cows."

  Worst of all, Lujan, who, as the enforcer of the Endangered Species Act is charged with acting as the foremost protector of wildlife in the nation, is of the opinion that not all endangered species should be saved. "Do we have to save every subspecies?" Luhan asked a reporter during a May 1990 interview. "The red squirrel is the best example. Nobody's told me the difference between a red squirrel, a black one, or a brown one." In a statement that invokes the memory of Reagan-era Interior Secretary James G. Watt, the rabid antienvironmentalist, Lujan said that the Endangered Species Act is "too tough" and should be rewritten.

- Before his forced resignation in late 1991, White House Chief of Staff John H. Sununu undisputably ran the show. He aggressively overwhelmed all Cabinet-level opinion that did not agree with his own. A nuclear engineer by training, Sununu was openly hostile toward environmental protection concerns throughout his tenure, and engaged in what amounted to a fierce personal vendetta against environmentalists.

Sununu never believed in the greenhouse effect. He installed in his personal computer a simple version of the climate models that the National Center of Atmospheric Research runs on its supercomputer, and was obsessed with trying to prove the scientists wrong in their forecasts of global warming.

- Office of Management and Budget Director Richard G. Darman openly expresses contempt for environmental protection, and routinely shoots down environmental regulations claiming that they will be too expensive.

  Darman takes almost any opportunity to denigrate those with opposing views on the environment. In a speech he gave at Harvard University in May 1990, for example, Darman said that the United States should not abandon its market economy and economic growth to clean up the environment. "Americans did not fight and win the wars of the twentieth century to make the world safe for green vegetables," he said.

- Vice President Danforth Quayle sided with environmentalists only 34 percent of the time during his tenure as congressman and senator from Indiana, according to the League of Conservation Voters. A lifetime of antienvironmentalism apparently helped him get his other job as chairman of the President's Competitiveness Council, a deregulatory group that routinely guts environmental regulations-in-the-works at the behest of big business. Quayle inherited the job from his predecessor, George Bush, who faithfully operated the deregulatory machine during the Reagan administration.

  The council's members are Richard Darman, Attorney General Richard Thornburgh, Treasury Secretary Nicholas Brady, Council of Economic Advisors Chairman Michael Boskin, and Commerce Secretary Robert Mosbacher. John Sununu also sat on the council until he resigned.

- Secretary of State James Baker, who, like the President, is a former Texas oilman, had a legal document drafted removing himself from the White House global warming debate on the grounds that his participation could affect his substantial oil and gas holdings and therefore would constitute a conflict of interest. Baker, however, did not excuse himself from managing the Persian Gulf crisis, or from helping to frame Bush's National Energy Strategy for the nation, on the same grounds. Still, Baker had often backed up the proenvironment stance of William Reilly, and by so doing, incurred Sununu's wrath.

- Bush's appointment of Delos Cy Jamison as Director of the Bureau of Land Management, often derided as the Bureau of Livestock and Mining, was a predictable disaster. Jamison, whose agency oversees most of the nation's public lands, is an avowed antienvironmentalist. He formerly served as an aide to former Interior Secretary James Watt, and an advisor to Rep. Ron Marlenee (R-MT), two of the most aggressive antienviron-mentalists in government over the past decade. Jamison has carried on the tradition of his predecessor, Reagan-appointee Robert Burford, in favoring the exploitation of public lands by ranchers, loggers, mining companies, and other private interests, over environmental protection.

Jamison opposes attempts to raise fees for grazing on public lands, defends the General Mining Law of 1872, and opposes wilderness designation for federal land in Alaska. ("Nothing is happening to it just sitting there," he once said.)

Jamison has proposed that the threatened northern spotted owls of the Northwest be captured and relocated in order to allow logging to continue in the 10 percent of ancient forest that remains. Jamison wants to continue below-cost timber sales in BLM-managed forests that the U.S. Fish and Wildlife Service has recommended be preserved as critical habitat for the owl. In September 1991, he asked Interior Secretary Manuel Lujan to convene the "God Committee" to decide whether the BLM can go through with its logging proposal.

Grade: D

"We cannot govern by listening to the loudest voice on the extreme of an environmental movement. And I did not rely heavily on them for support in getting elected President of the United States. And I'm not going to be persuaded that I can get some brownie points by appealing to one of these groups or another. . . .

"[Environmental groups] haven't seemed happy with me for a long time. And I'm not too happy with them."

—*President George Bush, Houston, July 1990*

• • •

BUSH ADMINISTRATION GRADES:

Global Warming: F
Ozone Layer: B
Clean Air: D
Energy: F
Transportation: F
Defense: C
Oceans: D
Antarctica: B
Public Lands: F
Wetlands: F
Forests: D
Animal Rights: F
Genetic Engineering: F
Endangered Species and Biodiversity: D
Political Appointments: D

Final Grade: D